Caroline Forbes

Simon Winder is the editor of several anthologies, including the highly praised *Night Thoughts*. He works in publishing in London, where he lives with his family.

EDITED BY SIMON WINDER

Night Thoughts

Sea Longing

The Feast

*"My Name's Bond . . .": An Anthology
from the Fiction of Ian Fleming*

The MAN WHO SAVED BRITAIN

The MAN WHO SAVED BRITAIN

A PERSONAL JOURNEY INTO THE
DISTURBING WORLD OF JAMES BOND

SIMON WINDER

PICADOR

FARRAR, STRAUS AND GIROUX

NEW YORK

www.picadorusa.com

Picador® is a U.S. registered trademark and is used by Farrar, Straus and Giroux under license from Pan Books Limited.

For information on Picador Reading Group Guides, please contact Picador.
Phone: 646-307-5259
Fax: 212-253-9627
E-mail: readinggroupguides@picadorusa.com

Grateful acknowledgement is made for permission to reprint excerpts of the following material: *Casino Royale* copyright © Glidrose Productions Ltd. 1953; *Live and Let Die* copyright © Glidrose Productions Ltd. 1954; *Moonraker* copyright © Glidrose Productions Ltd. 1955; *Diamonds Are Forever* copyright © Glidrose Productions Ltd. 1956; *From Russia with Love* copyright © Glidrose Productions Ltd. 1957; *Dr. No* copyright © Glidrose Productions Ltd. 1958; *Goldfinger* copyright © Glidrose Productions Ltd. 1959; *For Your Eyes Only* copyright © Glidrose Productions Ltd. 1960; *Thunderball* copyright © Glidrose Productions Ltd. 1961; *The Spy Who Loved Me* copyright © Glidrose Productions Ltd. 1962; *On Her Majesty's Secret Service* copyright © Glidrose Productions Ltd. 1963; *You Only Live Twice* copyright © Glidrose Productions Ltd. 1964; and *The Man with the Golden Gun* copyright © Glidrose Productions Ltd. 1965. *Octopussy* copyright © the Literary Executors of Ian Fleming 1965, 1966, reprinted with the permission of Ian Fleming Publications Ltd., www.ianflemingcentre.com. All works by Ian Fleming.

Library of Congress Cataloging-in-Publication Data

Winder, Simon.
    The man who saved Britain : a personal journey into the disturbing world of James Bond / Simon Winder.
        p. cm.
    ISBN-13: 978-0-312-42666-8
    ISBN-10: 0-312-42666-6
    1. Fleming, Ian, 1908–1964—Criticism and interpretation. 2. Bond, James (Fictitious character). 3. Politics and literature—Great Britain—History—20th century. 4. Literature and society—Great Britain—History—20th century. 5. Spy stories, English—History and criticism. 6. Espionage in literature. 7. Spies in literature. I. Title.

PR6056.L4Z94 2006
823'.914—dc22

                                                                                  2006010024

First published in the United States by Farrar, Straus and Giroux

First Picador Edition: October 2007

10 9 8 7 6 5 4 3 2 1

FOR

BEJW

. . . but there is also such a thing as ersatz happiness, perhaps happiness exists only as an ersatz . . .

Günter Grass, The Tin Drum

Bond cursed into the sodden folds of his silk handkerchief and got going.

Ian Fleming, On Her Majesty's Secret Service

Contents

Introduction

Eating Old Jamaica at the Tunbridge Wells Odeon

I am ten years old, sitting in a suburban English cinema. On the screen a man with a large chin and black roll-neck sweater pushes through jungle foliage. He crouches behind a gravestone and takes out an enormous pistol. A white woman has been tied to a post and a black man dressed in animal skins is laughing crazily and wielding a massive poisonous snake. Around them hundreds of voodoo worshippers are screaming and convulsing. The man with the large chin starts shooting the black people, who are too busy rolling their eyes and waving old cutlasses to offer proper resistance.

To be honest my memory goes a bit hazy at this point. In a moment of bravado before the film I had bought a jumbo Old Jamaica, a weird 1970s chocolate bar filled with rum essence and raisins. It had struck me as a sophisticated treat, little realizing that its only target market was in fact aspirational ten-year-old boys. Anyway, the reality of feeling sick, the perception of being drunk, and the confusion of the notionally West Indian flavour of the treat and the loosely West Indian setting of the film conspired to overwhelm me. Leaving the voodoo worshippers to their fate I staggered to the toilets. Thirty years later, rum essence still flings me back—like some reduced-to-clear Proust—to that cinema and what proved to be a transformative encounter with a man with a large chin.

Writing this is peculiarly painful. The film in question was *Live and Let Die*, and its hero, James Bond, has since that moment deeply affected my life. For me that film pushed open the Golden Doors of sex and death, revealing a world of sophistication and cruelty previously unimagined. Sheltered by a prior movie diet of such duff material as *Tales of Beatrix Potter*, a ballet film featuring a dancing frog, I suddenly had discovered a film packed with steel-clawed black giants, alligators, speedboats and girls whimpering, "Oh, James." The Two Bad Mice prancing about hitting a little plaster fish (which of course, at the time, I had absolutely loved) became overnight something thought of always but spoken of never.

I went to see *Live and Let Die* again a week later, this time spurning the siren song of the Old Jamaica: it was a flawless gem. Every scene conveyed so much—the brutal cunning of the villains, the decency and wit of Bond, the glamorous American and West Indian locations, the miraculous music. Happy years followed of reading and reading again all the Bond books, tracking down the older Bond films, preparing myself spiritually for the next one, *The Man with the Golden Gun*.

The painfulness in all this is of course that *Live and Let Die* is dreadful. In a moment of lunatic parental outreach I recently bought the DVD to watch with my own twelve- and ten-year-old sons. I had not seen the movie in many years and this planned piece of quality nurturing left me mute with grief. The film was a mean-spirited and offensive shambles, too stupid really even to be racist, too chaotic to be camp. Worse, the film was the first to feature Roger Moore—a faintly louche manikin, famous as the Saint and, with Tony Curtis (then going through one of his cyclical career low-points), one of the Persuaders. Moore was to spearhead the progressive degeneration of Bond over a further seven films. Now I can see that I encountered and fell for Bond at the precise point, 1973, when he was spiralling out of control.

And yet for many years he *had* been important—important to millions of people in all kinds of ways, a uniquely powerful, strange presence in British life since his invention by Ian Fleming in the early 1950s. Wholly oblivious, I had as a ten-year-old bumped into his most embarrassing avatar, but my entire upbringing had been in effect soaked in the world in which Bond had thrived and in which he was understood. In this time—before Bond films were ever shown on television—double bills of old ones would tour cinemas, playing to vast steaming audiences, seeing the films, like myself, over and over again almost as a religious undertaking. I was simply then the latest among whole populations of men and women (well, mainly men to be honest) who had stood in line for the Bond experience. Our school games were soaked in Bond, our talk was endlessly about the films and about the cruelty and sex in the books: Bond was a sort of currency, albeit, and quite unknown to me, one in steep decline on the open market.

This book is an attempt to get to grips with Bond's legacy and with the worlds in which Bond *really* mattered—not to a helpless ten-year-old ding-a-ling in the early seventies but to the generation who had fought in the Second World War and who in vast numbers read the Bond books in the 1950s and saw the Bond films in the 1960s.

I hope to explore with reasonable seriousness the trauma faced by Britain in the 1940s and after—a far smaller trauma than that of mainland Europe, but profound nonetheless and one that could have been terminal. The link between Bond's invention and his overwhelming success and the horrors faced by Britain from 1939 onwards are close and interesting. Ian Fleming, a cynical upper-class waster galvanized by and briefly endorsed by the emergency of the War, reacted to the gradual, but sometimes vertiginous, implosion of Britain when the fighting had ended by creating the Bond books. These proceeded to find their vast niche as part of a general right-wing reaction to the humiliations and failures of British life. I want to re-create some of the stifling British obsession with the Second World War, which still cannot be shaken even today, but which once permeated all aspects of life and was dominant throughout my own childhood. Toys, film, novels, memoirs about the War were everywhere, and through them strode James Bond, the secret hero who calmly carried the values of that war through a treacherous and ungrateful Cold War world.

Inevitably this book must lean heavily on a sort of ancient archaeology—here are the remains of a door post, here a possible site of cult ritual. So much has changed and so rapidly that it is hard to get right inside the original impact of the books or the films. Morals have changed, movie gun noises are much more reverberant, sex has got sexier. The Cold War has, weirdly, completely vanished, leaving behind such peculiar debris as *From Russia with Love*, a book and a film which will appear as strange to future generations as abandoned Kazakhstan rocket silos or fallout shelters.

As a memoir, this book is fragmentary and scraped together from very slightly interesting bits and bobs. My life has just not been melodramatic enough to take up more than a few pages. I had a cheerful childhood packed with affection, no specific features to incite sympathy and no adventures to speak of. As history it will anger many, filled as it is with shocking generalizations and lack of documentation. I share that anger. This book was written in large part because I want to convey, perhaps in an overdrawn form, some of the ways in which Britain has changed—and by following James Bond show some of a vanished world which he in various ways pulled together.

The eight chapters are roughly chronological, pursuing Fleming's, Britain's and Bond's lives from the 1930s to the 1970s with occasional comfort-breaks to deal with specific themes. I have tried to give just enough background on Britain and its empire to make events around and after the War intelligible. While carefully researched, this material is breathtakingly selective and loaded with no doubt facetious and callow interpretation of a kind that will have historians shrieking to heaven for vengeance. I should really emphasize that I am not a professional historian and that anyone who has devoted their life to a serious study of this period should probably see about swapping this for something else.

A further obvious point is that this is a book only about some people some of the time: for every individual concerned about Britain's international prestige or the global nuclear threat there were countless more simply getting on with their lives. It is a simile used before, but it is like Brueghel's painting *Landscape with the Fall of Icarus*: a shepherd stares at the clouds, a plough-man ploughs a field, a merchant ship hurries by, and down in the corner Icarus crashes—with a tiny *ploof!* of water—completely unremarked into the sea. Clearly the end of the British Empire was for very many people an unremarked and tiny *ploof!* but for many others, continuously or intermittently, it was much more.

Devoted contemporary fans will be driven to distraction by this book. Going to a premiere of the last Bond film, *Die Another*

Day, at the Empire Leicester Square, I had to say that I was unmoved by what happened on the screen. Tiny voices whispered that *Die Hard* did this better, that *Face/Off* did this better, that even Vin Diesel's *xXx* did this better. I'm afraid that some years back I parted from the Way and feel relieved at having done so. But Bond's later abasement should not cloud what he used to be and movies featuring John Cleese as Q and an invisible car cannot sully the immense pleasures of the books and the early films.

This then is part memoir, part history, part a meditation on being a fan/not being a fan. The little telltale phrase, though, in the last paragraph, "going to a premiere," will of course tell you all you need to know. I am not exactly cured. Like a hopeless modern version of Goya's *The Sleep of Reason Brings Forth Monsters*, I lie slumped at my desk with disturbingly well-thumbed copies of *Diamonds Are Forever* and DVDs of *Octopussy* (for God's sake) flapping about my head. But that I think still applies to British men in general—if diminishingly so—who still walk a little differently, dream certain dreams, and are somewhat comforted and sexually a little odder than would have been the case without the imagination of a man born into a very different sort of Britain.

Note

Books and Films

Ian Fleming (1908–1964) wrote fourteen James Bond books: *Casino Royale* (1953), *Live and Let Die* (1954), *Moonraker* (1955), *Diamonds Are Forever* (1956), *From Russia with Love* (1957), *Dr. No* (1958), *Goldfinger* (1959), *For Your Eyes Only* (short stories, 1960), *Thunderball* (1961), *The Spy Who Loved Me* (1962), *On Her Majesty's Secret Service* (1963), *You Only Live Twice* (1964) and the posthumously published *The Man with the Golden Gun* (1965) and *Octopussy* (short stories, 1966).

The films are *Dr. No* (1962), *From Russia with Love* (1963), *Goldfinger* (1964), *Thunderball* (1965), *You Only Live Twice* (1967), *On Her Majesty's Secret Service* (1969), *Diamonds Are Forever* (1971), *Live and Let Die* (1973), *The Man with the Golden Gun* (1974), *The Spy Who Loved Me* (1977), *Moonraker* (1979) . . . I'm sorry: I just can't go on it's all so terrible. They're roughly the same, come out at irregular intervals and tend to have the word *Die* in the title.

There are also three oddities: a hypnotic American television version of *Casino Royale* made in 1954; the pitiful spoof *Casino Royale* with David Niven and Woody Allen (1967), which derived its rights from the earlier television contract; and *Never Say Never Again* (1983), a pointless offshoot of legal disputes about ownership of the *Thunderball* screenplay.

The MAN WHO SAVED BRITAIN

Chapter One

"NIGHT AND DAY"

MY MOTHER used to tell me how her clearest early memory was of sitting on the front step of her family's house in South-East London, aged six, eating a honey sandwich and watching as planes zoomed over her head, engaged in fighting the Battle of Britain. I often think of that encounter and the thousands of times I had gazed at my mother who had in turn gazed at one of the defining moments in the world's history, but who was as much concerned with the taste of the honey as with the Spitfires.

My grandmother—my mother's mother—experienced the War and specifically the Blitz quite differently: as terror piled on terror. She still talks today with incredulity of the three months during which every night brought an air raid, of giving birth during a raid, of the people and houses randomly annihilated around her own neighbourhood. She and my mother (safely tucked up for the rest of the War on a farm) both remembered too a world substantially without men—of families filled with missing sons, brothers and fathers, of a country which by 1945 had some four and a half million men in uniform scattered around the world.

Every country's recent history provides different forms of trauma. It is absolutely the case that the British experience of the Second World War was not remotely as horrible as that of Poland, say, or Russia. There was not the physical annihilation experienced by Ukraine or even anything approaching the subtle but acrid horror of occupation undergone by France or Burma. The 300,000 or so British dead matches roughly the American figure, although the latter was almost exclusively military whereas the British was about a fifth civilian. In the scarcely credible cauldron of the War these are tiny figures, swamped by—say—the Bengal Famine alone.

But just as the death of a patient in the next hospital bed has no serious bearing on an individual's own dangerous and invasive operation, so Britain's "benign" War experience was in the end completely traumatic and terrible. Indeed the whole idea of the "good war" has been developed to generate both a sense of moral certainty that was in practice under siege for much of the conflict and to allow those who experienced the War to hide their eyes from the vast gulfs that had surrounded them.

Fundamentally the War, despite its being won, consisted for Britain of a ceaseless nightly Blitz of humiliations, compromises and setbacks, and these did not stop with 1945 but kept up a relentless battering until well into the 1970s. The country that reeled into the European Economic Community in 1973 was, with Ireland, the poorest member state, an ashen, provincial, polyester sort of country, no longer recognizable as the victor of 1945 and a million miles from the self-image British people had nurtured for themselves for generations.

The strange obsession Britain has with the Second World War, now almost unique in the world (with the interesting exception of Russia), has profound roots, therefore: it was the last point at which there had been a deep sense of purpose and value, crystallizing around the two peaks of the Battle of Britain and D-Day and forgetful of the horrible failures that otherwise marked much of the War experience. The pace at which Britain then "decompressed," from being the triumphant victor over Germany and Japan and the world's largest empire in 1945 to being a shorn, flailing, International Monetary Fund beggar in 1976, perched resentfully on the fringe of Europe, makes an extraordinary story. Most countries en route to such a debacle would have stirred themselves to shoot a few of their rulers or organize a Latin American–style coup. This was certainly the traditional European approach, whether in Berlin, Vienna, Paris or Moscow. But somehow in Britain the revolutionary left were never more than a fringe of a fringe and there was never a faintly plausible caudillo waiting in the wings (even the comic/sinister Lord Mountbatten turned down such an idea).

There were many reasons for Britain's different fate, but none in themselves seem quite enough: an unprovokable sense of deference; the food; the weather; the quality of BBC programming (if you took to the streets you might miss something good); a non-political police and civil service (or at least non-political in comparison with most European countries). These were immensely fraught, febrile decades with almost every year loading on further shame and chaos, handled by a political class in thrall to history, exhausted and embittered. But through that devastated landscape walked a fascinating, symptomatic figure—the totem or lucky charm: James Bond.

Before laying out some suggestions as to how we should see the Second World War and its aftermath, it is important—

or at least quite interesting—to get to grips a little with Bond's remarkable creator.

WHAT SORT OF a man was Ian Fleming? What do we need to know about him to understand his creation? Thanks to his photo sessions with Cecil Beaton and Horst Tappe he has left an indelible image. Many writers are associated with smoking in their most iconic portraits (Auden, Simenon, Camus—the last's image more compelling surely than mere social pressures as a reason for lighting up), but none with smoke itself. Fleming's skin, textured like that of a giant tortoise, is almost hidden by smoke in Tappe's late photos: indeed there is so much smoke that it is as though his neck has caught fire. The weirdly compelling, flat, contemptuous face, the clenched teeth on the cigarette holder, the mean, shadowed eyes, all seem to imply a man of ferocious purpose. Tappe's saurian anti-smoking ad is one of the essential icons of the early 1960s. Reproduced on millions of Pan paperback covers—overlaid with such lovely quotes as "Brrr . . . how wincingly well Mr. Fleming writes" and "Muscularly brilliant . . . not for prudes"—the photo implies less that Fleming is Bond than that he is himself a sort of criminal mastermind—a coughing version of Blofeld.

And yet in other, less widely used photos the effect is less happy. In one bizarre session Fleming is shown looking down the sight of a revolver, the gun-barrel pointing at the camera, looming and massively distorted. He looks like a dotty old novelist camping it up, which of course he was. Rather than arranging with a nod of the head for some merciless killing, dropping into place one more bloodstained piece in some vast jigsaw of terror understood only by himself, Fleming was in reality merely tapping out nonsense on his portable typewriter in Jamaica whilst slurping cocktails and muttering querulously about socialism.

After their deaths almost all writers are remembered by photos taken late in life. Pictures of them when younger, when indeed they may have written their most memorable books, always seem to appear as unrealistic previews for the crumpled or craggy later versions. Shaw, Tolkien, Beckett, Waugh are doomed always to be wonky and gnarled. Accident has spared us the spectacle of the frog-like, scrumpled property billionaire Camus enjoying a joke with his friend President Chirac. Pictures of the younger Fleming, without the thousands of impacts from drinking, smoking and matrimonial screaming matches, have no real plausibility. He looks as he was: a handsome but banal philandering toff; self-confident but only through staying within the vast ramparts of class disdain; intelligent but only because the usual arbitrary scraps of elite education had stuck to him. In fact he is very much like Bond, but minus the action and adventure and plus the golfing chums.

Before the War, all the interest attached to his remarkable brother Peter, journalist, adventurer, hero author of the magical *News from Tartary* and *Brazilian Adventure*. Indeed Ian Fleming was almost a parody of a less talented younger brother. Clearly his family upbringing *was* surprising and interesting—because it produced Peter Fleming—but there didn't seem enough left in the bag for anyone else.

HOW SHOULD WE understand the past? Historians have to create a coherent narrative (the meaning, after all, of the word "history"), but inevitably this creates limits and frustrations.

The past does not roll out like a motorway building project. People often do not notice what is going on—they are too tired, too old, too young, too stupid, looking in the other direction. Inevitably history becomes what the historian chooses to point out. History is also, of course, hindsight— each event lived then as a set of choices blurred by prejudice, greed, panic and habit tidied into a plausible sequence.

Countries can become very crowded with history, and the British national obsession with it should tell us much more about the nature of what has happened to us—and continues to happen to us—than it does. The merely folkloric or picturesque historical interests of many countries and the careful aphasia of others show that history itself will deal a great range of cards which different nations either pore over or discard. Britain is a country with so much "live" history that it sometimes threatens to engulf it.

However defined, historical events broke into twentieth-century British lives in highly disturbing ways, where the blameless private unfolding of family stories and the grand narratives of the two world wars intersect. Through the timing of births my family was almost unaffected, beyond the mysterious death of a great-uncle in Ceylon while in the RAF. Other families' timings and decisions could result in their being ravaged to pieces by the dates 1914–18 and 1939–45, with mere fragments stepping into what proved to be the post-war world. Fleming for example had, just before his ninth birthday, to hear that his father (a dashing friend of Churchill's and a Conservative MP) had been killed on the Western Front. In the Second World War a brother was killed in action and a long-term girlfriend killed by a bomb in London. For very good reasons we put such terrible information aside all year except on Remembrance Sunday. What is for many a day of pleasing, attenuated melancholy is for millions completely unbearable.

LOOKING AT Fleming's life in the 1930s I feel a little Red commissar inside me thumping his desk and waving around a revolver. The sheer imbecile levels of privilege, the thoughtlessness, the parasitism are astounding. Fleming wandered through life as a sort of walking reproach to capitalism as a rational system based on competitive Darwinian struggle. In many cradles of European civilization it had been okay for at least a hundred and fifty years to carve up people like Fleming and set fire to their mansions as a legitimate form of central heating. Somehow in Britain they survived. Robert Fleming & Co., the bank from which the family fortunes derived, was at the heart of a vast spider-web of imperial interests, from Anglo-Texan cattle millionaires to Anglo-Iranian Oil, the company that later became BP. Around the world many thousands of people were toiling in effect for the bank to create an awesome, dazzling, infinitely complex structure which had lurking in it somewhere a little up escalator for the fortunate Ian Fleming.

After leaving Eton he mucked about in the army for a bit, spent some time in the Alps at a special type of school, worked for a while at Reuters news agency, got a job as a stockbroker because his mother knew the Governor of the Bank of England . . . You expect a scene like the climactic moment in the great film of *Frankenstein* where the enraged villagers all rush along, yelling and waving flaming torches, intent on burning everything down. When he's not shooting stags he's flying to France to play golf, when he's not skiing in Austria he's leafing through imported French pornography in his bachelor pad. A serialized, strip-cartoon version run in a Soviet children's newspaper would have been spurned by its young readers as crudely implausible.

It is this British upper-class imperviousness between the Wars which is now so striking. The civil wars in Ireland and Spain, the street-fighting and hatreds sprawling throughout Europe, the quintessential newsreel image of the era of tiny male figures in hats and overcoats running in panic down ornate chilly boulevards: these are all held at bay. The unfolding horrors of Nazi Germany and the USSR had no resonance outside an ineffectual British fringe on right and left who never seriously threatened or even perturbed a ruling-class core who, behind the bluff, pipe-smoking fraud of Stanley Baldwin and his "National" government, could weather epic levels of unemployment, colonial unrest and even a king's abdication.

Fleming effortlessly floats along on all this, working his way through endless specially made cigarettes and upper-class women. Of course, in the end everyone has to be grateful. Britain spends the 1930s in effect manipulating or using up a tremendous range of international assets, exploiting its weakening but still key role in finance, emigration and trade to cushion itself against some of the worst aspects of the Depression. This sense in which Britain was using itself up would become cruelly apparent in 1940 but until that point was reached—a point neither wished for nor imagined by anyone in the whole population—there was a stability which, as scared or angry crowds surged through Barcelona or Paris or Vienna, is extraordinary. And if this stability was bought at the price of a few thousand Ian Flemings then that was surely an acceptable price. The communist or fascist critiques of European capitalism had a validity in many countries but only a very limited one in Britain. Nobody really wanted Buckingham Palace to become People's Sausage Factory No. 1 and the palace's painfully feeble-minded and marginal inhabitants were never in the least danger. Nobody even, on the approved Continental model, took a shot at them or waved around a dagger of retribution. British capitalism and society retained immense reserves, however pressured. Indeed, it could be claimed that the solidity of the British system, based on a great global framework of money and language of astonishing resilience and complexity, of which the island itself was merely a focus point, was perhaps always unbeatable by Germany: itself an isolated and almost landlocked piece of a small continent with no global reach of any serious kind at all.

This sort of solidity or stolidity which shaped Fleming's whole world and the country around him was both impressive and distasteful in almost equal measure. The foam-flecked mouth of my internal Red commissar can quite readily be bought off by a nice cream tea at a National Trust property. No critique of Britain's life, even one as cruelly intelligent as, say, George Orwell's, could come up with a means of creating some level of social justice without risking the terrifying fate of Russia or Germany. It was only in the fleeting moment of triumph in 1945 that a timid but thoughtful bid could be made to overhaul the status quo but, as we shall see, this was rapidly tamed and rechanneled by the same huge forces that kept Britain, at great moral cost, safe in the 1930s.

The immediate and completely frightening nature of the great emergency of 1939 is overwhelmingly coloured by our knowing what happened (we survived) and this gives a specific narrative flavour *now* not enjoyed *then*. Identifying these distortions can in effect be a definition of an entire kind of history, far more than some plodding re-re-recounting of events. If Fleming spent the 1930s for the most part mucking around, there were others who were grey with anxiety.

IN A WORLD saturated with media and with Internet access to a welter of images, each historical period reinforces even further its dominant flavour: Louis XV's must always be crowded with terrific cloaks, hats, dresses and sword-pommels even if in practice it was more usual to be dead in a ditch; the Mogul court was a magically refined place, but undoubtedly filled with many hundreds more vigorous individuals than the two or three seated, poised with small flowers held between their fingers, favoured by some of its painters. This is particularly cruelly the case around the lead-up to the Second World War.

When we think of the politicians and soldiers of the early twentieth century they suffer under huge disadvantages, not the least being that they were obliged to carry out their duties in black and white. It is startling how massive the impact of black-and-white photography and film is on our sense of the period. Victorians and Edwardians detonate with painted colour—their arrogance and relentless sense of purpose like the firework finale to a two-and-a-half-century-long tradition of English ruling-class portraiture. Millais, Sargent and others were revelling in a shorthand established under the Stuarts. Regardless of the poor posture, listlessness or imbecility of the subject, a reliable job could be done. There is a Sargent portrait of a governor of Singapore in the National Portrait Gallery, all cream, gold and bursting moustache, that can hardly be contained: half imperial grandeur and half Studio 54. Our heads are filled with pre-twentieth-century images that emphasize colour. As the last century progressed, however, this tradition collapsed and the twitching black-and-white newsreel or stuffed and groomed official photograph took over. The effect has been incalculable—we live with a sense of politicians taking on a specific gloomy tone, allied to the querulous voices preserved but also distorted by the recording equipment of the time. The medium conspires to make everyone look shifty and pettish—or shiftless and petty—to a degree that just cannot be true. In his towering portrait by Millais, the brutal late Victorian warrior Lord Kitchener looks fabulous, a creature from myth, destroyer of infidels and Boers, humiliator of the French. But in black-and-white film in later life he looks comic, or idiotic in a sinister way. At the opposite end of the spectrum, the rare colour photos of Hitler look obscene and disturbing. He seems almost normal, like a human being—as though he has got away from the "correct" cosmological set of evil attributes under which he functioned in black and white. That the British statesmen of two world wars and the Depression should be in black and white all the time is simply too appropriate.

Were they worse politicians in themselves than their brightly coloured predecessors? Perhaps not. The interwar politicians are generally viewed as incredibly mediocre but Victorians could get away potentially with very little talent, sitting on most of the world's money, resources, land and technology and being able to decide casually over drinks on actions that would eviscerate some far-off country at the cost of almost no British casualties.

It is impossible not to think with awe of figures such as

Lord Kitchener or the megabrain Lord Salisbury. Their very stance implies a clockwork-regular, post-breakfast bowel movement of overwhelming proportions, generated while humming snatches of "Immortal, Invisible, God Only Wise." They stalk out of their devastated bathrooms with a mental note to send a stiff telegram to the French. These frightening and rather weird figures have all gone by the 1930s and it is not surprising that with such changed circumstances their successors look haggard and jerky.

NEVILLE CHAMBERLAIN sits at the heart of our bafflement with the 1930s. In newsreels he twitchily gestures at crowds or pauses awkwardly for the camera. It is as difficult to get any more of a sense of him than by staring at some extinct alphabet. The figure known to voters then, the commanding, iron-fisted modernizer of the Conservatives, the safe hands in a crisis, the magician cheered by crowds on his return from Munich, has vanished and this near-consensus view of the time has now completely evaporated. His clothes look silly, his moustache looks silly and we know him, or think we know him, to be a failure and a fool.

Winston Churchill creates a different kind of bafflement. His wartime images are now permanently burnt into our brains, with his slightly mad pugnacity rightly provoking an overwhelming sense of gratitude. But before the summer and autumn of 1940 he stood for everything backward and contemptible about Britain—a drunk, discredited, elderly aristocrat hating not just the Nazis but also the working classes and Indian independence and embracing a whole host of perverse and unhelpful causes. The breaker of the General Strike and mocker of Gandhi, Churchill inspired confidence in nobody and should have retired in the early thirties. Indeed, it could be argued that his wild public attacks on Hitler helped discredit the position he championed—just as everyone would cough and shuffle away when he began to sound off on some further elaborate scheme to arrest Indian nationalists.

But of course Churchill as a horrible old relic is as unrecoverable as Chamberlain the stern masterbrain. We can stare and stare at the newsreels and see Churchill simply preparing himself for greatness, waiting in the absurd shadows of MacDonald, Baldwin and Chamberlain to rescue the country. That he really does do so is one of the central facts of British life in the twentieth century, but it also confuses, distorts and conceals much else.

MY GRANDFATHER had been active in Conservative politics before the War and when in his house, as a ten- or eleven-year-old child, I would often be cornered and lectured at for hours with his stories of F. E. Smith, Austen Chamberlain (who looked like the Penguin from *Batman*) and others. He had one story of how as a boy he had gone to a Birmingham flower show with his father and shaken hands with Joseph Chamberlain, the dazzling Edwardian imperialist, who, confined to an invalid carriage, was judging an orchid contest there shortly before his death. This one tale aside, to my dismay I cannot remember *any* of my grandfather's hundreds of stories (or possibly dozens put on a repeat cycle). I sat there, hot-faced with boredom and resentment—and with no sense at all, of course, that he would himself have been filled with a matching sense of self-loathing at being reduced to talking at such an audience. Or perhaps he was motivated by a wish to pass on his perceptions to a world beyond his lifetime, in which

case my inattention has served him dreadfully. I have no idea
now how many of these stories were from his own experience
or how much these were simply tales out of Tory circles. My
own disgust for the whole milieu doesn't for a moment,
though, stop me from crying with frustration and much else
that my grandfather is now long dead and can no longer be
asked *What was it like then?* and that my mother is now long
dead and can no longer be asked *What else can you remember
apart from your honey-sandwich anecdote?*

BRITISH WEALTH and success had for a century been quite
cheaply bought. After the apocalyptic twenty years of war
with revolutionary and Napoleonic France, Waterloo had
marked an immense increase in British power. This power
and prestige had been maintained around the world through
constant if small-scale warfare. It is odd to think that the
Royal Navy was, with the peculiar blip of the Crimean War,
little used in the century after the defeat of Napoleon except
to chastise painfully easy targets such as slavers, Turks and
Chinese. It ferried troops and administrators around, went on
scientific expeditions, but rarely fired at anything much. The
navy was so huge and so technologically ahead of its com-
petitors that its mere existence made it very hard to imagine
anyone attacking Britain in any sustainable way—much like
the United States now. Most of Europe was marched across at
some point in the nineteenth century, much of it repeatedly,
leaving dead liberals lying in heaps, but Britain remained
inviolate, both physically and to a striking degree intellectu-
ally. The great nineteenth-century developments of mainland
European politics, the perception of a life-and-death struggle
between capital and labour, the rise of anarchism, of virulent

anti-Semitism or anti-clericalism, all passed Britain by while convulsing France, Germany, Russia and Italy. It is extremely strange to think that while the United States tore itself apart in civil war, while Italy and Germany became newly united countries in a series of spectacular battles and uprisings, while France was invaded, its army destroyed and Paris turned into a communist bastion ultimately blown to pieces by regular French troops with some 5,000 *communard* deaths, Britain drifted on with effectively no history (meaning "exciting events') at all, beyond specific innovations in industry, fashion, cakes, etc.

Of course Britain imposed plenty of "exciting events" on other countries, and its history lies elsewhere. But with the fluky exception of the Crimea it restricted its actions to punitive expeditions to extend control of Africa, India, Australasia and China—areas which British technology meant were effectively unable to fight back. One of the oddities of thinking about the British Empire has always been the assumption that somehow—compared to other empires—it was rather benign or even liberal.

Recently wandering around the military chapel attached to Les Invalides in Paris, I found myself feeling completely nauseated by the captured battle standards that decorate it. The horrible face of *French* imperialism seemed readily accessible there. Mainly Chinese or Vietnamese, these standards (some just little squares of cloth with a stitched single ideogram) had been "won" in some lopsided, late-nineteenth-century bloodbath with syphilitic, feverish French troops using repeating rifles and naval guns against feudatories clad in vermilion silk and armed with matchlocks and lucky hats. But my revulsion is purely an inherited one: British people have *always* lived with this image of the French Empire as disgusting and somehow illegitimate—licentious, cruel, underhanded and tinpot. This was how it was described by the Victorians themselves and my gorge was rising as part of a multi-generational response to Britain's black legend of French (and, of course, earlier Spanish) imperial wretchedness.

The clear value of these other empires' unacceptability was that somehow it helped make Britain's own more clean-limbed, unmucky and even-handed. And yet if a graph could ever be constructed for ammunition expenditure around the world in any given year after Waterloo it would be dominated (except in very specific patches such as the American Civil War) by bullets streaming from British weapons, cutting down rulers and their armies around the world. In modern terms Ghana, Pakistan, Sudan, New Zealand, innumerable regions of India, Burma, Afghanistan, Ukraine, China, Ethiopia, South Africa, Zimbabwe and Egypt (and I'm sure I have forgotten somewhere obvious) were all lashed by unanswerable firepower and technology, generally with as little serious intellectual rationale as any conjured up by Attila's Huns. Any local setbacks, such as General Gordon's in the Sudan or the Indian Mutiny, were viewed as almost unbelievable moral outrages to be crushed with completely deranged levels of violence. With the exception of a handful of bribed, lolling sultans and doomed chieftains pulled into Britain's orbit by trade or by fear of other colonial rivals, *nobody* ever agreed voluntarily to be ruled by some very odd people in red coats backed by a supporting cast of fever-ridden missionaries and some of the world's most grotesque Walrus-and-the-Carpenter-style traders. When we focus on all the fun things (trains, docks, English-language courses and so on) that filled the Empire, this immense violence (backed up of course by unlimited reservoirs of self-righteousness) tends to be forgotten or even excused. The French Empire on a map seems to offer a withered little parody of the British Empire and indeed offers an entertaining geographical game (Vietnam as against *the whole of India*, New Caledonia as against *Australia*, Chad as against *Nigeria*, and so on and so on) but it also holds up a mirror that shows how when we have no national or patriotic stake ourselves in a specific part of the world we can probably see much more clearly the sheer horror of European engagement with it. In effect we dare to mock the French for having done so much less harm than ourselves.

After about 1900, however, after one Georgian century of exciting, seat-of-the-pants dominance, and then a Victorian one of easy, arrogant dominance, everything changed for Britain. It had one last (and spectacular) throw when it gained control over most of the world's diamonds and gold in the Boer War, but it paid a huge price. Not only did that war cost vastly more in lives than had ever been imagined, it also helped generate a near apocalyptic atmosphere in Germany, whose rulers realized that the entire planet, outside a gloomy, cabbage-oriented little chunk of northern Europe, was to belong to a sprawling Anglo-America. The Boer War also suggested more generally both to allies and enemies that British strength had for some time been massively overestimated.

The price to be paid for this collision course was, of course, the First World War, which Britain and its allies won only through an overwhelming and finally Pyrrhic effort. Staring at the ruined international system of 1918, with 800,000 of its own dead, with a supremacy based only on the temporarily even greater ruin of its opponents, Britain's rulers must have felt both stunned and helpless. Now, with none of the technological, financial or military advantages it had enjoyed in the nineteenth century, Britain had to forge ahead, knowing that it had to defend both itself and its often frivolously gained colonial commitments pretty much everywhere against an appalling range of enemies. Territories picked up by a handful of malarial planters more or less for a laugh or by some naval expedition sent to correct some ancient and now long-forgotten slight suddenly turned into unlimited, indefensible (in two senses) liabilities.

Not only did the end of the First World War find Britain as an exhausted victor unable to keep a peace that few of its opponents valued, but because of its victory Britain was oddly unreformed. Nobody would wish any country to go through the nightmare let loose across most of Europe in this period, but everywhere new and notionally more modern forms of government were springing up and consolidating. While across Europe his opposite numbers and relations were being shot or exiled, George V still glumly collected vast albums of stamps featuring miniature pictures of himself and inveighed dimly against Impressionism in art. If the Napoleonic Wars had in the end endorsed as successful a British state little changed since the Revolution of 1688, then the First World War offered, *just*, a further endorsement. It is certainly true that the early twentieth century saw the British aristocracy being shoved aside by non-aristocratic elements, but in an early-twenty-first-century world in which arbitrary selections of semi-retired people continue cheerfully to wrap themselves in ermine and sit in the House of Lords, this is not a startling development on a scale that other European politicians would recognize.

In the early twenties it seemed briefly that Europe might restabilize around British and French enforcement and American money. The attempt to re-create the lost Edwardian financial world fell to bits, however, in the Depression and evaporated the only scenario that would have allowed Britain to survive: the hope that everyone was getting too wealthy to bother about things like, for example, wars of revenge. It also left Britain with two enormous and unattackable enemies with different reasons for not liking British global influence: the Soviet Union, whose whole point was to export revolution to countries often controlled by Britain, and the United States, whose founding beliefs were anti-colonial and nationalistic and whose good will to Britain did not extend to the British Empire. That these countries became Britain's allies against the two empires of Japan and Germany that did the immediate and overwhelming damage to Britain in 1939–42 did not make them necessarily anything other than *very* provisional friends indeed.

It is therefore almost as though technology knew what symbolically it had to do: flickery black and white was needed to portray all the world's statesmen—but it was particularly appropriate for Britain's. The speed of Britain's diminution was breathtaking. Everything that had seemed to make Britain a superpower before the disastrous summer of 1914 now conspired to make it impotent. The modernization that it had pioneered now swamped it as others caught up. The huge populations of the Soviet Union and the United States threatened it; the huge populations of India and China now made the future of empire completely problematic. Any further war was by all standards unaffordable for Britain.

WHERE DOES James Bond come from? He may have been invented in the early 1950s, but his roots lay for the most part in Ian Fleming's reading between the wars.

At the simplest level he was named after an American ornithologist, famous for his work on West Indian birds and whose name had the right, straight, tough air for Fleming's hero. But what about his antecedents? This is a very murky area. At massive psychological cost it might be possible to rummage around indefinitely in the world of pre-War pulp fiction, but Bond's *Homo erectus* or indeed his Piltdown Man could easily be lurking pretty much anywhere.

The very obvious antecedents lie in the strange late-nineteenth-century and early-twentieth-century world of "Imperial Leather" fiction. It is strange enough that so many people in the early twenty-first century rub themselves down in the shower with a soap called Imperial Leather (some non-British readers may simply refuse to believe this) without any specific sense of unease that, nude and vulnerable, they should be reaching for something that so neatly implies a specific form of British sadomasochism. The word combination "Imperial Leather" seems so clearly to conjure up some vision of a hideously mutilated trooper's naked corpse pinned to the saddle of his horse, stumbling through the burning Sudanese desert, that it comes up a bit short as a mere toiletry. Possibly many of its users simply assume, reasonably, that it is "Imperial Lather." In any event, "Imperial Leather" fiction's finest hour was probably H. Rider Haggard's novel *King Solomon's Mines*, which, as a sort of hymn to the magical worlds of southern Africa, transcends any genre, but in its heart of hearts is a disturbing and nasty book with blacks doomed to be either loyal or treacherous and invariably credulous, and whites domineering and ruthless but on balance strangely noble. As a source for Ian Fleming's work it is interesting because much of the book's power comes from its sense of place (which Fleming would parallel in his love of the United States and the West Indies). It is also one of the first books to associate military equipment and erectile tissue in the Bond manner. Haggard is very good at talking about supplies, cartridges and rifle manufacturers and the Bond books get some of their power from the same source — the sense of ballistic expertise, of Fleming cross-examining various obsessives to make sure that all his talk about sniper rifles and magazine size was correct, however absurd.

Another clear influence is John Buchan, who created much of the formula — plucky, no-nonsense British hero (Richard Hannay), mad villains, exciting chases, right-wing agenda. Interestingly, both *King Solomon's Mines* and Buchan's *Greenmantle* feature a messianic white hero who will be the inspiration and leader for countless Africans and Muslims respectively: a strangely naked fantasy of how on earth Britain could carry on ruling much of the world. The clearest debt Fleming has to Buchan is the criminal mastermind obsessed by the pleasure of anarchistic destruction rather than gain. Figures such as Lumley in the splendidly demented *The Power-House* ("As I read your character — and I think I am right — you are an artist in crime") do much the same thing, complete with the sort of unhinged disquisitions on the banality of civilization that Blofeld or Mr. Big would enjoy so much. It seems wholly symbolic of how the world had moved on—and a kindness—that Buchan should have died in early 1940, just too early to see the British army's overwhelming disaster in France. And just too early to see General Sir Edmund Ironside, the Chief of the Imperial General Staff, whose earlier heroic and exotic career had inspired Buchan's most famous books, playing such a leading role in that disaster.

Beyond Buchan is the locked sub-basement of writers such as Dornford Yates and "Sapper" (Herman Cyril McNeile). Their books are effectively unreadable now, so it is hard to conjure up how they were ever of any value. In any event, unlike Buchan or Rider Haggard, these were writers of very low ambition and so can hardly be overly castigated because long after their deaths their social and racial attitudes seem a bit quaint.

There is also the aristocratic quest novel—the enormous bestseller being Anthony Hope's *The Prisoner of Zenda*, which generated an endless sub-genre. These are echoed undoubtedly in Fleming's work—not least through the sort of exchanges which make it plausible for the villains to discuss their plans "as one gentleman to another" rather than simply killing Bond on the spot. The great difference of course is the level of ambition in the villains—Graf von Nortibitz or Baron Nastikoff on the whole want to do pretty low-grade things like impugning a lady's honour or stealing a glass sword rather than, say, murdering the entire population of Miami Beach. The pleasure of "Ruritania" and its related countries is the feeling that they are a toybox come to life (echoed nicely in Fleming's own *Chitty Chitty Bang Bang*) and this in the end is *not* the atmosphere of the Bond books, except perhaps towards the end, with Blofeld in his loony Japanese castle. It is impossible not to feel, though, that beneath the crumpled grey uniformity of their post-war-international-criminal clothing Fleming's villains do not hide a little bit of the lemon-yellow uniform, spurred boot and glittering monocle of their predecessors.

The other very obvious precedent is provided by Sax Rohmer's Fu-Manchu novels. Now I am completely happy to concede that Rohmer's contemporary Arnold Bennett was a very great writer and Rohmer was a national disgrace, but if you tug the lid off *Anna of the Five Towns* there is a far less powerful smell than that emitted by, say, *The Daughter of Doctor Fu-Manchu*. More can be learned from these books about a notionally bluff and self-confident imperial Britain than almost any other source. As with Fleming, Rohmer may be basically unserious, but his books and his enormous success, pouring out novels and film adaptations for decades from 1913 onwards, are fascinating—a pullulating heap of racist neuroses about secret Chinese plans to destroy the "white race" married to an infinite capacity for inventing ingenious new murder methods. And who can in all honesty not warm to these stories with their trapdoors, silent poisons, dacoits and secret cellars bursting with lethal fungi ("'It is my fly-trap!' shrieked the Chinaman. 'And I am the god of destruction!'")? Researching this book has not by any means been all fun and games, but Rohmer's books ("'They die like flies!' screamed Fu-Manchu, with a sudden febrile excitement") are a clear compensation, however patently unacceptable by most criteria. It has to be said that Dr. No appears a relatively run-of-the-mill, almost clerkly figure compared with his equally medically qualified predecessor. Fleming steals directly from Rohmer in the fiendish giant-centipede scene in *Dr. No*, but more frequently there are more straightforward echoes of both subject matter and prose style ("her lips, even in repose, were a taunt").

Far more appealing is to plot some sort of antecedent in Graham Greene and Eric Ambler, both politically alert left-wing writers, making use of the thriller format to make interesting didactic points. Ambler's spectacular novels, particularly *Journey into Fear*, *A Coffin for Dimitrios* and *Cause for Alarm*, have many Bond elements: interesting locales, omnipresent and omniscient dark forces, appealing heroes. The background of Fascist Europe in the 1930s is more palpably felt in Ambler than in any conventional British novels of the period, most of which carry on as though there is no international crisis at all—or indeed as if foreign countries do not exist. *Cause for Alarm* is both a wonderful book and a primer in late-thirties paranoia—a paranoia which in practice turned out to be pure documentary realism.

If Fleming could simply be seen as the descendant of Buchan, Greene and Ambler, we could all relax, but there is one hideous relative, long confined to private, secure care. In my brighter moments I think of Fleming as Ambler's inheritor; at darker times however he is the beneficiary of the extraordinarily prolific Captain W. E. Johns. Johns invented Biggles, a British pilot of an uncertain age who flew his way through dozens of adventures from 1932 onwards in a chaotic melee with Hun swine throughout both world wars and beyond, backed up by his friends Algy and Ginger. These books really are genuinely worthless. Sometimes I wake up, eyes staring sightlessly, caked in sweat, buffeted by the insight that nobody wants: Is Bond just Biggles with a cock? Is any claim for Bond's significance flat in the dust from the outset? I have some dim memory of one novel featuring Biggles strapped to a rock with squids hauling themselves out of the water to eat him, surrounded by derisively laughing Malay cut-throats, but to fact-check this would mean reading through such acres of drivel it would make a stronger man than me crack.

It is definitely fair to say that there is a bit of Biggles in Bond, but I hope to show there is something more. Fleming's books may be a deranged cocktail made from Imperial Leather, fungus-manipulating Chinese super-criminals ("with a brow like Shakespeare and a face like Satan"—stop!), Ruritanian swordsmen and square-jawed Hun-bashers, but they transmuted into something much more interesting.

FLEMING'S FRIVOLOUS and narcissistic enjoyment of the late 1930s was entirely characteristic of Britain as a whole, aside from the politicians and soldiers staring in increasing panic across the Channel. As the economy gradually recovered, Britain, like a handful of other countries such as Sweden, stumbled onto the future: a consumerist, light industry/clerical/hobbyist future. Stanley Baldwin's genial, lazy persona hovered over a nation listening to the radio, smoking pipes, using Hoovers, fiddling with bicycles and cars. Driving into London from Heathrow Airport still remains the quintessential British 1930s experience—the rows of large if somewhat flimsy houses, the Gillette razor-blade factory, the strip developments provoked by greater mass car ownership. This is the world derided by George Orwell in his novel *Coming Up for Air*, but we can now see its appeal—the pleasures of electricity and tarmac, talkies and weekends. Of course it was not very heroic but it was the world to be discovered by the rest of Western Europe after 1945 and the rest of the rest of Europe after 1989. There is a limited narrative drama in buying things on hire-purchase or popping into Woolworth's, but the humdrum was something that would come to be valued overwhelmingly as events unfolded and Britain's peculiarly vulnerable role as a global superpower without the resources or ideas left to support itself came into plain view.

FOR ME AND many others Cole Porter's "Night and Day" sums up a great deal about the 1930s. This poor old song has been so heavily picked over that it seems a shame to mention it again. Is it a song of obsession or of relaxed infatuation, is it happy or sad? How could such perfect lyrics be matched to such perfect music? For me, from the perspective of now, it stands for all the possibilities that could have been there in the 1930s. Fred Astaire's magical singing implies a whole world of intimacy and tranquillity: of private life, of sex, of dreaming. It is a preview of pop consumerism, of just being left alone. It is the cocktail-shaker world of Fleming and his bored cronies, but it is also democratic, happy, modern and popular. Britain was very far from being a blameless bystander in the 1930s. It was still willing to use overwhelming violence—most recently in Palestine—when its interests were threatened. But Britain was also a country that had been severely frightened by what modern war meant and that was starting to realize the serious consequences of being a great power after a century of what now seemed to have been a frivolous and easy supremacy. As a new war loomed in 1938, all of this manifested itself in a desperate wish to be left alone that became dysfunctional. The orgiastic crowds that greeted Chamberlain's humiliating and cowardly behaviour at the Munich Conference and his acquiescence in the destruction of Czechoslovakia, one of Europe's last remaining democracies, seem in a way almost admirable and sane. Nobody in Britain wanted to be a superman, no one wanted some form of race-blood *Götterdämmerung*. They wanted to chose curtain materials and watch Hitchcock movies.

Whenever I hear the recording of Chamberlain's weirdly peevish and unconvincing declaration of war it seems nearly impossible to remain standing. What icy despair his words must have provoked as they crackled from myriad radios, proclaiming the end of all hope.

Chapter Two

THE STUFFED COBRA

For every male child even as late as the early 1970s, when I became a fully sentient part of that total, the Second World War was everywhere. Every game, every conversation, every television programme seemed in some way to spring from the War—a ceaseless round of Airfix model planes, *Commando* comics, *Dad's Army*, military games, Action Man and dreams of visiting the Imperial War Museum, a form of childhood that had been consecrated in Britain since the War itself.

I have a vivid memory of one happy summer reenacting the RAF's epic Dam Busters raid in our living room. I never had quite enough Lego bricks to make more than a single Lancaster bomber and only that through roping in all sorts of implausible shapes which undermined any sense of documentary truth. Lego then remained true to its relentlessly decent Danish roots and great care had been taken to use jolly colours and no shapes that could be construed as even slightly weapony. This was fine for the tots of Denmark, wiling away happy hours clicking together model nursery schools or yogurt factories, but in the murkier world of British childhood, where the crying need was for models of coastal gun batteries or V-2 launch sites, Lego bricks fell well short. In any event, the little nubbles on the top of each brick that allowed it to be joined to its neighbour meant that any weapons system was not only brightly coloured but strikingly nubbled.

Anyway, my Lancaster bomber instead of having a bouncing bomb had a small glass marble which I skipped/bounced across the floor—a faintly plausible dark-green carpet—into the mighty Möhne dam, thereby fatally crippling the Nazi war effort. The dam, after many experiments, was made of a row of old Ladybird board books, ideal because they could be slightly opened and set up like thin simple tents. They looked, of course, a bit silly, but fulfilled the role admirably by falling over if hit with sufficient force by the bouncing bomb.

So, with appropriate radio chit-chat between the tense pilots and tremendous engine noises, the festively parti-coloured nubbled model plane banked steeply over the green carpet, dodging heavy flak, incredibly flying only a few inches above the ground—the fruit of months of training: too high and the bomb would sink, not bounce; too low and the plane crashed—the crew pouring sweat. The plane released its glass marble. It was away: bouncing once, twice and blasting a hole in the Möhne dam that flooded the whole valley. Engines shot out, the Lancaster tried frantically to bank away but instead slammed into the dam, scattering blue and yellow fragments everywhere and knocking flat *Farmyard Friends*, with its painting of a duckling having a bath on the front.

When I think of the sheer brain-churning mental effort that made such hopeless materials into something my ten-year-old self was totally absorbed by I feel profoundly grateful for the arrival of computer games and other vastly more worthwhile things. The ease and pleasure of playing *Grand Theft Auto* or

Medal of Honor must open up vast areas of intellectual space in today's children.

I always think of that crashing Lego plane as summing up the sad state of post-war British life and the Second World War obsession, but it was just a small part of a very rich brew. *Commando* comics and heaps of others were crammed with stories of derring-do and had a succulent, lip-smacking enthusiasm for sub-sub-Goya violence that makes them now extremely disturbing to read. The carnage they portrayed and the sense that the British (and the occasional American) were crusaders hacking their way through a swamp of square-headed or yellow foes, that no death was too bad for such filth and that a wry sense of humour got Tommy through, put children very directly in touch with a debased version of wartime propaganda. I remember one story in the Burmese jungle where a soldier described as a "plucky cockney" holds back hordes of Japanese, eventually doing so only by swinging his rifle butt at them, before disappearing beneath waves of soldiers presented as buck-toothed, slit-eyed maniacs screaming "Banzai." The remarkable British general in Burma, William Slim, had in 1944 reminded his men that their enemies in the jungle were not humans but "insects." It now seems very odd that the normal invective of a wartime emergency was carried over into the world of suburban children thirty years later.

War games were also essential—every grass incline a slit trench, every stick a rifle, every pinecone a hand-grenade. Every playtime seemed to be devoted to loving reconstructions of El Alamein or D-Day, so loving indeed that one child had a gold front tooth to replace one knocked out during an overenthusiastic Defence of Tobruk.

All these activities were tied together by the Imperial War Museum—a sort of Potala Palace for southeastern male British children, crowded with real tanks and planes, elaborate dioramas and grisly memorabilia of a kind that gave visits there an air of exceptional pilgrimage. And beyond this, of course, was the elaborate kingdom of Airfix soldiers. These tiny, inch-and-a-bit-high plastic troops celebrated a vast range of countries and uniforms: Russian infantry, U.S. Marines, Afrika Korps (everyone's first romantic encounter with the German language—who could not love an organization called the *Afrika Korps*?) and so on. Amusingly these had been made and modelled to somewhat different specifications at different points in Airfix's history so the Parachute Regiment had magnificent, detailed uniforms and weapons and beautifully sculpted features whereas (a bitter disappointment) the British Infantry Support Group were dwarfish, blobby-faced and to a slightly but noticeably wrong scale. There was even a very dull RAF Personnel box stuffed with tiny people pushing boxes of things and standing about with spanners—their only saving grace was that they could be used as dead civilians in the Lego wreckage of some Nazi-torched town. For thousands of children these soldiers almost defined the idea of "playing indoors." I remember once with a friend amalgamating astonishing numbers of boxes of soldiers to create a minutely detailed Anzio landing on the admittedly undulating and somewhat fluffy red carpet in my bedroom.

What was it about the British experience of the Second World War that created this frankly pathological situation by the 1970s? The stuff above could go on indefinitely: at least the reader has been spared fond details about a doll called Action Man and his astonishing array of plastic guns—and the infinity of board games, television programmes and newspaper memoirs that crowded in from every side. For very obvious reasons German children were not playing with such toys, indeed very few children around the world were. It is hard to imagine many Americans in the 1970s doing pint-size reconstructions of Iwo Jima—they were too busy enjoying the present day. Of course, boys love weapons, love war movies and love anything involving fighting, but it was the incredibly detailed specific experience of British attitudes that now seems so odd and which has, of course, in the twenty-first century converted itself into a bottomless appetite in the now adult population for books on the Second World War, following their childhood indoctrination.

How can we understand this odd behaviour? And how does James Bond stalk through it in such a strange, providential way?

THERE MUST SURELY BE a great book to be written about the British experience of the War. A book that would somehow unite fighting in different theatres of combat, working in a tank factory, in a hospital, in a steel mill, down a mine, flying U-boat patrols over the north Atlantic, racing to abandon sinking ships, manning an anti-aircraft gun; a book that would be about the private and the public; a book that would allow the vast complex of the wartime economy to be shown, with flows of shipping and factory output and troop movements and calorie intakes arranged in ever more zany, multi-coloured charts like some unrealizable, profoundly disturbing, forever trapped-in-development computer game.

It is one of the most blatantly strange aspects of modern Britain that almost nobody has attempted or even glanced at a book approaching such an idea. The Second World War for the British has to do with personal anecdote or with military campaigns—never with ideology or economy or any of the issues routinely studied in relation to the Nazis or Soviets. Schools and universities crawl with courses studying the Nazis, many of this country's most brilliant academics pore over the entrails of Hitler's regime, while Britain's own experience of the War and the surrounding years goes almost unstudied. Instead, serious thought is replaced by a small range of shorthands: loveable *Dad's Army*, the clever nostalgia of *Brideshead Revisited*, the POWs escaping from Colditz, and so on. Or there are boring projects like "The 1940s House" where a modern family live in the manner of a wartime family, which of course they can't do except at the level of eating Spam—for obvious if regrettable reasons the producers recoiling from the necessary bit of realism in, for example, randomly killing someone in the volunteer family.

Britain's obsession with the War shies away from anything approaching the detailed understanding that we now have of Hitler's Germany or of Stalin's Russia. There are a tiny handful of writers—Angus Calder and Paul Addison are almost the only ones that come to mind—who have been consistently and valuably interested, but otherwise it is a blank. School exams and degree courses almost ignore any study of Britain in the War. No conversation is complete without some discussion of D-Day or Dunkirk or Churchill's greatness, yet it all occurs against an extremely hastily sketched-in backdrop. Could it be that when we routinely accuse Americans of being historically blind or over-selective, we are ourselves much less alert than we would like to believe?

*

For Ian Fleming, the War meant a total change in his life and that was true for virtually the entire population. For many this change was a very unwilling one. The remarkable scenes of mass fervour in 1914 were, for very obvious reasons, nowhere matched. The sense of gloom in Chamberlain's voice as he announced the outbreak of hostilities was a fair reflection of a country trapped in an unmanageable welter of impossible commitments with no ideological back-up to enforce any view of the upcoming conflict. France and Britain are strikingly similar in this respect: weary victors of 1918 adrift and declining, frightened by the fascism and communism that had been summoned up by that ruinous victory. But for some, such as Fleming, there was an old-fashioned and as it proved inadequate sense of honour about 1939: that here was a chance for a new generation to take up the appalling sacrifice of the previous one. This was not a view, interestingly, much shared by those who had actually fought in 1914–1918: most British commanders and many British politicians shared with the French a dread of what was to come. The Germans on the other hand had concluded that victory was possible and could be gained by technology and by an overwhelming yoking of national and military goals apparently missing in the Great War—an emphasis that makes Germany at the outbreak of the earlier conflict, with its funny spiked helmets and antique Prussianisms, quite wrongly look almost quaint. The British concluded that nothing could be worth a repetition of what had happened—the two decades of anti-Versailles arguments, of Sassoon's and Owen's poetry, of *Goodbye to All That*, of a profound pacifism which meant that, even as Hitler was ripping up every treaty, many still focused all their hopes on the Geneva disarmament talks—all this gave Britain no basis for fighting. What to us now seems a grotesque series of failures—the refusal to do anything faintly impressive about the Japanese invasion of Manchuria, the Italian invasion of Abyssinia, the German and Soviet roles in the Spanish Civil War and then, the cherry on the cake, the agreement to Czechoslovakia's dismemberment—must be seen against this backdrop. It is astonishing just how many allies and potential allies Britain had scattered all over Europe, all weaker than itself and all looking to be led by the First World War's principal victor. But no lead was coming and one by one the Germans turned and ruined every one of them. The acrimony and uncertainty this generated we still live with today—the amazing luck and heroism of the late summer of 1940 that turned Britain into a beacon of hope has to be seen against years of connivance and betrayal, perhaps best summed up in the figure of Sir John Simon, a politician who managed somehow to be both slimy and desiccated, and who haunted the 1930s, always seeming to pop up somewhere with some grotesque sell-out proposal.

Of course what is very hard to deal with when looking at this period is the sense that this British turning from violence and a national fear of death is wholly admirable. There were still areas where ruthlessness was possible—the ferocity with which Montgomery and others put down the "Arab Revolt" in Palestine, for example, but overall it is clear that Britain no longer believed in the sort of brutal enthusiasm for warfare of the kind that had held it in good stead for centuries. The British in India are not a very admirable gang between the wars but what is interesting is that the massacre at Amritsar (1921) was so widely condemned and felt to be unacceptable, whereas only a few years before Tibet had been blithely invaded and the entire Raj had been built over many years on one long bloodbath of on the whole cheap victories cheered on merrily at home. The negotiations with Indian nationalists in the 1930s may have oozed bad faith and the repression by the British was real, but it belonged to a different world from, say, the 1937 "pacification" of Nanking by the Japanese, which left a quarter of a million Chinese dead.

British imperial attitudes had *never* been as engulfingly ferocious as those of the Japanese or Nazis, but there was a definite moral blankness. The Royal Marines monument in the Mall in London stands in for many others in its casual savagery, with its bronze relief of the 1900 attack on Tientsin, showing a seemingly helpless Chinese being run through with a bayonet while most of his colleagues flee in a cowardly way. Clearly there was something immensely violent and callous about the British government (and this of course is to skate over the terrifying, locust-like behaviour by British settlers everywhere since the seventeenth century) but British popular reaction to the First World War was broadly a feeling that this could not happen again. The indelible images of that war—most potently of course of the Western Front but also of such astonishing spasms of violence as the British repression of the Irish Rebellion of 1916 which left central Dublin looking like Ypres' twin town—and the relentless emphasis in the 1920s on Remembrance Sunday, the colossal array of monuments to the dead (the largest investment in funerary commemoration since the time of the Pharaohs) combined to mute the bloodthirstiness of British history.

This huge ethical change had two effects. The first was to make Britain completely useless as a resolute foe to Nazism (this role fell to the Soviet Union). The second was

to make Britain as the War progressed into a genuine democratic alternative to Nazism. Before the catastrophe at
Dunkirk, Britain seemed unable to articulate this, even
feebly, both because its Conservative and backward-looking
leadership rightly feared such logic but also because you
cannot come up with convincing reasons for doing something if you don't want to do it. Britain fought in 1939 only
because it knew it had no choice left except that of becoming
a feeble Nazi vassal. It had progressively waved goodbye to
unappetizing allies such as Italy, to more appealing ones
such as Austria and Czechoslovakia and, with most other
European nations now making deals with the Germans, it
had either itself to succumb or to fight. The one fundamentally correct assumption of the late 1930s, that Hitler and
Stalin would have to fight each other, was also now messed up
for two years, in part by the woefully cackhanded efforts
of the British to ally with the Soviet Union. In a crowded
field the story of the British mission to the USSR is one of the
most pathetic—leading Stalin in 1939 to realize, correctly,
that Britain simply wished to trick him into fighting Hitler to
save Britain the trouble, and thus fomenting the astonishing
Nazi–Soviet Pact. And so, shorn of almost all allies and with
almost no cards to play, Britain, with a similarly depressive
France, was cornered into fighting. It doesn't in any serious
way detract from the real heroism and courage of what many
British people achieved in the War to see the origins of that
involvement as highly problematic and the country's beacon
role as grudging and almost accidental.

IF THE 1930s were an argument for having people like Ian
Fleming dragged before People's Courts then the War itself

showed the real opportunities of Britain's system. Entirely through connections rather than merit Fleming found himself in naval intelligence during the War and he seems to have been brilliant and expert in that role. With all the entitlement, arrogance and panache of his class he poured out ideas, pulled rank, oiled Anglo-American relations and generally became an interesting part of the impressive if strained machinery that pulled Britain through.

His only active service was in helping refugees flee France in 1940 but he was also bobbing about offshore at the quintessential pointless British disaster of the "Dieppe Raid," a deranged attempt masterminded by Lord Mountbatten to test German defences—which were tested only in as much as they clearly worked very well, leaving some 1,000 dead on a beach to no gain whatsoever. Fleming had good ideas and bad ideas, but he was besotted with the small action—with the idea that guts and personal ingenuity could win through. This love of special forces, of commandos, of spies was the bane of American and Soviet planners who saw that the War would be won through the use of a sickening juggernaut of industrial output, but it was central to the British self-image. This was very odd considering that Britain had pioneered in every way the use of technological, financial and military superiority to smother the planet for generations and was to use during this war the ultimate expression of that expertise—the area bombing of civilians in cities—even as the plucky individualists were being casually picked off by bored German sentries. Fleming was intimately involved with groups of specialists that were to be sent into occupied Europe behind the British army to comb through installations for secret weapons and gadgets in a sort of ultimate expression of military hobbyism. It was a reasonable fantasy for a power in decline, that had learnt the price of mass warfare in 1914–1918 and didn't intend to go there again. Fleming was at the heart of that fantasy — coming up with all kinds of bizarre schemes that relied on individual pluck and initiative and which, while reasonable as part of a genuine policy of total war, were in the end irrelevant to the War's outcome.

My favourite Fleming scheme was the fake radio station that broadcast misleading and subtly disheartening information of various kinds to U-boat crews and which seems to have been fully manned and running for at least two years. The idea that some quite scarce British German-speakers were siphoned off into such an abstract project seems unimaginable. But this love of special forces, of the individual boffin who cracks some military problem, of the single, isolated hero whose initiative saves the day, remained a tremendously important part of the British psyche. The harsh reality of millions of British soldiers and factory workers grinding Germany to fragments through attritional technology was, in the minds of many, importantly offset by this much happier idea. It has threaded its way through the intervening years, through endless war movies, through the nationally unique obsession with the secret services and through the latest generation's obsession with the SAS, whose origins in the Desert War dig into the same artesian well of pluck as Lawrence of Arabia in the First World War or Orde Wingate and his Burma-jungle troops in the Second. It is a bit leaden even to say it, but of course this chivalrous, romantic, freebooting, aristocratic world finds its most famous outlet in Ian Fleming's post-war invention.

*

THE GREAT Anglo-American machinery, in which Fleming was a microscopic but perky cog, which ground through the Mediterranean, south Asia, the Pacific and western Europe and which burnt to the ground most of Germany's and Japan's cities and civilization, was a startlingly different beast from the Britain that had footled and screwed up in 1939–41. In late 1944 Fleming went on an exuberant global jaunt on behalf of the Admiralty that summed up so much of Britain's extraordinarily transformed position. He flew first to Egypt, home of an enormous British army, the Suez Canal Zone now forming one of the largest military bases in the world—the home of an army which now, for the imperially minded, was at a stretch that would have seemed incredible to the Victorians: dominating the Red Sea, holding the previously French and Italian colonies of Syria, Lebanon, Libya and Somalia and humming with plans to bring them under permanent British control.

He then flew on to Ceylon, now a key British base and part of a cat's cradle of bases that crisscrossed the Indian Ocean, making the very few semi-independent countries in the region wholly dependent on British goodwill. Again, countries which had always eluded Britain's grip were now free to be disposed of at will—Madagascar, a French possession successfully invaded by Britain in 1942, and Iran, jointly ruled with the Soviets and home to the enormous British oil facility at Abadan, one of several bases that ensured the Persian Gulf was also uncontested British territory.

Fleming then flew to India to see his brother Peter. India was certainly in some disarray and anti-British feeling was considerable, but with the focus remaining on the defeat of Japan, British power-projection was formidable, with the Japanese army in Burma reeling from defeat to defeat and an elaborate plan for the invasion of the whole of southeast Asia underway—a plan that was to result the following year in a mad final efflorescence of British rule in countries as diverse as Vietnam and Java.

He then flew on to Australia, the whole trip being in pursuit of how best to organize a substantial British fleet to aid the Americans in the Pacific, now that the War in Europe was winding down. The British Pacific Fleet of 1945 put the Royal Navy in a very junior role in relation to the U.S. Pacific Fleet, but nonetheless marked the most substantial return of Britain to the Pacific in a generation. In due course all the British colonies scattered across the Pacific and much used and abused by both Japanese and Allied forces throughout the War were returned to Britain, making it once again the largest colonial landlord in the Pacific (as it remained too, in a somnolent way, in the Caribbean).

After flying through Pearl Harbor and on across the United States, Fleming arrived back in Britain to supervise the special units he ran at the Admiralty designated to fan out across Germany in the wake of the British army looking for secret weapons, unusual experiments and so on. And here of course was the most extraordinary thing of all—an enormous British army right at the heart of Germany. This was the strategic outcome that had come to be viewed as inconceivably mad and implausible by British Imperial planners towards the end of the First World War and which had made the Armistice seem desirable. It was the continuing sense that the successful invasion of Germany was simply too surreal a possibility that had haunted the crises of the 1930s and the Phoney War. And now, here was Germany, the country that had for more than thirty years pressed down on British policy-makers as a sort of nightmare, completely and irredeemably crushed. With troops throughout western Europe, with British military rule coming to northern Germany, and looming administration over chunks of Berlin and Vienna, with its armies also dominating the Adriatic and the Aegean, Britain for a few months realized a global reach which would have been a fantasy to anyone at any earlier point in its history.

Fleming had a brilliant time on his great global tour and well he might. He seems to have spent it in a riot of sex and drink and fine dining, in between discussions about how to expand and consolidate British naval assets around the world. The possibilities—on all topics—must have seemed endless. Not only were Germany and Japan wrecked utterly, but Britain's traditional European colonial rivals were shattered too—other empires existed only at Britain's say-so: Italy's vanished completely; France disappeared permanently from the Middle East; the Dutch, ruined and exhausted by the Occupation, never had a serious chance of reimposing themselves in southeast Asia.

Of course this was all an illusion, as was to become very rapidly clear. Almost all the manpower came either from British recruits eager to return home or from Indian volunteers who had no interest at all in fighting Ho Chi Minh or policing Abadan. The British High Command was riddled with anxiety that whether in Jakarta or Athens, Trieste or Jerusalem, Addis Ababa or Rangoon, the British were even in the short term unwelcome and in the medium term were sitting ducks, reliant on two huge factors way outside Britain's control—the ability of the Americans and the Soviets to, in their different ways, really dictate events.

With the dropping of the atomic bombs many people in

Britain just wanted all the danger and excitement to end. Some, particularly in the Labour Party, were excited by the idea of south Asian independence as a concrete expression of what the Second World War had come to be fought for. Others, many others, simply resented being shot at and given horrible illnesses in hot countries when they could be at home. But some were profoundly upset by what they saw as a threatened unravelling of everything that had made Britain great. Fleming's elated tour marked a moment of real triumph in the face of overwhelming horror, a result that we can all still marvel at. But it also contained all the seeds of the end of the British Empire and the bitter wistfulness among many that would—to turn from the cosmic to the more frivolous—ultimately create Fleming's own enormous fan base.

All this is important to understanding the Britain that emerged after the War and the Britain which Bond did so much to buoy up. Every other major European combatant under such a weight of failure and humiliation had buckled completely. This meant going through a terrible fire that created a new order in that country—sometimes several changes of order—by 1945/46. Everywhere there were vast convulsions going on—whether in Germany or France or Italy, or across the Middle East and Asia. Regime change was almost universal and astonishing. Someone sitting in outer space who fell asleep in 1935 and woke up fifteen years later would have been completely baffled. The impoverished, semi-occupied semi-colonized mega-disaster of China was en route to being the unified communist superpower we now live with. The USSR had a seemingly endless aggressive future. The United States could do what it liked with little reference to any wartime ally. The enemies which had needed such efforts to destroy,

Germany and Japan, now appeared strangely small and feeble compared to the three behemoths. Britain's future, on hold during the emergency of national survival, was again threatened on every side.

SHORTLY AFTER starting work in the mid-eighties, I spent a happy few months living with an uncle and aunt in the English countryside. I had not known them well before and they turned out—like everyone—to be tangled up in the British Empire.

My uncle had done his national service at the time of the invasion of the Suez Canal and the Cyprus "Troubles," had been trained in all kinds of things by the army with limited application in later life and was shuffled about geographically like many other recruits in this confused and weird period. His wife, however, was much more firmly imbedded. Her father had been a magistrate in the Punjab and at independence had decided to stay in Lahore as a justice for the Pakistani government. Before independence, the rest of his family took ship back to England: one daughter was doomed to become my aunt.

The picture she gave of England as it loomed out of the cold, dirty fog in the forties was one of complete horror. Having grown up with the usual impedimenta of ayahs, peacocks, jungly flowers, bright colours, monsoons and privilege, my aunt landed in an England completely monochrome, icy, dreary and devastated. For those who had lived in England throughout the War the late forties were merely a further round of grimness (rationing and shortages but with at least the killing stopped), but for someone who was a young girl, raised on stories of English wonderfulness in a part of India far from the War, the almost science-fiction freakishness of what she actually encountered was overwhelming. This was a country with no fuel, no food, no money and facing total ruin.

Through a strange coincidence I once spent some days working in Lahore, and I went to visit the grave of my aunt's father, who had died in Pakistan in the 1950s. It was in the European cemetery some way from the old centre of town, well kept and appealing. A gardener cleaned up the grave, we put fresh flowers on it and that was that. I felt a complete fraud being involved at all: he was not a blood relative and I knew too little of his story to be moved. It was very strange though to be the first relative, however ersatz, ever to visit his grave. It was a brief encounter with a world which could still be described by people who had experienced it and yet it had been a world in which departure meant for almost everyone an immense rift, where it was quite normal to die thousands of miles from "home" and where the news of death would arrive through a cold telegram.

SINCE THIS imploding world was the world in which James Bond appeared, it needs to be delineated quite carefully. Despite the greyness and chilblains, the late 1940s are generally viewed in a favourable light and some remarkable things were indeed done. It is impossible on any sane scale not to feel an overwhelming sense of wonder at the achievement of Clement Attlee and his Labour government. Their humane single-mindedness in making sense of the horrors of the War through the creation of a new social order based on fairness and inclusion rather than class-hatred and coercion makes all other post-war governments seem pitiful. Here was a unique chance to change the country, and the chance was seized. Schools, state ownership of major industry, progressive taxes and the National Health Service: a new Britain emerged in whose shadow we still remain—albeit minus all the major nationalized industries and plus a train system that now functions like Thomas the Tank Engine on crack.

As many of the key members of the Labour government had been part of the wartime coalition there was in practice only a small change of tack—it was certainly a much more "organic" handing over of power in 1945, perversely, than when the Conservatives under Churchill took it back in 1951. Attlee's hypnotic lack of charisma makes him a vague figure now, but all first-hand accounts make it clear how dynamic and purposive the government was in this strange period. Perhaps it can best be understood as the half decade when it became clear, but only slowly, that Britain was in deep trouble. South Asian independence came seemingly from a position of strength. In the eyes of many liberal British, having fought alongside India in defeating the Japanese, it was logical that India should now rule itself. Many in the Labour Party had a long-standing enthusiasm for Indian independence. It was assumed in 1947 that Britain would remain a powerful enough country to be a partner with India and a military presence in the region into the indefinite future—it was only afterwards that it became clear how deluded this notion was.

The decision to build a British atomic bomb also seemed a plausible and rational action once it became clear that the United States would not share its knowledge. With Britain's global network of interests to protect, having nuclear weapons was almost uncontroversial. From a military point of view they were, before the world of enormous missile arsenals, a helpful extra. MacArthur had certainly believed this during the Korean War when he had wanted to use them against Chinese cities (although, of course, he was sacked for this enthusiasm). But again, as Britain's international role dissolved, the weapons became ever more absurd—ultimately seen as simply an invitation to the USSR to reduce this island to ash as a side effect or precautionary measure.

The great efforts of the Labour governments in the end came to too little—or certainly not enough. Financially Britain was in ruins, with enormous debts, millions of servicemen to demobilize and industry geared only to turning out endless heavy bombers. The sole breathing space was provided by the fact that most of Europe (Britain's traditional competitor in many markets) had been flattened. This breathing space was to prove very unfortunate as it lulled the urgent sense—which pressed on Japanese, French and German businesses, for example—that industrial reform and reshaping were needed. Perhaps it was just not possible for the Labour government to do more without taking on the sort of coercive, dictatorial powers which would have made the whole enterprise obscene.

But for every voter who was elated by Labour there was another revolted, for every voter who felt thrilled that the asinine, gold-braid world of Britain was at last being thrown on the bonfire there was another eager to pull it from the flames. This reaction rebuilt the Conservatives— with their usual short memories voters quietly forgot the lies, cynicism and failures of the thirties (and indeed, to be fair, the feebly pacifist Labour Party of the same period) and clustered around Churchill. If Churchill had only retired this might not have happened in the way it did, but the immensely old and distracted Churchill remained and behind him lurked all kinds of Old School gargoyles.

WHEN I WAS a small child we went on a family holiday in western Scotland. We were under somewhat pinched circumstances at the time and sat for day after day, as the rain poured down, in a converted stationary caravan. I remember my parents' despair when we came slurping and squodging back from some rain-soaked expedition to find that the wonky little fridge (called the "Snow Queen," as we never ceased to reminisce) had caused the tonic bottle to first freeze and then explode in our absence. The day that was to have been at least partly cauterized for my parents by gin and tonic therefore ended with clearing up the debris, throwing away the frozen eggs and flexing and warming the plastic packs of dreary ham that remained for dinner. The trip was not an overwhelming success but had its compensations, including the pleasure of first discovering the islands of Rum, Eigg and Muck, which we could not see off the coast because of the driving rain, but which we could at least imagine from delightedly looking at them on the map.

One day we visited some distant parental friends in Oban, on the west coast. The grey, battened-down houses, the cold, the sluicing-down rain offered no preparation for the sharp transition of walking through their front door. The entrance hall's main, astonishing feature was a grotesque stuffed diorama of a mongoose and an Indian cobra fighting, the mongoose baring its tiny teeth in mid-dance from side to side, its sickening opponent rearing up, as is traditional, all hood, scale and fang. At some point somebody had knocked the whole thing over and children had repeatedly mucked about with it. This rather rubbishy taxidermist's concept had therefore quite by accident taken on a more cosmic air, just as the most feeble old statues become ennobled by a bit of moss and rain damage. The mongoose and cobra seemed to have been locked in death-combat forever, regardless of missing eyes, missing fur, or the word "Jamie" clearly written on the snake's scales. The whole house was a temple to south Asia—a riot of conflicting Buddhas, Ganeshas and images of the Taj Mahal (in the British tradition of decoration as unintended interfaith outreach), rugs, soapstone boxes, marquetry and assorted hideous bits of brassware.

This sort of contrast between grim, dreary Britain and arbitrary interior fantasy is replicated in hundreds and thousands of homes. Indeed, it is nauseating to think of just how many elephants were needed to make all those elephant-foot umbrella stands. There have of course been vigorous domestic reassessments going on in recent decades—surely some spasm of revulsion must have put the mongoose-cobra combo into the Dumpster by now. But middle-class houses remain crammed with imperial offloads—faintly obscene African sculpture, Chinese hangings, Malay knives, Persian carpets. And of course an infinite range of day-to-day goods— West African cocoa, Demerara sugar, Canadian flour, Assam tea, Australian wines and so on, the direct comestible progeny of so many years of appropriation, slaveholding and violence.

This immense framework, this process whereby over centuries great chunks of the world were repopulated and reconfigured by British settlers whose almost insectoid blankness and rapacity will surely to some later global generation make them appear far, far worse than the Mongols, fell to pieces. It is the single biggest fact in British life in the late 1940s and throughout the 1950s and yet it now barely impinges on our consciousness—it is not taught, it is barely read about: but for the generation this book is concerned with it was the overwhelming thing. If people understood in 1945 that Britain had won the War only because the United States and the USSR had won it with them, then they certainly did not understand that the consequence would be the demolition of the British Empire, a cornerstone of national identity, hopes, fears and opportunities, in the space of about fifteen years. A genuine and imperishable beacon of democracy after 1940, one of the "Big Three" victors in 1945, ruler of about a quarter of the world, Britain became by 1960, in the words of one derisive American friend of mine, "a dying island on the edge of a cold, small continent."

THE ASTOUNDING and, before 1939, wholly unexpected winding up of the British Empire generated more change around the planet than had the Second World War. German-generated horror, with the exception of Atlantic U-boats, never stepped outside one corner of Eurasia and the top of Africa; Japan's extraordinary if evanescent riot through Asia still left much of the continent untouched. Indeed one of the very odd features of the War was that its two ferocious new imperialists were never strong enough to attack the countries that most threatened them. In summer 1940 it became clear that Germany simply could not invade or destroy Britain or get anywhere near any of its colonies beyond the Channel Islands and possibly Egypt, and neither the Nazis nor the Japanese had the remotest idea how to attack the United States. Aside from sinking some shipping, occupying some small, barely inhabited islands in Alaska, dropping a grand total of four small bombs on Oregon and (amazingly) sending thousands of lacquered paper balloons loaded with incendiary bombs drifting on wind currents (which killed six people on a Sunday school outing), Japan had no capacity at all to attack a country that economically and militarily dwarfed both itself and Germany. The Germans mucked about with plans for rocket-driven one-way suicide bombers which might have done some slight damage to New York, but which were never remotely close to being operational and would have in any event been irrelevant. However appalling therefore the mayhem unleashed by Germany and Japan, it lasted for a very brief period and directly impacted only specific areas. A historian from the safe distance of, say, the twenty-third century would probably have to conclude that the most far-reaching event of the twentieth century was not the First and Second World Wars themselves but their consequences: the collapse of Europe and the end of the European empires, and overwhelmingly most important, the end of the British Empire.

It is extremely strange to think that a process initiated after the War by Britain and ended for the most part twenty years later generated change across all continents, completely transferring power in the end (by my rough calculation) to some sixty-four new nations—from whoppers (India, Nigeria, Pakistan) to tiddlers (Tuvalu, St. Kitts)—and changing the aspirations, geography and politics of much of the Earth. The effect of this change within Britain was massive and profound trauma—it enraged millions of British who neither understood it nor saw how they could create for themselves a new identity without the Empire: a conundrum which suffuses the Bond books and films and still haunts us today.

The first great stage in dismantling the Empire was the

departure of the former "settler" colonies. Australia, New Zealand, Canada and South Africa had all fought with Britain in the First World War and had shared in the annihilatory disaster. As with Britain, the dawning of the Second World War saw them dubious about the entire idea of military might. While they all participated equally vigorously, the events of 1939–42 effectively turned them into entirely separate nations. As junior partners to Britain they were consistently abused and humiliated by a British military command that often seemed to be in the hands of some dedicated freemason group whose entire role was to wind up international good will and cooperation. The high-profile catastrophes around the world, where New Zealand, South African and Australian soldiers were compelled to surrender in their thousands to smaller forces, generally through British ineptitude, were breathtaking. For the rest of the War these countries were fighting not as genuine colonies or dominions but as part of the general "United Nations." As the War ended and the Cold War began all these countries made other military plans, generally involving the United States and generally with cheerful but only limited reference to London. There was still cooperation, but these were all now entirely independent countries with personal or pragmatic or silly (the Queen) links with Britain.

The second immense shift was south Asian independence— India, Pakistan, Ceylon (Sri Lanka), Burma (Myanmar) and what is now Bangladesh. This is a very uneasy subject as it is genuinely unclear how damaging Britain's role wound up being. It is certainly very important to the history of Britain's benign end to empire to state that the massacres that ended up killing at least half a million people were somehow unconnected in any way to Britain, because they happened just after independence. Mountbatten, the last Viceroy of India, was always very pleased with the way he had handled it and quite content in his refusal to use British troops to prevent inter-communal violence. Was the hasty carve-up into Muslim- and Hindu-ruled areas of the former Raj inevitable or was it the result of incompetence and chaos? The horrible result of Partition—the mass killings, the resettlement of millions of people—has in the end to lie partly at Britain's feet. Certainly Mountbatten's idiotic award of Kashmir to India does. Certainly the failure to give independence to India in the 1930s had dreadful consequences as it allowed religious nationalism to grow and a world war to be fought which killed many Indians (it is inconceivable that the Japanese would have attacked Burma and India at all if they had not been British territory).

Sitting in the early twenty-first century, in a now pleasant, prosperous, engagingly multi-cultural, slightly irritating offshore piece of Europe, the real issue seems to be to understand imaginatively how Britain could ever have ruled such countries at all. It is hard to say whether the idea is comic or nasty or just weird. It is certainly remote. The general implosion of colonialism, including the Soviet Empire after 1989, now seems so unavoidable that individual actions or decisions become irrelevant. But for many British people at the time it seemed far from being so. The enormous networks that, directly or indirectly, had sustained millions of lives came to pieces between 1941, with the Japanese invasion of Malaya, and the independence of Kenya in 1963, the last important colony to go beyond the thorny oddities of Hong Kong and Rhodesia. Entire towns all over Britain were profoundly entangled in colonial trade, colonial supply, emigration, officialdom and so on. Where I grew up in southeast England, admittedly in a town with *particularly* strong links with India, antiques shops were and still are jammed with recycled junk from south Asia—all fond mementos of something that stopped very suddenly in 1947. For hordes of British people this was not an inevitable process but the result of a series of blunders: the repulsive, unpatriotic behaviour of the Labour government, probably in the pay of Moscow, making a mockery of everything that Britain stood for. It remains odd today to think of the thousands of British troops who died in Burma to "liberate" a colony which only ever benefited a few oil, rice and teak merchants. But it was part of a wider framework which had seemed to many legitimate and when, in 1948, Burma became independent, it generated in many British people a sense of shame and disgrace: the idea of the "forgotten" army, of the War against Japan as a piece of futility. This poorly focused sense of treason—that Britain was somehow tricked into giving up the booty of centuries rather than having it drop from its nerveless hands— carried over into all aspects of public life and its ripples continue into the present. It generated a bitterness and loss of identity that found solace in, among other things, certain high-quality action books of the 1950s.

WHY SHOULD we be interested in history? Many people are not. Perhaps the great majority live very thoroughly in the present—children have a horizon only centimetres from their toes, many people through exhaustion and daily need can think little about the past or the future, many others live largely in the future, through religion or ambition, personal or familial. To be interested in the past is both a specific activity and a very vexed one: history is as likely to be a source of toxins as of pleasure. The obsession with "a place in history" which has animated all dictators, the role of totalitarianism as a prime source of nurture for crumbling heritage, is perhaps unhelpful, whether it is Mussolini's vast viewing platform in the Colosseum or the Shah's hopeless attempt to ally himself with the ruins of the Persian Empire. Indeed, the degree to which almost all the human past seems to be a confrontation with the profoundly illiberal, with slave empires, deranged monuments, staggering cruelty, forces a kind of discipline on the history reader: if a little bit of the reader does not want to be Xerxes or Nero or Cortés then what is the point of sinking into this stuff? What does it say about us that we all walk through local history museum reconstructions of Neolithic families building huts laughing with boredom but head straight for the bronze shields and battleaxes? But equally to read about the fall of the Incas or the Taiping Rebellion or the settlement of Ireland at a purely tut-tut level (what has been brilliantly tagged as "boo-hoo history") is disastrous. Is this cruelty hardwired? If it is a human characteristic then how does each national history, including of course Britain's, some-how comfort itself that others (Mongols, janissaries, Aztecs) exemplify "cruelty" where one's own national forces (red-coats, tars) and experience don't?

At some level history really is useless: to comment on history is as wan an activity as yelling at the players in a tele-vised football game: they can't hear you, they don't care and it's already too late. For me this latent sense of horror is always best summed up by the villain in Umberto Eco's medieval fantasy *The Name of the Rose*, trapped in an underground passage. Nobody rescues him because by the time they can dig him out *he will have died* of asphyxiation. History and the application of history to the present shares this night-mare, with an almost unbreakable mesh between ourselves and present, unfolding events that cannot be torn through. What value does a reading of history have? Its great value has to be, as a historian recently summed it up, to "criticize, criticize, criticize." For me, nothing can be more valuable than this constant patrolling around an always shifting kaleido-scope of events and decisions, both in themselves (they explain why we are here, doing what we do, earning what we earn) and because their interpretation is in effect a cross-examination of the present and of ourselves.

Staring at Britain's performance as a country in the twen-tieth century, we are all in effect yelling at the screen. It is useless because the actors in the drama cannot hear but it also raises endlessly interesting questions about what the actors *should* have done, and why we should want them to have done those things—in other words what sort of country would we prefer to live in today? That this is irresolvable and dies with the death of each of us does not make it illegitimate or masturbatory, although of course it can be both. That every individual's religious quest dies with him or her does not make that quest stupid, and the same is true of history: we can never resolve or conclude on any subject, except in a spirit of pub-bore certainty, but the exercise of thinking, for example about the nature of the crisis of the late 1930s, is infinitely fruitful. There are thousands of historical issues which have similar meditative value and these are different for every society, individual, time and place. The decision *not* to be interested in history is also an important one as it implies in relation to one's own national past that something there is poisonous or simply too vexed. Many contemporary European countries have an aphasic feeling about their recent pasts because those pasts are too raw or too humiliating. Britain, on the other hand, has uses for its past which are narcotic and insidious.

Any criticism of specific historical actions has to involve positing an alternative. One of the most interesting problems for me is staring at the Britain that fought the Second World War and imagining some of these alternatives and how disturbing they would be. For example, Britain's almost total military failure in every offensive it attempted against everyone except the Italians between 1939 and late 1942. Watching the magnificent Noël Coward movie *In Which We Serve* is a case in point. Made during the War, this is a highly nuanced, realistic and moving account of a ship being sunk off Crete in 1941 and the memories of the helpless survivors as they are strafed by Nazi aircraft on a waterlogged raft. What is most striking now is that Coward managed to write, direct, compose the music and star in a film which could feature him as a ship's captain surrounded by panting, oil-coated sailors—perhaps the modern era's most elaborate and expensive homoerotic tableau. What is also remarkable is that the values of self-deprecation and decency it exalts are completely hopeless. In the face of the annihilatory predations of the Germans and Japanese this sort of tea's-on-the-table niceness is both irrelevant and, even at this distance, terrifying to watch.

I always used to think, in common with millions of other children, that there was something fundamentally wrong with British uniform design in the first five years of the Second World War. Why was there no theatre of war in which the British looked faintly convincing: why did the Eighth Army in their shorts and socks appear so unmartial while the Afrika

Korps were so desirable? Why did the BEF in northern France simply *look* such a walkover for the Wehrmacht, or General Perceval at Singapore even in photos *before* the Japanese attack look like a beaten man in his appalling tropical costume? By 1944 the situation has improved no end and the D-Day paratroopers or the Fourteenth Army in Burma in their jungle hats look super. But this discontent with military appearance, married of course to actual military performance, shields a far greater anxiety. Would we want these soldiers to succeed? An alternative history in which the Nazis are quite readily beaten is an alternative history where we are in fact more ferocious than they, more committed, more fanatical, more willing to break treaties and violate borders. Are France and Britain, as genuine democracies however flawed in 1939, effectively doomed by that fact to be beaten? Is the survival of a non-Nazi Europe therefore the accidental gift of the United States and the USSR? *In Which We Serve* has simply no future in the reptile-brain world of 1940s Europe: what we admire about ourselves in Britain is what should have doomed us. Our involvement with understanding our own history therefore becomes seriously vexed—a successful British army fighting its way into Germany in 1940 could only have been an even more violent, bitter, Nietzschean outfit. The complete failure of independent British arms before the arrival of Soviet and American help becomes rather admirable, therefore: a sincere alternative to the new Race Empires, albeit an alternative containing rather considerable risks.

JAMES BOND is useful in thinking about all this because he provides the most all-pervasive wistful alternative, a sort of vulgar threnody on ideas of Britishness, the ultimate ersatz for compromised, difficult reality. As we yell at the television we have both to see what is happening on the screen and listen very carefully to what we are yelling: Do we really want to have dominated Europe ourselves, rather than Germany? Were we preserving our island independence—or were we preserving (as the Americans suspected) a way of life based on parasitic strip-mining of much of the planet? Do we really want the British Empire to have survived into the present? At all the turning points or non-turning points of the twentieth century, what would have been a better outcome? It is impossible not to conclude that Britain has been almost uniquely fortunate, that it has done much less than it thinks to deserve its good fortune and that there has been a substantial, if manageable, price to pay.

SOMETHING VERY STRANGE happens to British culture after the War. The culture of the present or the near present is almost impossible to write about, as there is simply too much glare, too much going on to make worthwhile generalizations. But it is very striking from the safe distance of now how British culture blooms around 1945 and then curls up and fails completely in the fifties. This is particularly true with films— the impetus provided by the partnerships and habits of the War itself and the funding and audience that went with it generate a sort of landslide of great work: *A Matter of Life and Death*, *Great Expectations*, *Hue and Cry*, *A Canterbury Tale*, *Kind Hearts and Coronets*, *Brief Encounter*, *The Red Shoes*, *Whisky Galore!* all come pouring out—imaginative, subtle, clever, populist, various. But then it all goes wrong—somehow this world folds up and disappears, with even the great Michael Powell by 1956 making boring rubbish such as *The Battle of the River Plate*. It is very tempting, and perhaps true, to feel that this is linked to the excitement of victory, the excitement with the new Labour government, followed by a feeling that everything was going wrong: that victory had led nowhere and the British future was one of gloom, rationing, mediocrity, of being a battered fragment in the general European disaster, of a world in which there was no place for *The Red Shoes*. It is of course impossible to make this link, beyond a general conviction that serious cultural work is more readily made by very exuberant or wackily imploding cultures but not by ones simply toppling over sideways. And the cinematic exuberance masks a deeper desperation: the inability of British literature or culture more broadly to wrestle interestingly with the War—the lack of any enduring, widely read novels, for example, beyond perhaps *Brideshead Revisited*, that could explain what everyone had just been through. No Mailer, no Céline, no Grass, no Heller, no Beckett, no Böll, no Grossman, no Sartre—no Steinbeck, even. In a marked contrast to the First World War, the Second does not generate any lasting British response—plenty of military memoirs and fascinating diaries, generally published many years later, but otherwise remarkably little that anyone turns to today as a shorthand for the experience. It is strange and rather sad that high culture should have so comprehensively failed to define the subject of everyone's conversations, everyone's reminiscences. As Britain settled into a thirty-year wallow in popular memory of an Age of Giants, it provoked no more vigorous response than such bitterly regretful satires as *Sword of Honour* and *The Military Philosophers*. In the end it seems to me impossible to come up with an adequate reason for there being no British *Catch-22* or *The Naked and the Dead* or *Dangling*

Man beyond an overwhelming feeling that the entire country was going over a waterfall by the late forties and early fifties, which made any response useless. The great films dry up, the literature is silent or introverted to the point of madness (I'm making a specific point here—I worship Ivy Compton-Burnett, but it is impossible to see her on her occasional forays into Kensington as engaging, even faintly, with the greater world). One last, exhausted effort in 1951 got everyone to the Festival of Britain, with its strange but beautiful burst of Scandinavian modernism, and then the country seemed to fall silent.

ONE TRADITIONAL wealthy English response to the cold and despair of Britain had been to winter abroad, as so many more were to do over the following half century. In the course of his duties with the military during the War, Ian Fleming had gone to Jamaica; he was entranced and once the War was over built a new winter home there.

As Fleming sat over the coming winters at his gold-plated typewriter knocking out a Bond novel a year, elated by his own cleverness, delighted by his growing success but also haggard, self-hating and ever more convulsed with boredom at his own creation, what real claim does he have on our time? The lives of Britain's ruling layers were closely entangled and probably any given figure could appear to be at the centre of a web of significant relationships. Some solitary scarlet-faced maniac in a remote aristocratic pile could on the basis of in practice distant, disgusted but influential relatives seem to be the Establishment's puppet-master. Fleming's position, though, *is* very startling. Growing up, Fleming was surrounded by figures from finance and the military, was aware of his late father's friend Winston Churchill, was part of the peculiar elite that sprang out of Eton. He spent years flitting in and out of his widowed mother's coterie of artist and writer friends and had a half-sister whose father was Augustus John. His brother Peter was an immensely successful writer, and Ian had an acquaintance with many journalists and writers way beyond the confines of his—on the face of it—vacuous public and private life. The War then put him on the outer rim of the inner circle of power, specifically linking the imperial, naval and military worlds with those of intelligence and special operations, linking too the British and American worlds in new, useful and surprising ways (ways which apart from anything else were to make him wind up in Jamaica). In the 1950s he became that most characteristic product of Late Empire—an offshore cynic, angry, self-damaging and filled with disgust with the state of the world. Fleming was never an important player in Britain's ruling class but he was omnipresent and known to circles who would otherwise have been quite ignorant of each other. His newspaper work in the fifties expanded his range even further, with all kinds of people telling him secrets or semi-secrets, relying on him, passing things on. With his elaborate self-image, his collection of first editions, his sadomasochism and his relentless drinking, Fleming was almost a bohemian figure. But equally, with his high-society contacts, his crisscrossing of the Atlantic, his sadomasochism and his relentless drinking he was characteristically "Establishment."

Fleming's chameleon nature, once this hit its mature form as he was writing his books, can seem very appealing, but often he feels like a chameleon that has been used in some disturbing, if groundbreaking, laboratory experiment. Equally engaged and interesting talking to old intelligence chiefs in

London or to New York lawyers or to Jamaican neighbours, a novelist and a journalist, a man who split his life between three countries with side trips to many more, Fleming burnt out and died in his late fifties in a perhaps unsurprising manner.

This is in no sense a biography, but however multifarious Fleming may have been he is incomprehensible without some grip on the personality of his extraordinary wife, Ann Fleming (née Charteris; then O'Neill; then Rothermere). Clearly a great figure, Ann Fleming is poorly served by photographs, where she invariably appears querulous and slightly mad. They give no hint at all of how rich and powerful men would beat their heads against marble tabletops from thwarted desire at a mere word from her. Admired and hated by an enormous circle of notional friends, Ann Fleming hurtled through British life during and after the War, and just her more significant lovers run a startling gamut of political positions, from her second husband, Lord Rothermere, owner of the *Daily Mail* (the par-excellence paper of Britain-goes-to-the-dogs right-wing bitterness), to Hugh Gaitskell, the leader of the Labour Party denied the role of prime minister by his sudden early death in 1963. Fleming first met her in 1939 when she was still married to her first husband, but little came of this until after the War, when they became seriously involved. In the wake of a late miscarried child in 1948, Ann's marriage to Rothermere collapsed and she eventually married Fleming in Jamaica in early 1952 with Noël Coward as master of ceremonies. Some days before, Fleming had sat down to start writing *Casino Royale*. Their marriage was chaotic and filled with violence, with Ann Fleming deriding Ian Fleming's books as "pornography" and running off to see more seriously extreme friends such as Lucian Freud, who could only have been derisive of Fleming's clubman views and tastes. Ann Fleming had a breathtaking ability to create trouble and complexities for herself and these came to a head in 1963 with Hugh Gaitskell on the verge of death in London and telegrams from Fleming in Jamaica asking her to fly over after tests that showed he had himself only a short time to live.

It is hard to exaggerate Ann Fleming's importance to the Bond books. They were clearly written both at her urging and in order to impress her, which in different moods they succeeded or failed in doing. If anyone could wreck Fleming's fortress of self-regard it was she and despite endless screaming rows about each other's lovers they seem an oddly endearing pair—horrible and humiliating to meet, but fun to contemplate at a safe distance. And in any event very remarkable, as the result of their relationship was James Bond. If we can be baffled and grateful that a Polish-born riverboat captain in the Congo Free State should have become the Joseph Conrad who wrote *Heart of Darkness*, there must be a case for being as dazed that someone so *deeply* embedded in fast-decaying British imperial life should have become, from a position of immense, strange knowledge, that life's great memorialist, fantasist and emollient.

Chapter Three

CORONATION CHICKEN

THE BRITISH 1950s are kicked off by two enormous events with a much smaller one tucked in between: the two enormous ones are the return of the Conservatives to power and the coronation of Elizabeth II. The much smaller event is Fleming's finishing and publishing *Casino Royale*. All are closely intertwined, however.

I once saw an interview Anthony Eden made in the mid-1960s for the great French documentary about the Occupation, *Le chagrin et le pitié*, and it is like watching someone from a different planet. His accent was extraordinary, a sort of bleaty warbly noise. What he says is moving and thoughtful, how he says it implies a sort of hyper-officer-class world picture, of discreet patrician amateurism within a frame long broken in the rest of the world. That he should in the interview be speaking French but with a completely uninflected English accent is almost too good to be true: any quarter-way motivated French patriot would be obliged to gulp with anger and disbelief at this incarnation of *rosbif perfide*. What Eden, of course, represents as the incredibly decrepit Churchill's second-in-command in the new Conservative government of 1951 is that world of the thirties, which the rigours of the War and Labour's 1945 election victory were meant to have exorcized but which now grimly sprang back into place.

Eden always drew credit for having in the end resigned from Chamberlain's government in early 1939, but as with many other Conservatives, his change of heart looks very late in the day. It now seems incredible that such a figure, bland, peevish, morally bankrupt, should symbolize 1950s Britain. The Conservatives who stalked back in 1951, including the immensely powerful, almost unbelievably compromised R. A. Butler, were substantially the same gang, facing the same problem: a very traditional ruling class simply unable to engage with a world unravelling far faster or more irreversibly than had seemed possible even in the late thirties.

It is hard not to reach for some tidal metaphor to describe Britain in this period: that 1945–50 had marked a high water of reform and thoughtfulness and that this tide then began to go out quite heavily until in 1951 the Conservatives just squeak back into power on a minority vote. But who voted for them? Who could possibly have turned once more to a crew who had let everyone down so often, a party who—ancient leader aside—could take so little credit for almost anything that had occurred? This is where Ian Fleming's work becomes so valuable. Of course we can never know exactly who read the books, but we can guess intelligently.

My early memories are filled with the stifling nostalgia for the Second World War that filled my parents' newspapers. I was brought up in a Conservative household by parents who were in no sense violently ideological and who were more than willing to be critical of "their" government. My mother's views at that time, the late sixties and early seventies, were reflected by papers such as the *Daily* and *Sunday Express* and were suffused with an overwhelming sense that "things were going wrong." I have often thought about those strange papers which really fed quite remorselessly on a sense of bitterness and anger over a poorly defined "they" who had let everyone down. "They" could be the Soviets, of course, but also oily Europeans, vulgar Americans, vicious Africans (I remember a lot on the Rhodesia crisis—including a cartoon of Robert Mugabe as a mad gorilla in a circus cage, with Ian Smith, the white leader, dressed as a ringmaster holding the cage's key with a caption along the lines of *Thank goodness I've got the key*), shirkers and cheats of all kinds—in fact virtually everybody.

This is a vast, clear strand in British life that goes oddly unnoticed. In the years I lived in the United States I never once encountered anything approaching this strange tic, and it does not seem a serious force in countries such as Italy or Germany. Le Pen, of course, taps into something related in France and for similar reasons—and I bet there's lots of it in Russia, which now shares much of Britain's old psychosis. The *Express* has fallen away somewhat but still one of the most influential papers in Britain is the extraordinary *Daily Mail*, which carries on this tradition and still sells millions of copies, where no day goes by without some story of foreign welfare cheats destroying decent Britons, where the main story almost invariably involves some overwhelming bit of bitterness. This was beautifully encapsulated (although to be honest it is beautifully encapsulated almost every morning) by the main *Express* headline in June 2005, NOW THEY WANT TO SCRAP OUR HONOURS SYSTEM, the THEY and the OUR being such fascinating givens.

The 1950s saw this tendency in British life really find its feet. A whole category of people became decisively embittered.

They hated the Socialist government of 1945, hated the loss of India, hated the feeling that Britain was no longer Great and were worked up about the United States, about which many had, to say the least, complicated feelings. This bitterness has been a huge theme in British life ever since, fuelled by the series of disasters described in this book. These people clung to Churchill, who should have retired in 1945, adored the royal family, emigrated in substantial numbers and hated every twist and turn of the permissive society as it unfolded in the fifties and sixties. They were not fools in any sense but they were doomed by political, military and economic events to experience the next decades as a roller coaster in a condemned fairground they had not even asked to visit.

Middle-class patriots—and Britain defined itself by its patriotism, recently so vigorously displayed in the War—were glum things to be in the 1950s. Everything they hoped for was expressed in voting for Churchill in 1951 and backing the long run of Conservative rule to 1964, but they were to be utterly disappointed. The Conservatives may have been backward-looking and with a madly inappropriate view of Britain's new position in the world, but they were flexible and smart enough to know they could not roll back the welfare changes brought in by Labour. They could not be the openly reactionary party many of their more picturesque MPs and voters wanted them to be and, through their war experiences, they often in practice shared Labour's obsession with state-fuelled modernization.

Instead of dismantling everything, they treated the new system of public healthcare and national free schooling with a sort of friendly neglect. As imperial issues withered away and healthcare, transport and schooling became government's main concerns, Britain was left with a zany system in which the MPs of the Conservative Party, who ruled cumulatively for thirty-five years from 1945, would not themselves have dreamed of using either the public health system or public transport (beyond first-class carriages on trains) and would have been socially ostracized if they had sent their children to state schools. This left a long-lasting, very peculiar split where the Conservatives, often blue-blooded figures of astonishing dimness or over-articulate fatalism, continued to attract support from a broad base — partly aspirational but also, and more important, bitter and angry about the whirlwind ruining their world.

EVERYTHING THAT suggested Britain's profound blood-poisoning was summed up in the coronation of 1953. The remarkable length of Elizabeth II's reign has accidentally sheltered us from fully noticing the gigantic changes that have gone on in Britain (indeed James Bond and Elizabeth, flung together by chance, offer almost the only continuity). We have also been sheltered from the horror of having to watch another coronation, of course. The flyblown pantomime of such an event, the horrific sense of decrepit, fawning pseudo-feudalism: how can we possibly survive the next coronation without popular revulsion setting in? In 1953 the system worked, just. George VI had been a chain-smoking cipher of no clear accomplishments, but he had in a very limited way (if wholly eclipsed by Churchill) symbolized Britain at War, going a long way to efface the damage done by his politically disturbing older brother.

There was a sense of shock at his early death, gratitude for that symbolism, and enthusiasm for his daughter, whipped to a frenzy by all the stuff in places like the *Express* about the

"New Elizabethan Age." The coincidence of the conquest of Mount Everest immediately before the coronation, which was viewed as a fresh British triumph (albeit its two heroes being people who were not from Britain and in a part of the world in which Britain no longer had any political power), added to the excitement.

The coronation became a vindication for all that Britain had gone through in the War and for the British system, now (just) back in the hands of the Conservatives. George VI's coronation in 1937 had been a bizarre event, following the abdication, disgrace and exile of his brother, and loaded down with brocade-crusted, stooped flummery and for most of the world a disturbingly obvious contrast to the spine-chilling power of the Nuremberg Rally held the same summer. Elizabeth II's coronation was just as bad, as it continued to imply a system that required no change.

To watch the colour footage of the event now, with all the rubbishy orbs and chrism, its whole sickening air of servility, is to see something that should (preferably peacefully) have been disposed of many years before. The victory of 1945 had not been created by lords in funny cloaks. Britain continued to exist as it did through enormous technological and military effort, good luck and having been on the same side as the United States and the USSR. Worse, it represents only one side of the British experience—the conclusions that many fighting the Second World War drew, that a future lay in admiring and imitating America or Russia or engaging in the new Europe, were made a monkey of by the coronation. Still worse, it had everyone eating "Coronation Chicken," a dystopian dish involving curried mayonnaise, parodic of both the limits of British cooking and the ways in which debased versions of Indian things impinged on British life. Britain's future in 1953 could have been celebrated in modern and optimistic terms—but the future envisioned by the coronation appeared to lie instead within the comforts provided by myopic, heraldic feudal infantilism and by yellow chickens.

WHILE RESIGNED TO the idea that probably the readers of this book will be limited to those who already have some interest in Bond (are you there? are you still with me?), the aim is to use Bond merely as a thread to tie three curious decades together and not get lost in pointless plot summaries or mere fan's notes. Not wanting to presume prior knowledge, therefore, here is a very brief outline of the books themselves.

Fleming's first Bond novel, *Casino Royale*, was written in 1952 and published in 1953 and the novels then came out at roughly year-long intervals. Indeed, one of the points against Fleming is his mechanical approach to his own work—even down to length. *Dr. No*, for example, is set up beautifully, with a compellingly expressionist villain and lair and an incomparable picture of aspects of the West Indies, but all this elaboration comes to nothing as the story is hastily ended in rubbishy battles with giant squids and anaemic, under-realized rationales for No's wickedness. No's death, suffocated under tons of guano, provokes applause, but there is no way round the fact that Fleming has simply reached his word limit and can't be bothered to go on. The pile of typed paper is nearly the right height—time for a big drink.

This style of output is a bit dismaying, as is the uneven quality of almost all the books: if Fleming hit a dull patch he tended to keep plugging along rather than going back to fix it. I am certainly not suggesting that his books are masterpieces, although *From Russia with Love* at the very least is exceptional, and many people make a special case for *Casino Royale*.

Live and Let Die followed *Casino Royale* in 1954 and introduced the two principal staples of the series: surprising locations (the United States and the Caribbean) and the megalomaniac villain, in this case the black American gangster Mr. Big. As with Graham Greene's study of Beatrix Potter's work and his identification of darker and lighter phases in her output, one can also categorize Fleming's work, but more in terms of worse and better phases. The next two books, *Moonraker* (1955) and *Diamonds Are Forever* (1956), are definitely worse: they have entertaining features but come very close to routine—they are absurd in uninteresting ways and seem to imply that Fleming had little ambition for his creation, failing to build either on the invention of Bond himself and his world in *Casino Royale* or on the "baroque" villainy of *Live and Let Die*. *Moonraker* is set entirely in England, the last time Fleming would make this mistake, and certainly has incidental pleasures which it would be sad to lose (such as the moment when Bond taunts his Nazi Werewolf adversary Drax for having sucked his thumb at public school) but the texture is thin and the story stupid (I mean stupid in a stupid way rather than stupid in an inspired way). *Diamonds Are Forever* restores the exotic locations (New York and Las Vegas) and is therefore helped on its way, but the villainy is banal and the set pieces uninvolving. It absolutely fails to explain why an Englishman would play any role in foiling such low-key gangsterism.

If Fleming had stopped at this point (and the books were not so successful that it was necessarily advisable to continue) he would be one of dozens of writers such as Rex Stout, James

Hadley Chase or Ngaio Marsh who are merely names now, and not very interesting ones—except by the very narrowest of definitions, whereby Ngaio Marsh has to be one of the most interesting names ever.

Something happened, though, when he wrote *From Russia with Love* (1957), which has an Eric Ambler–like plot, a wonderful location (Istanbul), spectacular villains at full throttle (SMERSH! It is amazing that this organization, which sounds so quintessentially Fleming, was a genuine part of the KGB) and lovely plotting. After veering about uneasily Fleming had at last pulled himself fully free of old tropes (gangsters, Nazi shockers) and embraced the future—the Cold War, the parallel fictional world he was to elaborate with such crazy and pleasurable effect with schemes of vast daring and cosmic fiendishness. The book is also helped by featuring a long train trip. At some level anything involving a semi-sealed form of transport with macabre passengers can't go wrong, whether it's the disgusting ship in Ambler's *Journey into Fear* or the train in Hitchcock's *The Lady Vanishes*.

Following *From Russia with Love*, Fleming then turned out *Dr. No* (1958), *Goldfinger* (1959) and *Thunderball* (1961) and created the entire world that has been enjoyed, copied, parodied and derided ever since—pliant, inventive girls, villains of unspeakable ambition prone to monologues and grand, glamorous locations suffused with Cold War paranoia. Then, like some decathlon champion, having dazzled the world in sport after sport, Fleming did the equivalent of killing a judge with a crazily mismanaged javelin throw by writing *The Spy Who Loved Me* (1962), a shameful disaster he himself later disowned. He then recovered with his best novel in "straight" terms (but, alas, we do not read Fleming for his "straight" qualities), *On Her Majesty's Secret Service* (1963), and struggled along with the splendidly zany *You Only Live Twice* (1964), with his villain Blofeld now reduced to tricking suicidal Japanese into using his "garden of death." Now very ill, Fleming squeezed out the weak and posthumously published *The Man with the Golden Gun* (1965). He had also written various opportunistic (or to be fair, even more opportunistic than his major novels) short stories, which were collected as *For Your Eyes Only* (1960) and the posthumously published *Octopussy* (1966), neither of which add much beyond some fun minor twists.

This was Fleming's complete output, aside from two works of nonfiction, *The Diamond Smugglers* (1957) and *Thrilling Cities* (1963), which really are just old journalism of an unreadable kind, and, of course, the children's book *Chitty Chitty Bang Bang* (1964), which, through the devotion of the Bond film producers, was made into a strange, rather queasy film, albeit with Sherman Brothers songs and the actors who played Goldfinger and Q (neither looking happy), as well as the truly horrific Dick Van Dyke.

Would these books be read today without the films? This is both an obvious question and an irritatingly irrelevant and unanswerable one—the books and films are knitted together seamlessly, and British popular culture exports can be compared only with the Queen, the Beatles, the Rolling Stones, *The Lord of the Rings* and Harry Potter, an odd gang. For half a century Bond has been a shorthand for Britishness in a peculiar way in a huge range of cultures and languages. Elvis, Mickey Mouse and Darth Vader are clearly more powerful American figures, but in the general world of popular-culture symbols few beat Bond for either familiarity or longevity.

However horrid an experience *Die Another Day* (a wearisome amalgam owing nothing to Fleming) might have been, it was still one of 2003's most successful films, half a century after *Casino Royale*'s publication. This must be telling us something about Bond's having a place in our imaginations beyond that of any more workaday hero.

CASINO ROYALE is a book all about privilege, but privilege of a very marginal and almost grimy kind, and it shows the reality of British life with a startlingly greater clarity than the coronation. The action is entirely based in and around the dull, failing Normandy coastal town of Royale—a sort of hopeless Deauville. One can imagine that French casinos circa 1950 had been through rather a lot—the previous decade having seen a "mixed crowd" at the tables. The nature of Bond's privilege is to be at Royale at all. Currency and travel restrictions meant that the Channel, the barrier essential in 1940 to keeping the Germans out, was now quite as actively penning non-military British people in. The very wealthy, or those with friends in France, could make arrangements to get round the restrictions (which stayed in place in various ways until the 1970s—yet another example of how strange the recent past was), but for virtually everyone France, even blustery, sour northern France, had become as exotic as Shangri-la. Fleming could not have chosen his location more cleverly: he would need to ratchet up the flow of exotica with each of the later books (until by the end Bond is mucking around with Japanese lobster eaten live as it crawls around his table), but Britain's frame of reference had shrunk so small by the early fifties that Royale was quite enough.

The book teems with now almost invisible digs—indeed

the whole idea of the casino with its theoretically limitless stakes and winnings must have seemed derangedly heady to the book's first readers. And the Anglo-American relationship has never been better summed up than when Felix Leiter hands a broke Bond an envelope crammed with lovely new banknotes, allowing him to carry on playing cards with the villain, Le Chiffre. For me the heart of the book, though, must be the scene when Bond tucks into an avocado pear. An avocado! These were exotica in 1939 but they could at least be bought. Avocados really became available again in Britain only in the late 1950s and had a desirability status akin to that felt (rather more democratically) for bananas by East Germans. The sense of the exotic which Fleming had to work for really hard in later books is won here with a mere oily tropical fruit on the windswept Channel coast. Oddly, during one of the many horrible, diarrhoeic currency crises that ravaged the international value of the pound (this one in the late sixties), avocados were specifically mentioned (along with strawberries and vintage wine) as imports to be restricted under the draconian "Operation Brutus," mercifully never implemented.

Immediately with *Casino Royale* Fleming sets up his central point: that Bond knows and the books pass on to the readers valuable scraps from the master's table. This expertise spreads in every direction—it implies some absolute knowledge about food, about sex, about foreign countries, clothing, drink: it is the fantasy that inspires all guide books and is one of the chief (if more pathetic) reasons for travel today—and it is ushered in by Fleming in *Casino Royale*: the first great hymn to consumerism, sneeringly presented to a readership with nothing yet to consume, cowed by years of rationing and restriction. The avocado is waved in front of readers with all the glee of a man who is himself living it up in the Caribbean, thousands of miles away. After a while even the two slightly bizarre scenes where Bond eats toast imply that he probably eats it in a more discriminating and intelligent fashion than anyone else. Even his toast appears aloof and unfeasibly marvellous.

AT UNIVERSITY I was lucky enough to be taught history for a term by a man reputed to have been a "spymaster." It was never entirely clear why he was believed to be one. After all, if it was common knowledge among a strikingly callow group of nineteen-year-olds then it suggested a security breach even more grotesque than those habitually endured by the British secret service. This rumour made life extremely hard for an entirely admirable man. Like everyone he taught, I would sit before him reading out my latest under-researched essay, stuttering with excitement as I waited for him to pop the question. There was disagreement about the form of the question: Some of us favoured, "How do you feel about serving your country?"; others, including myself, were sure he would say, "Could you ever . . . kill a man: if it was your duty, I mean?" Hours were wasted arguing about the best response. The first seemed simple enough: a manly and slightly stumbling, "Well, sir, I find it hard to put into words—but don't we all, in a sense, serve our country every day of our lives?" The second was more difficult as it could be viewed as a trap—a means of tricking people into mentioning the words "James Bond," which would result in the conversation's hasty end, a means of weeding out obviously mad loose cannon in an increasingly bureaucratic age. But the second question could also be a bluff:

an attempt to winkle out a homicidal recklessness that could then be harnessed to national needs through ruthless training.

Of course, none of us were faintly interested in joining anything so risible as MI6, but how we yearned to have that first interview, gagging with laughter as we signed the Official Secrets Act with a pen which, hopefully, could also be used as a flamethrower. Needless to say, my entirely wasted term with this tutor never resulted in any such question being popped. As the term came to an end, those whom he taught viewed one another with increasing paranoia and indeed we would all practise a sort of gruff hesitancy that implied we knew more than we could possibly let on. This later meant that as we settled into a range of, on the face of it, banal and parasitic jobs—law, publishing, journalism—there was always *a chance* that one of us, or indeed (in some despairing variant on *The Man Who Was Thursday*) all of us, had dissimulated and that we would at some point embarrassingly bump into each other in East Germany, all trying to garrotte the same communist.

What the tutor himself thought of all this of course we will never know: the security breaches around his alleged role were so massive that he had presumably heard about it himself long ago. Perhaps he wiled away the thousands of hours as we recited boring essays by practising his mysterious manner and leaning forward hesitantly to rattle us into thinking the special question was en route. Certainly whenever he would praise some point ("That is really very perceptive") we would have breathing difficulties waiting for the follow-up (". . . in fact you are rather an exceptional person. How do you feel about serving your country?") and perhaps he knew this and kept himself sane this way. *Perhaps* he was unwittingly at the heart of the only really successful British spy operation—successful because accidental, whereby it will in the end emerge that, tipped off by numerous leaks, the Russians poured millions of rubles, some of their best agents, a Romanian gypsy dancer and a collapsible helicopter into attempting to infiltrate what was genuinely just an essay seminar on the reasons for the failure of the Second Crusade.

I mention this story because it illustrates something very odd about Britain—that its elite structure seems or seemed to imply a close and valuable link with the world of espionage. This clearly had been the case in the quite recent past. Around the time I was at Oxford the only secret service operative known to have been recruited—because he turned into a minor news story—had been a tubby oddball who as a student had dressed in SS uniform. Photos showed him to be an almost Monty Python–like security risk, and the fact that someone somewhere had indeed asked him the question rather knocked the last of the bloom from the secret service rose. But the intellectual and social calibre of British spying had in the past been traditionally very high, even while all the most famous spies turned out—which of course is why they were famous—to be working for the Russians.

The extraordinary story of Burgess, Philby and the rest has been told too often to be repeated here. As the Cold War ultimately ended in ways that made nonsense both of their ideological commitment and their treachery, much of the anguish around the story has evaporated or become hard to reimagine. Now, however, it seems very clear that Ian Fleming's role in the debacle was an odd and interesting one. The hysteria around the news of treachery and Maclean and Burgess's scarcely credible successful escape to the USSR dogged several already deeply depressed British governments.

They became some of the most damning news stories from 1951 down to 1963 (when Philby, with great insouciance, made his escape, too), with later, completely weird aftershocks like Sir Anthony Blunt's unmasking in 1979. Incidentally: the Keeper of the Queen's Pictures being a known Communist spy, is there no level of corrupt, zany peculiarity to which this country does *not* aspire?

The one really major exception to this shambles proved to be the great code-breaking operations, beginning in the early twentieth century and reaching their apogee with Bletchley Park and Ultra. This whole enterprise was shrouded, however, in such absolute secrecy that it only really came out in the open in the 1970s. So one of the key areas where Britain really could be proud and which had an overwhelming role in winning the Second World War was shut away during the crisis and collapse of the imperial state. Thus a highly success-ful British spying operation (which of course continued in mutated form throughout the Cold War) was unknown and only the screw-ups and pratfalls were in the public domain.

The spy scandals and the Bond novels formed an elaborate double act whereby "spy mania" fuelled enthusiasm for Bond while enthusiasm for Bond led to ever greater hysteria about spy traitors. The very clear, attractive and reassuring portrait of Her Majesty's Secret Service invented by Fleming was so convincing that the glamour around the real thing has some-how remained intact. The shorthand of the films (the shot of Westminster, the sound of Big Ben chiming, cut to pleasing, oak-lined office with pipe-smoking "M") has carried on the good work. No British spy-related story is without its uplift-ing James Bond reference: the fame of MI6's duff ziggurat headquarters on the Thames, the identity of its latest director (invariably "the new 'M'"), the general sense of reassuring infallibility totally at odds with what little we do know about their true actions. Perhaps the most recent evidence of MI6's uselessness—over Iraq's weapons programme—will at last tip the balance, but since the 1950s, in the minds of very many people around the world, Britain is preeminently the country of brilliant spies with brilliant gadgets, with the gimcrack truth, thanks to Fleming, limping far behind.

IT IS PROBABLY true to say that in the hierarchy of reasons for Bond's endurance his villains perhaps stand highest. It is quite hard to find fully comparable figures in earlier fiction, not least of course because plans for genuine global domination become feasible only in the wake of Hiroshima. An entirely new level of apocalyptic imagination becomes available to all sorts of writers and Fleming, along with Tolkien perhaps, makes best use of it.

Mr. Big in *Live and Let Die*, the second Bond novel, is the prototype for all others. The racism with which Fleming describes Mr. Big is undeniable: there is no doubting that he is meant to be scary because he is black but also because he is American and because he is, like Goldfinger and the other Fleming villains, so beguiling with words. He is the first to give one of those self-exculpating speeches which have so often been enjoyed and burlesqued ever since: "Mister Bond, I suffer from boredom. I am a prey to what the early Christians called 'accidie,' the deadly lethargy that envelops those who are sated . . ." Or even better: "Each day, Mister Bond, I try and set myself still higher standards of subtlety and technical polish so that each of my proceedings may be a work of art, bearing my signature as clearly as the creations of, let us say, Benvenuto Cellini." This marvellous, sonorous stuff could go on forever. It is impossible not to feel oneself urging Mr. Big to hurry up and kill Bond rather than dally in this way and wind up getting eaten by a leopard shark. The web of megalomaniac words is given to readers as a stark contrast to the bureaucratic desiccation of M, with Bond strung up in the middle, moral because British, criminal because a state-armed murderer.

This sense of tremendously clever men, caged in by the dreariness of the diurnal, planning vast and devastating schemes more for their own pleasure than for any rational gain, so flatters and cheers the reader that it is enough on its own, in my view, to justify Fleming's literary career. There are clearly precedents: Dr. Fu Manchu undoubtedly lurks in the background, aspects of Moriarty, Quilp, the Professor in *The Secret Agent*, Melmoth in *The Way We Live Now*, but the Olympian grandeur is new, specific to its time and specific to Fleming.

After a while it becomes clear that Fleming is far more besotted with the villains than with Bond: the impossibly ruthless Emilio Largo, dabbing his forehead with his Charvet handkerchief soaked "with the musky scent of Schiaparelli's Snuff"; Rosa Klebb in her blood-spattered smock rushing down the corridors of SMERSH so as not to be too late for a torture session; Blofeld in his castle of suicide in *You Only Live Twice* (extolled thus by his sidekick, Irma Bunt: "You are indeed a genius, *lieber* Ernst . . . It is as if one of the great fairy tales has come to life. A sort of Disneyland of Death. But of course . . . on an altogether grander, more poetic scale"). This crazily inventive empathy for evil is a complete pleasure to read now, and clearly speaks to something inside all Fleming's readers. Who would not want Dr. No's Caribbean lair, Blofeld's Alpine fastness, Goldfinger's Kentucky stud? Even as we are picking our noses or clipping our toenails there is a piece of us saying, "Mr. Bond, all my life I have been in love. I have been in love with gold. I love its colour, its brilliance, its divine heaviness."

WHY DID the British Empire come to an end at the *exact* point when people started travelling in jet airliners? How did something that had mutated and grown for at least four centuries fold up completely in the fifties? Perhaps the technological reasons will become obvious in a few more decades and we are simply too close to see them, but a curious mutation of distance and time goes on in the early fifties that is at the very least suggestive.

It is true that during its existence very few people saw any of the British Empire unless they had direct business with it and perhaps the technological changes that allowed lots of people both to crowd in and have a look and to travel around pointing out its ugliness was enough to kill it off. Until almost the end the people who left Britain for the Empire tended to leave for good—to go to Australia or to Canada was to disappear to new planets for all but a very small elite. Farmers, engineers, miners, the new Vancouver or Perth middle class, poured out of Britain—still a flood of hundreds of thousands a year throughout the 1950s. Some made money and in small numbers cheerfully returned home, many more made money and cheerfully remained, and quite a few simply got stuck. With the folding up of the British Empire (and increasing restrictions on migrants) in the 1950s the idea of Britain as a country which you tried quite hard to leave went partly into abeyance. Soldiers and administrators moved around, but the former in any number only on special occasions—and certainly many fewer people altogether than now fly back and forth to Greece in any given summer. And, of course, they all went by sea on journeys which now seem almost insanely long, taking weeks to get anywhere. An aunt emigrated to Australia at the beginning of the seventies and we still have the picture of her, in a very charismatic coat and hat, waiting anxiously at the Southampton docks for her ship: incredible!

For the non-emigrant Empire the 1930s saw the brief era of "jazz-age colonialism" when intercontinental trains, liners and flying-boats, the sealed spaces so crucial to Agatha Christie novels, allowed the very wealthy to drop into Alexandria, Mombasa, Penang or Shanghai. It had been hard but just possible to imagine as legitimate and quite exciting the just post-Conrad world of, say, Malaya back in the 1900s with its strange, isolated, semi-nativized, quite often dying European planters and traders—a ruthless and mercenary bunch, but also courageous and a part of a wider world of Bugis, Chinese, Malays, Indians and Arabs all trading away and either making piles of money or getting killed. Somehow, after the First World War, though, when families start coming out on ocean liners, visitors pop in and out and everything stultifies into a cold, dull, race regime it becomes irrevocably nauseating—the mere parasitic battening onto countries genuinely transformed by the vast work of earlier generations. But this too was a ship-based world still, a world of ports, sailors, docks, quarantine, telegraphs, dredgers—a world which has now been handed over entirely to freight rather than passengers, beyond the scattering of leisured folk on the *QE2*.

All of this changes in the 1950s: *Is* there a link? Perhaps it lies in the handover of technology from Britain to the United States, and specifically it lies in the Comet story. All the problems facing Britain in the post-war world come together in the terrible Comet jet disasters of the early 1950s.

Although sinking beneath the weight of German, American, Russian and Japanese strength and ferocity in 1939–45, Britain still maintained a remarkable and versatile military-industrial complex. It was not as though Britain was wholly stultified—it was simply battered and exhausted. It had the strength to initiate key aspects of what became the Manhattan Project but it did not remotely have the drive or resources to bring it to fruition (if one can use such a jaunty word here). The aeroplane industry was the one major exception. In the First World War, Britain had been the world's largest aeroplane manufacturer and despite huge cutbacks in the 1920s and early thirties it was still absolutely at the cutting edge and a close competitor with the Germans. As the hideous summer of 1940 unfolded, all Britain's obsolete or misguided planes (e.g., the Fairey Battle—not a war-winning name or aircraft) and their brave but baffled crews were destroyed in a few days, leaving both Hurricane and Spitfire fighters and in advanced stages of research and completion the Wellington and Lancaster, aircraft which for sheer size and brutality the Germans never came close to matching, as they found their cities devastated to a degree they had never been able to approach in their own aerial attacks on Britain.

This aggressive and successful interest in planes meant that the British military sponsored Frank Whittle's invention of the jet engine, and later the creation of the Allies' first operational jet fighter, which unfortunately came on stream just as there was no Luftwaffe left to shoot down—but by its existence made all other planes obsolete. Some of this excitement can still be felt in David Lean's strange film *The Sound Barrier*, which, despite a central story of murky tedium, captures perfectly this British love affair with planes, with ecstatic footage of test pilots at high altitude flinging around propellered Spitfires at the beginning and jet-powered Vampires at the end. For a country that had seen itself rescued from destruction in 1940 by its aircraft designs, the new world of jets seemed immensely potent.

The Comet stood as the great focus for all this, the symbol of British modernity, filmed in *The Sound Barrier* with camerawork that is almost erotic. The world's first jet-liner, it first flew in 1949 and had its first commercial flight in 1952 on the tremendously imperial and symbolic Johannesburg route, stopping off in British territory in Rhodesia, Uganda and Sudan before going on to Lebanon and Italy. Like every other British initiative of the time, however, it went wrong, with the inauguration of a new kind of horror, the passenger-jet disaster, as four Comets either crashed on takeoff or disintegrated in midair. All planes were grounded, and by the time exhaustive tests showed that metal fatigue had caused the crashes, the Boeing 707 was born and the British civil industry wasted away. After the War Britain had appeared a close second to the United States as an aircraft maker, but by the 1960s, in every area except engines it had become insignificant. Not helpful was a Conservative minister in the late fifties having a vision that the future belonged to military encounters between short-range missiles, not manned aircraft, sidelining fighter research in favour of missile research (also later scrapped).

The great, daft monument to the final convulsions of Britain as a civil airliner manufacturer was of course the

Concorde. If ever there was a clear example of wistful, post-imperial compensatory spending it must be this. Put through by Harold Macmillan with almost no serious discussion at all, Concorde wound up costing around £1.8 billion for fourteen small aircraft used only by hobbyists and slightly hilarious businessmen. Admittedly this was not a solitary British aberration: the cost was shared with the French, who were in the throes of Algerian independence and bracing themselves for close to a million angry white settlers and pro-French Algerians shipping into their southern ports, and also therefore having a need to chew on some absurd techno uppers.

The fifties and sixties are otherwise a wilderness of budget nightmares, cancelled projects and general embarrassment, ending in a much reduced industry, certainly not one that was at the cutting edge of anything much. The only interesting, indeed revolutionary, project remained the amazing HOTOL from the early eighties. This half-plane half-rocket was meant to be blasted at huge speed into the air, where it would smash through the atmosphere like a squash ball and zoom round in orbit before hurtling, red-hot, into Sydney International after only a few hours, and right on time. Could this plane have flown? Would passengers have valued the saved flying time if it meant being converted into strands of jelly, albeit jelly (as the nauseated, ashen Australian cleaning crew would discover) still loosely gripping the glasses that had contained their complimentary cocktails? Who would have volunteered for the first test flight? We will never know: not least because for twenty years I have in fact completely misunderstood the HOTOL project, the craziness of which had intermittently preoccupied me since it was finally cancelled by Thatcher. Only on finishing this book did I discover that far from being a comic way to liquidize self-important executives, it was in fact a crewless satellite launcher of no great interest (it seems to have worked by pouring billions of pounds of subsidy money through its special engines). Britain's final mad dream of dominating world flight, even if it could no longer dominate the world itself, had in fact shuddered to a halt with Concorde but kept going for a few more twilit years in my ill-informed brain.

As people began then to fly around the world on business or pleasure in the 1950s to an unprecedented extent, they were to be conveyed in non-British planes, just as wars were to be fought on the whole with American, Russian and French planes. The European empires dissolved as mass tourism began.

Fleming himself flew voraciously, not just London–New York–Jamaica but wherever he could, operating at the very cusp of what could be achieved in a dizzyingly expanding industry. His nonfiction book *Thrilling Cities* is a sort of hymn to this new ability to pop into a metropolis, savour it and then move on. Bond's flights in the books have a delighted sense of newness ("The sixty-eight tons deadweight of the Super-Constellation hurtled high above the green and brown chequerboard of Cuba") that must have been very vivid to its first readers. In the early films, the Bond theme blares out simply because Bond is going through customs, having got off a plane: a very far from commonplace event for most filmgoers in the early sixties and well worth playing music for.

IN DECEMBER 1952, a horrible smog hit London: a disastrous mixture of river fog and coal smoke became trapped over the city, smothering everything in a dirty yellow mass.

It was sometimes impossible to see more than a few inches and everyone blundered and retched their ways home through streets of immobilized buses, trams and cars.

My mother would sometimes tell the story of how, as a young secretary, she picked her way through this hideous fog, so dense and harsh that it killed some four thousand people and shortened the lives of many more in insidious, immeasurable ways. She was in her late teens and part of the army of shorthand and typing secretaries who once filled large cities and who now seem as quaint as lavender sellers or cat's-meat men. She described the cold foulness of the smog, the dirtiness, the way it reduced lit street lamps to small spheres of brown-yellow light, ruined clothing and filled hair, and her despair at ever getting through the miles to her parents' home: a simple commute inflated at a stroke into a nightmare. As she stumbled on, a nattily dressed older man from the City in a pinstripe suit and a bowler hat—a further antique, as remote now as if he were wearing doublet and hose—appeared out of the gloom. He walked with her much of the way, chatting and being encouraging as they dodged through the murk. He then waved and vanished.

My mother clearly valued this story and it is one of the few things I know of her life in the 1950s. In an odd way I have always felt grateful to the man in the bowler hat—I first heard about my mother in the smog when growing up and I have kept the initial child's instinct of happiness that someone had looked after her and that she was safe. I have also kept in some small part a sense that it was only she and this possibly slightly sinister gentleman fighting the smog, as in a fairy story, when of course it was millions of Londoners often in far worse circumstances. Indeed, keeping the smog as a personal story is very important as otherwise it would be beyond human strength not to view it as a nauseating, overwhelming symbol of Britain in this period: a temptation that this narrative resists.

This London of smog and typists and trolleybuses and men in bowler hats became four months later, with *Casino Royale*'s publication, gradually filled with Ian Fleming's first readers. My mother caught on to him early and read each book as it came out. She remembered vividly the shock at the end of *From Russia with Love* where it seems Bond has been killed, poisoned by Rosa Klebb's fiendish knitting needle, though reading it now this ending is so vague as to positively invite Bond's recovery. It is as though Conan Doyle had left Professor Moriarty and Sherlock Holmes battling on the edge of the fatal Alpine waterfall with the latter wearing a crash helmet, a life jacket and an inward smirk, with a rescue helicopter clattering overhead. But back then, when first published, it really did seem the end for Bond. When he returned the next year, in *Dr. No*, my mother recalled a sense of overwhelming relief—as though a friend had pulled through a bad illness. It was around this point that the books began to take on a burgeoning hyper-popularity, each book operating on a grander scale than the one before and in turn selling to fresh readers all the previous books in the series.

THE BRITISH governments of the 1950s now give out an overwhelming sense of weariness. This was less true at the time because there was such a hail of events that they appeared quite busy, but it was only the seemingly busy behaviour of a corpse being tugged around by dogs. These were all desperately old and baffled people, brought up in a world that assumed Britain was the apple of the world's eye. Attlee, Churchill, Eden and Macmillan had all fought bravely in the First World War to defend their country and specific values which had then been mocked by the unfolding disaster of the Depression and the rise of countries fearfully inimical to British greatness. They had in their different ways tossed and turned through the 1930s and on the whole had *not* drawn the conclusion of figures such as Chamberlain, Halifax and Simon that capitulation was the only way forward. They had not, however, proved in any real sense more perceptive than the appeasers. The latter prided themselves on their rationality: this proved catastrophic in dealing with Germany but it was at least based on a sense of the limits of British power: Halifax's views, for example, on India's future were always vastly more perceptive than Churchill's. The problem that racked them all was that two world wars had been far too high a price to pay for Britain's place in the world.

There is an interesting debate among historians about how much the British Empire ever mattered to Britain's population as a whole. There was of course an enormous network of people for whom it mattered a great deal, whether at the level of parents receiving letters from a daughter in South Australia or shareholders receiving dividends from South African mines. But whether someone making, say, handcuffs or bullets in the West Midlands cared specifically about their destination or whether knowing at school where Johor or Nyasaland were on maps really shaped people's lives it is impossible to say. It certainly had an effect on emigrants but they, in most cases, well, emigrated and tended to develop a sense of slightly affectionate contempt for Britain which so irritated those left behind. Soldiers and sailors were always important and their movement from crisis to crisis defined the headlines continuously from the opening of the Second World War through innumerable interventions until such things finally petered out in the late sixties in Malaysia and Oman. Their numbers reached a high-water mark of some five million personnel spread around the world in 1945 but this was drawn down rapidly, once Germany and Japan had surrendered, and then reduced even more rapidly as country after country suggested they could do without their presence, with an upward blip for the Korean War (where some fourteen thousand British troops were engaged). Asia remains scattered with endless camps and graveyards, now long abandoned by their sweaty and irritable British garrison troops. I once visited a bookseller in Pune, in the Western Ghats, whose shop was on the edge of the old cantonment. He cheerfully showed me a back room piled with hundreds of desiccated, yellowed Penguin books—the consignment for the troops that had arrived just after they had left in 1947 (and including, as I remember, a novel by Sylvia Townsend Warner).

The overwhelming fact about the British Empire in the twentieth century, however, was that in two world wars it had drawn in millions of British people to fight for it and, frequently, get killed. It is a small tragedy in light of what happened to other countries, and indeed in light of what Britain itself did to some of those countries. But it was nonetheless a real one that the amusing gunboat expeditions and high jinks of the nineteenth century gave Britain effectively unlimited liabilities in the twentieth. The husbands and sons who in their thousands upon thousands found themselves dying of fever on the Euphrates, killed by camp guards in

Thailand or drowning in the South China Sea, did so to protect a range of interests that generational echelons born only a few years earlier could warmly but dimly enjoy at no cost to themselves.

By the 1950s figures such as Eden and Macmillan (Churchill was effectively a superannuated blank for much of his nostalgic, inert final premiership) were staring at the wreck of everything they had believed in. Every year brought bad news—not just the loss of India and the rest of south Asia, but even China, an area so long despoiled with almost no effort by British interests, turned on its masters and, following Mao's victory in 1949, kicked Britain out of everywhere except Hong Kong.

This pattern was repeated everywhere—either nicely (Australia and New Zealand sensibly deciding to favour their own direct treaty links with the United States) or not nicely (in riots, violence and boycotts across most of the world). Attlee's Labour government had an ideological commitment to Indian independence that helped it to happen; Churchill, Eden and Macmillan had nothing to help them beyond a sense of bitterness and depression that their lives and values had in the end been made fools of by the progress of history. What *was* the right way to react to Britain's chaotic decline and the wilderness of imperial issues which heaped up in their in-trays?

This is one of many points where the value of reading history becomes awkward. The key questions have to be: did they finesse Britain's collapse intelligently and was there another way to do it? These are, of course, unanswerable. There is something illusory and repulsive about Britain in the early and mid-fifties that is unshakable—whether it is the nuclear tests or the Suez invasion or the failure to take the

European Community seriously or the ferocious destruction of the Mau-Mau rebellion. What we cannot see now are the difficulties Eden and Macmillan faced and the uncertainty about the future. We can now see that European race-based empires were all finished and attempts to prolong them revolting and mad. We can also see that modern-day Britain was preset to become a strange, hybrid, medium-sized country strung out between Europe and America—a country that would have been utterly unrecognizable to a visitor zoomed forward in a time machine from 1955.

There were, of course, plenty of people around in the 1950s who had a different sense of the future—whether protesting against the Bomb or filling Trafalgar Square in outrage at the Suez invasion. None changed Britain's future, as they were ignored by the rulers. They did do huge (and positive) damage internally, though, to the assumption that British values lay in projecting military power and generally swaggering about patronizingly. They provided a model for behaviour which was to have huge repercussions for sixties society, where it would also be ignored by governments, albeit governments now with a greatly weakened ability to damage the world much.

It is at this point that Fleming and Fleming's values come to the rescue: as the Conservative with a vision of how things might be better. As Britain's greatness went off a cliff with the chaotic mass decolonization of 1960, the books' sales went higher and higher, with *Goldfinger* and *Thunderball* the necessary palliative to a situation that for millions of ordinary voters (and not just Conservative ones, to be fair) was scarcely bearable. To read the newspapers of the time is to see a sort of paroxysm of national self-loathing—a bitterness that settled in at least until Margaret Thatcher's rule and in some areas beyond, in, for example, our attitude to the EU, or indeed, in some moods, to the United States. The Empire for whom so many had died only fifteen to twenty years earlier suddenly found itself with: nothing. Conventionally it was the army in Burma that had been called the "forgotten army" but almost every campaign of the two world wars outside western Europe now fell into the same category — including all the wars of the 1950s. There became a settled pattern of footage of panicked and angry British troops, tear gas, protests, trials, thunderous newspaper editorials, special commissions, all leading to the same result of independence, leaving as a residue only a handful of freaks (Gibraltar) or dozing whoopee cushions (the Falklands).

As a large part of the planet slipped from Britain's grasp one man silently maintained the country's reputation. When a secret organization with stolen atomic weapons planned to destroy Miami Beach it was not the Americans who would save the world, but a solitary Englishman, mucking around for wholly implausible reasons in the Bahamas. The beautiful Domino, key to the mystery, approaches him with the immortal exchange: "'And who might you be?' 'My name's Bond, James Bond.'"

ONE OF THE fossil claims to greatness of the Bond novels must be their treatment of the underwater world. If you had to search for a symbol for everything most remote from the immediate, make-and-mend existence of early 1950s Britain it would have to be a Caribbean coral reef. We are now so saturated with images of sharks and tropical fish that the dazzling parallel planet unveiled in *Live and Let Die*, *Thunderball* and *Octopussy* is now almost unreachable — except that Fleming writes about it so well and with such enthusiasm that the pleasure remains even without the novelty.

The conquest of water is one of the less noticed post-War achievements, but it has proved more imaginatively potent in many ways than the conquest of space. The latter has generated an entire genre but it was a genre that in many ways predated the actual achievement. Pre-war science fiction was as luxuriant and deranged as anything that has come in its wake—in a sense the actual penetration of space has been something of a disappointment. Surely much of the point (well, at least for children) of the moon shots was the hope that we would be treated to some final panicked communication from an astronaut as something nameless and dreadful came bursting through the hatchway. There was the disappointment of everything being completely sterile, allied to the bathos of astronauts seemingly chosen for their lack of imagination, dumbly playing golf on the moon. There was the total dullness of the escape capsule being heaved from the ocean and opened to reveal rather blank men with military backgrounds waving at us, rather than, say, all the space suits being found empty, except one choked to the brim with blood-soaked fungus. No, space has been buffeted by simply too many disappointments. Science fiction from H. G. Wells onwards had prepared us for space marvels that never emerged. The current desperate throws from astronomers suggesting there is certainly life in galaxies that would require many lifetimes to reach effectively ends the quest in bored hysteria. The monstrous, infinite malevolence of Mars kept us going through a very wobbly bit of our post-religious existence, and now it seems that all that lives there is, at best, some bits of moss (no tentacles, no eyes narrowed in mad hate).

What a contrast with the underwater world. This is a technology area, like television or jet planes, which makes the 1930s and the 1950s seem almost unrelated. That through all human history the sea has been a sealed surface, an absolute barrier to all beyond a few Gulf or Andaman diving communities, is now almost unimaginable. Submarines plunged through the water completely blind, surrounded by invisible wonders and horrors, the external underwater view beloved of U-boat movies of course being an impossibility.

I was once in a German photo archive and spent a freaked-out couple of hours leafing through a beautifully mounted presentation album given to the regional commander of the Nazi forces in Norway. The album dated from 1943 and was filled with pictures of the sort of dazzling "baroque" weaponry so beloved of the Nazis and which did so much to undermine their war effort in the face of relentless Allied mass-production of about a dozen simple things. Lovely, charismatic seaplanes and flying boats abound in the photos, together with lots of shots of happy, motivated young men building docks and airstrips, horsing around in the Arctic sun. The pictures appear to show a world where, astonishingly, the state simply pays for years of outdoors recreation. What is really disturbing about the photo album is, of course, that there is no hint anywhere that the purpose of all this activity was to build infrastructure to sink ships, drowning thousands of British and American merchant seamen trying to take convoys round Norway to supply the USSR. The quintessential figure at the heart of the album is the deep-sea diver in his impossibly heavy suit and robot-like helmet. If there was ever a symbolic representation of man's marginal, utterly vulnerable status underwater it is this figure, the brass helmet now doomed for evermore to decorate chandlers' and nautically themed restaurants. Presumably, like astronauts, the individuals chosen to wear these suits were picked for their lack of existential angst and stolidly went about their work oblivious to the frantic black abyss of madness that engulfed them. Early science-fiction illustrations propose these diving suits as models for space suits and they share the same sense of desperate clodhopperdom, of a marginal, tenuous presence fuelled by readily kinked air pipes. Even when used to brilliant comic effect by Buster Keaton in *The Navigator* (1924), the diving suit winds up just being stifling and frightening. To see these clunky figures, even knowing that they are methodically and inexorably putting together docks that will be springboards for killing merchant seamen, is to know that we have no place underwater. Images of life below the sea before 1945 or so were therefore highly restricted, too, picked together from stuff hauled mutilated and gasping to the surface, from contextless aquaria and from anecdotes and sketches. Perhaps the best, certainly the most lovely and persuasive, pre-war vision of life underwater was Disney's *Pinocchio*, which also established the beauty-in-the-midst-of-danger topos so dear to all post-war documentary makers.

All this changed dazzlingly through Jacques Cousteau's wartime invention of the aqualung, an invention kept secret from the Nazis in the Occupied French Riviera. Fleming's residence on Jamaica allowed him to participate in this whole revolution, also allied to mass use of rubber and plastics, begun in the 1930s, to make effective masks, fins and snorkel tubes. He was an enthusiastic diver, had dived with Cousteau himself, and his love of this brand-new world comes out in much of his writing. The underwater scene in *Live and Let Die* (written in the same year that aqualungs first became available in the United States) is a sort of fishy ghost-train of horrors as Bond makes his way across to Mr. Big's private island in the dark attended by barracuda, octopuses, etc., all doing their worst and behaving just as one would hope, a cavalcade of malicious seafood, before the pièce de résistance in which Bond is deliberately sprayed in fish guts to attract a welter of undersea predators. First reading this at age eleven, I found it chimed easily with an entire later genre perhaps best typified by Willard Price's *Underwater Adventure*, which memorably featured a hero zooming along on an underwater sled, pursued by a shark and with a vast octopus clinging to the tip of the sled, clambering sucker by sucker towards the hero, hoping to tear bits off him with its grotesque beak: a situation resolved only by a passing swordfish kebabbing the octopus and the shark's losing interest.

My early enthusiasm for Willard Price means that I cannot entirely blame Fleming for this, but nonetheless it is above all his descriptions of the underwater world that have caused me to waste so many hours splashing timidly around in a snorkel. Entire days of life have gone by swimming in warm but empty water—when I could have been reading or drinking—bracing myself for an encounter with danger which of course never comes. If someone goes into a tropical sea in a Bond novel the narrative *demands* the immediate presence of some dangerous fish. Indeed, it would be a banal disgrace if there were not one—just as Bond cannot talk to a girl without having sex with her or enter a casino without winning big. Most unfortunately this has so raised the bar for anyone entering the water as to make the actual experience a bit woeful. Every minute of watching small nervous dull fish in various locations has seemed to imply some hideous presence, some ravening, snaggle-toothed, Gorgonian jabberwock of a creature drifting up from the appalling depths, but currently just out of sight. Naturally such an apparition would not be wholly welcome, but there must be a part of any diver which yearns for such an encounter—when Bond swims in Nassau harbour alongside a barracuda it sets a standard to which anyone must aspire.

My greatest diving disappointment, in a crowded field, was at last to see an enormous dark circle on the sea bottom—a van-size semi-gelid monster studded with lures, bristles and teeth, the kind that ingests its prey with a wobbly convulsion of its entire body. My heart racing, torn between fascination and fear, I swam towards it, only to find that it was the shadow cast by a floating trampoline used by guests at the local branch of Jimmy Buffett's Margaritaville resort. Perhaps, indeed probably, the sea is simply so much emptier now than it was fifty years ago. Once, from the banal, un-Bondy safety of a glass-bottomed boat I stared down on the wreck of a fishing boat which featured a couple of massive stingrays, grey, malevolent and, with their great, thick, flexlike tails, like pieces of defective electrical equipment from some parallel universe. The seeming rage in their eyes could not balance out the fact that they were surrounded by acres of almost sterile water with plastic cups and bits and bobs drifting about in it—the trampy, marginal, grouchy survivors of a despoiled environment. It wasn't quite what I had in mind when first thrilled by *Underwater Adventure* and *Live and Let Die*.

But for his first, less jàded readers what Fleming was revealing was something entirely new, impossibly, almost achingly, overcoloured and riotous. He established definitively the little shop of horrors we have all enjoyed ever since:

the shark, the pain of treading on a super-poisonous stonefish ("sometimes it's so frightful [the victim's] eyes literally fall out of their sockets"), the relentless octopus, the greedy barracuda, with every creature understanding its cue and behaving just as we hoped it would.

But also he popularized, in the way that Cousteau did for nonfiction (or semi-nonfiction) purposes, the idea of democratizing the sea—that with a little bit of equipment anyone can see what had previously been the preserve of the odd millionaire with a glass panel to his yacht. This sense of freedom, of delight in buoyancy and bright colour, is a tone quite new to the human experience and nowhere better expressed than in Fleming's books, ushering in a new era which we now barely notice—the barracuda's "gold and black tiger's eye," the miniature octopuses feeding off the decomposing RAF crew, "dreadful, glinting, red-eyed comets that slapped themselves into dark corners"—nothing could be more enjoyable; the massive stingray "dark grey with that violet tinge that is so often a danger signal in the underwater world." This was a world a million miles from clanking Nazi welders—of drifting and waving among reefs rather than crashing and puffing through them. Much of Fleming's life in the end seems painful and neuralgic, but this seems wholly enviable—that he could see all these marvels without any of our own worn-flat, environmentally panicked over-familiarity.

Chapter Four

MANAGED DECLINE

WHEN THE SECOND James Bond novel, *Live and Let Die*, landed before an on the whole rather indifferent public in 1954, it teemed not only with wonderful underwater fantasy of a new kind but with Americanness. As Bond flies into New York he jumps across an almost indescribably vast divide—between a culture which by the fifties had little to look forward to beyond the next Benjamin Britten opera or *Lord of the Flies* and a culture that was striding into a dramatic and turbulent golden age of greatness. American culture always seems to be going through a golden age, but that of the fifties is scarcely credible. Where to begin? Is it Charles Mingus' "Goodbye Pork Pie Hat" or Perez Prado's "Havana 3 a.m." or Little Richard's "Get Rich Quick"? Is it *Lolita* or the magical rise of Tito Puente or (a specific personal weakness) Cal Tjader's Californian lounge vibraphone wonderland? Or *Invisible Man* or the Seagram Building or *North by North-west*? Or de Kooning or *The Adventures of Augie March* or Howlin' Wolf singing "I Asked For Water (She Gave Me Gasoline)"? Or Billie Holiday or *Rebel Without a Cause* or Jasper Johns? Or the Guggenheim or *The Rake's Progress* or Ella Fitzgerald? Enough! *Some Like It Hot* or *The Company She Keeps* or *The Searchers*? Really enough. Plus, of course, all the scientific research that would build towards the contraceptive pill, satellites, computers, the space programme and Pop Tarts—in other words, the entire modern world.

Fleming/Bond flew into this astounding stew and basically didn't really notice it. Bond is always rather uneasy in America because it is clear he can't compete. Fleming realizes this and gets him away from major urban areas as soon as feasible—Bond in New York talking stiffly with Felix Leiter and tutting about "hepcats smoking reefers" loses his cruel nonchalance, in a few moments mutating from cosmopolitan killer to pursed-lipped civil servant from the land of toad-in-the-hole. Fleming shifts him on to zones with a more simplified backdrop—carnival rides such as Las Vegas or the fetid comedy of southern Florida. Here Bond has the right, simplified scenery to thrive and none of the terrifying cultural background noise of New York or Los Angeles. There is also an air of incompetence or at least professional lassitude (as is strongly the case, too, in the Kentucky of *Goldfinger*) that gets round the obvious problem of local law enforcement. If Fleming had been foolish enough to send Bond to Chicago, say, or Cleveland (let alone Toronto), it is impossible not to feel he would have been arrested as an undesirable within moments, generating a rather dull adventure involving bail applications and prison food.

This dazzling New York world Fleming himself loved, albeit mostly at the level of smart hotels and excellent cocktails rather than as the heartbeat of a new Renaissance—but then as years go by it becomes ever clearer that things such as excellent cocktails are as symptomatic of a great culture as Jackson Pollock or *Junkie*. For visitors from careworn, shattered Britain, arriving in the United States in the early

1950s must have been akin to Dorothy's stepping into luridly coloured Munchkinland from monochrome Kansas. America had had some horrible years, with a Depression far worse than that experienced by Britain, but despite having had casualties roughly matching Britain's in the War, its home front had never suffered any real threat and its economy from the beginning of the War onwards had gone into hyperdrive—taking on an almost terrifying exuberance that pulled large chunks of the world along with it.

Every account of the British experience in the early 1950s now seems unbelievably depressing—a narrow, confused and cynical literary elite articulating a sort of corrupt despair. When I think of the fifties in Britain I think of writers engaged in grimly inexpert adulterous sex, generally interrupted in mid-session by arguments about whose turn it is to hop out of bed and stick another coin in the meter to keep the bar-fire going. America, beneath its Cold War/Eisenhower carapace, was a delirious, explosive vision of the future—the future we all now venerate and roll about in so happily. Britain is the lucky recipient of this, but in the 1950s this was not true at all. Bits very imperfectly started leaking through, but the results, except at the purely second-hand level of Elvis records or the movies, were only really to kick in during the following decade, a principal celebrant being, of course, the Bond movies, which draw so heavily on the things that Fleming himself didn't quite notice about 1950s America.

This is most ideally realized perhaps in the early scene in the film of *Goldfinger* (1964) where the camera lovingly dwells on Miami Beach, the swimming pools, the sunshine, the bathing suits, the vast hotel rooms, all topped off with a blaring big-band jazz soundtrack. We are now terribly used to

America—and Britain has taken on so many of its features—but in those moments of *Goldfinger*, we still get a glimpse into the America that made the books and early films so vivid, that must have made its original British viewers' eyes smart.

As Bond/Fleming sits in America and tucks into a mountain of crabs and melted butter, gorges on steak "so soft you can cut it with a fork" and slurps another giant martini it becomes an almost pornographic contrast with the cable-knit sweaters and briarwood pipes, trad-jazz-revival and milk-bar world he had flown away from. As Felix Leiter in the book of *Thunderball* watches from a helicopter through his binoculars a naked girl sunbathing on a yacht and yells to Bond, "Natural blonde," Fleming's original, chilblained, earnest British reader, with his uncontrollable flashbacks to the Burmese jungle and ill-informed keenness on Harold Macmillan, must have flung the novel across the room in despair.

FLEMING'S ATTITUDES towards America were very much of his class and time—but these attitudes in various forms continue to be very powerful in Britain so his manner is much less startlingly old-fashioned than his views on, say, race. Fleming knew America and Americans very well, not least because of his close involvement in the brief but extraordinary period of large-scale entanglement between the two countries in 1943–45. There is a very moving scene in Michael Powell and Emeric Pressburger's movie *A Matter of Life and Death*, made in 1945, in which a group of British and American servicemen and villagers in an English village are rehearsing *A Midsummer Night's Dream*—the sequence is only an echo of the main story (which is about a seemingly doomed romance between a British Lancaster pilot and an American radio operator) but was very self-consciously meant to stand for a specific moment of unity and to draw on Churchill's and many others' ideas about a new and permanent fusing of the two peoples. Fleming—shuttling between London and Washington, attending planning meetings, liaising here, there and everywhere— was one of the links in this great web that resulted most productively in D-Day and continues to have strange aftershocks in the tortuous "special relationship" today, its tangled roots buried deep in the military, treasury and intelligence.

This genuine fusion however was never to happen and from the British side Fleming makes it clear why. In the end he just couldn't stand it. He couldn't bear "Eldollarado," as he called it; he loathed playing second fiddle, being patronized and slighted and laughed at. He became adept in the way that so many thousands of other pliant British people did at taking Americans' money and then querulously deriding them in private. He knew where the future lay, liked some Americans very much, loved aspects of the culture (cocktails, pornography), spent many summers after the War staying with friends in Vermont, but found his and his country's unaccustomed role intolerable at heart.

A case could be made for Fleming's relationship with America being as much the spark for Bond as was his revulsion from socialist Britain. The books are drenched in this basic awkwardness—that Bond is in practical terms a solitary, and to be honest slightly dotty, emblem of Britain's secret might, whereas Felix Leiter at the CIA, who joins Bond in several of the novels and is a tedious presence in many of the films, is a mere interlocutor between Bond and a tremendously resourced organization. Fleming was also, of course, pulled financially into America's orbit and the earlier books (*Casino*

Royale, Live and Let Die, Diamonds Are Forever) were written with many American details, often rather fawning, in the
hope of cracking the American readership. As this strategy
foundered on American indifference, he moved more away
from U.S. locations, only to find himself suddenly a massive
success there towards the end of his writing life, which provided the incentive for him to write the diabolical *The Spy
Who Loved Me*—a book which, if there were any justice,
should have chased him right back out of that market.

As is invariably the case, Bond's perception of America is
also Fleming's and he follows a sort of tourist trail around
Manhattan, New York State, Florida and Nevada, interspersed
with scenes of sometimes brilliantly managed violence. Except
perhaps in Florida, the locations never really ring very true—
they rely too heavily on existing lore and books and movies.
Las Vegas in particular never feels like a place that Fleming
seriously visited, so stale and uninvolving is his take on it—
and the scene with Bond and girl on a little railcar being chased
by a gangster in an old-fashioned, cow-catcher-sporting American steam locomotive must rival Bond's battle with the giant
squid in *Dr. No* as "the scene most likely to suggest that these
books are in practice rubbish."

Fleming's bitterness towards America was very much the
bitterness of his class and generation, of course. The whole
point of Britain was its commanding role and as this fell to
pieces during and after the War, America was both a bright
spot (the rescuer) and a dark one (the rescuer with a profound
disregard for Britain's colonial role). Britain may have in the
early twenty-first century stabilized somewhat in its global
position, but the gag reflex continues to rack us now, particularly as all the arrogance and insularity that have been our

stock-in-trade for centuries now appear to have been transferred across the Atlantic. It was hugely important to the ideology of Britain that it be a decent country, almost outside history, a sort of sterile exemplar—a country which had decided views about other countries and which patronized or controlled them all. The unravelling of such assumptions in the twentieth century is still far from complete and America today still remains the area where that unravelling is most painful. All other countries view Britain through historical lenses as being admirable, hypocritical, conniving, inspirational, brutal, sexually comic, and so on, but we ignore them. It is America alone whose specific range of often derisive views we are painfully aware of and humiliated by. We share a language—but that language now allows us to hear our inadequacies carefully spelt out by a place far wealthier and more confident and with a vigorous tradition of invective and derisive humour: a nightmare, in other words.

Bond is driven mad by America's superiority—the cars are better, the hotels wonderful, the trains more pleasurable, the food yummier. The air of sexual release too is palpable. When Felix Leiter advises Bond that "mostly here we sleep in the raw" a mighty wind blasts through the whole British world of pyjamas, slippers and chilblain creams.

So demented does Bond become that at one point he raves that "the best things in America are chipmunks, and oyster stew," which must surely be beyond verification. In *Diamonds Are Forever* he offers American readers the happy lecture, "There's nothing so extraordinary about American gangsters . . . They're not Americans. Mostly a lot of Italian bums with monogrammed shirts who spend the day eating spaghetti and meatballs and squirting scent over themselves." This is followed up later in the book with comments on "Italian greaseballs who filled themselves with pizza pie and beer." One can imagine an increasingly thin smile on the lips of this book's original American readers and a happy affirmative grunt from the British.

IS JAMES BOND in himself a major fictional invention? I think one can answer fairly readily, "No." In and of himself he barely exists as a character and the constant, rather desperate mentions of his scars and his hair ("a thick comma") only serve to emphasize that there is nothing else to him—that the scars float in space rather than being attached to a plausible body. Bond is in every sense a shop dummy moved around by the chain-smoking, bow-tied figure struggling around behind him, trying to keep him upright, get his trousers off, and so on. It is as Fleming's surrogate that Bond takes on character traits, and it is impossible not to envy and enjoy the way that Fleming simply gets Bond to do stuff Fleming liked doing himself. Fleming liked golf; Bond likes golf. Fleming liked diving; well, so does Bond. He visits places Fleming likes, drinks the same drinks and, almost certainly, maps Fleming's own dislikes and enthusiasms. There is a bizarre scene in *Thunderball* where Bond fumes about his young taxi driver as he bowls through the Home Counties countryside: "It was typical of the cheap self-assertiveness of young labour since the war. This youth, thought Bond, makes about twenty pounds a week, despises his parents, and would like to be Tommy Steele [a chirpy singer of the period] . . ." And so on for several more lines. Is this really the man who has at this point saved the Western world several times, or is he rather an apoplectic older man over from Jamaica who hates everything he sees? Similarly, when Bond is described as liking "the solid, studied comfort of card-rooms and casinos, the well-padded arms of the chairs, the glass of champagne or whisky at the elbow, the quiet unhurried attention of good servants," there is a definite, pleasurable tear in the eye, the sort of droning satisfaction that would make even the most mildly liberal reader gag with revulsion and anger at the cliff-like immobilism and superiority of traditional English life. What makes these little interludes in the books so appealing is both the way that it is Fleming himself talking, decrying British Rail or socialism or English pub food ("Giant Toad and 2 Veg") and that he gives his readers such a clear view through the crystalline water onto the mad reef that was mid-century upper-class life.

BOND DOES NOT develop at all during the course of the books: he is effectively the same in *Casino Royale* as he is in *You Only Live Twice*, collapsing only at the end of that book before limping into the sorry diminuendo of *The Man with the Golden Gun*. Unlike in the films, though, he definitely gets hurt, revoltingly in *Casino Royale* with his balls barely saved, and punched stabbed drugged seared shot clubbed in ways that he definitely has to recover from. Of course a tremendous advantage of books over films is that a phrase such as "a few days in bed to recover" takes up only seven words whereas a scene of Bond patiently changing his wound-dressing, having a little more orange juice or needing help to visit the bathroom does not make brilliant cinema. That throughout the sequence of major books he starts each novel jumping up merrily (even if notionally a bit damaged in *Dr. No*), like a child after a minor playground accident, gives Bond an air of happy charm, of being a non-detoxed (toxed, perhaps?) Peter Pan figure who never accumulates self-knowledge or fear, whereas his modern equivalent would be suing the government for trauma within about fifty pages of *Casino Royale*'s opening. Indeed, a helpful sequel to the Fleming novels, rather than attempting merely to ape the existing formula, could depart quite drastically and consist mainly of Bond visiting a variety of specialists in between sessions with his lawyers and occasional anguished, tearful-yet-brave daytime television interviews.

For someone who has been so extensively mauled and who has scaled such heights, Bond is also oddly unrewarded, in a way that is never really explained. There is perhaps no pay scale for government-sponsored killers to negotiate around — and he seems comfortable enough in his Chelsea flat, looked after by the long-suffering May, Bond's "elderly Scottish treasure," who must presumably sit there gathering dust for months at a time until the door bursts open and her blood-caked gentleman reels in with some bizarre foreign houri on his arm. Indeed the government seems to have quite a good deal, as "off assignment" their lead killer mainly eats in the office canteen, fiddles with his car and enjoys golf and cards.

Bond has his peculiarities, though, presumably shared with Fleming. Indeed, one of Bond's odder sides is his fussy particularity, expressed in the movies only via his tiresome cocktail (if he is a secret agent why does every barman in the world know what he drinks?) but dwelt on lovingly in the books. Only one brand of hand-made cigarette (Morland, three gold bands), one bath essence for visiting lady friends (Floris), one food for dinner (scrambled eggs *fines herbes*), one newspaper (*The Times*—"the only paper Bond ever read"), even a brand for little pots of jam. Far from his being a merciless killer, at times Bond's hands seem to flap around in a wilderness of fuss.

Surely Oddjob or Klebb do not concern themselves with little pots of jam? But, of course, at almost every level Fleming is saying: that is why they are beaten. Backed by an infinite amount of scrambled eggs *fines herbes*, entire lakes of Floris and an army of elderly Scottish treasures, upper-class British wasters can take on the entire planet and win. Meanwhile, as the fifties progressed in the real world this was to prove very much not the case.

IF THERE IS one word associated with Bond, even in the outer reaches of not caring about Bond at all, it must be "gadgets." It is one of the areas where the films heavily encrust the books, like marine life covering the wreck of a once-glamorous schooner. In the books, they are startlingly scarce. Book after book goes by with nothing much beyond a car, a gun and a telephone. Fleming's Bond is always doomed to exist in a 1950s idea of the contemporary, with automatic toasters and transistor radios as the cutting edge, just as *Brave New World* is doomed never to have any computers at all and *2001: A Space Odyssey* is doomed to have computers that look comically 1960s. Presumably we are all fated in the end to suffer the crushing derision of the future: with every passed-over generation slumped in impotent rage as its grandchildren laugh at its steam-operated calculators and turnip-powered cars. This fevered technological-historical impatience will nibble anything to death and Bond is no more termite-proof than anything else.

When in the film of *Goldfinger* Bond greets Felix Leiter, then slaps his masseuse's bottom and dismisses her with the words, "Goodbye, Dink. Man talk," Bond is also slapping the bottom of and saying goodbye to any tenuous hope that a female audience might be watching. He is also slapping the bottom of and saying goodbye to a whole framework of ideas and assumptions that had once seemed so cosily in place and which have rotted away around a once harmlessly stupid little line of script. So with the gadgets, their lack was irrelevant then but painful now. Bond equals gadgets, but in the books they are simply not there. But then, in a further crumbling exercise, the gadgets that he does get in the films become laughable themselves. *On Her Majesty's Secret Service* contains a scene in which Bond opens a safe with the help of a computer *that has to be delivered in the hopper of a crane*. Nothing can survive such derision. Films which crave contemporaneity have to die by their failure to keep abreast of it.

Bond's total encounters with bona-fide gadgets in the books themselves are easily summarized: knives hidden in the heels of his shoes and a thick book called *The Bible Designed to Be Read as Literature*, which is hollowed out to conceal an automatic (both of these in *Goldfinger*), and a couple of simple frogman costumes. Otherwise Bond just rhapsodizes about his guns—simple weapons, either an automatic pistol or occasionally a sniper rifle. There is also a fun disquisition on ninja armament in *You Only Live Twice*, spiked chains and stuff, but these lead nowhere and Bond derides them. Can a piece of bamboo used for breathing underwater even count, in the proper sense, as a gadget?

The serpent in the garden, however, lies in the book of *From Russia with Love*: one simple little gadget that would end up so many years later giving birth to explosive cigarettes, underwater cars and the rest of the ill-conceived junk. "Q Branch had put together this smart-looking little bag . . .": the case loaded with ammunition, a death-pill and fifty golden sovereigns—as well as a tube of Palmolive shaving cream that conceals an automatic's silencer. The first Bond film, *Dr. No*, is gadget free; the second, *From Russia with Love*, is close to gadget free except for this case—but the huge pleasure it provoked launched Bond on a trajectory from the amusing gun-packing Aston Martin in *Goldfinger*, to the clearly quite silly jet-pack in *Thunderball*, to the collapsed, drunk-down-an-alley shamefulness of *You Only Live Twice*'s exploding cigarette. The crude thirst these gadgets generated meant that they always needed to be trumped, generating predictably awful moments in film after film. It is strange that Fleming himself invented only one real gadget—and that an agreeably Imperial Leather sort of ensemble—and that it should have generated such an array of mutant progeny.

THE STORY OF Commander Lionel Crabb is the bizarre and depressing parallel factual version of *From Russia with Love*, and once again highlights the immensely important wishful-ness of Fleming's writing. The public remains unaware of any specific British intelligence success at all in the 1950s outside the Bond novels—there could have been some, but Britain was poorly positioned to have them, as its operatives were being chased from country after country in the wake of the era's great global anti-European and specifically anti-British backlash. Commander Crabb, because his fate was so public, was a symbol of the humiliating reality of British intelligence.

Crabb had been a heroic, romantic figure in the War, most famously working in the Mediterranean to thwart the alarmingly successful Italian experiments with miniature sub-marines. The stifling, crude, nightmare world of pre-Cousteau diving is perfectly captured in the film *The Silent Enemy*, starring an implausibly peroxided Laurence Harvey and a completely weird Sid James, made in 1958 and prompted by Crabb's death. It is also a low-key but excellent precursor to *Thunderball*'s underwater fight sequences.

The exact details of what happened to Crabb are almost certainly doomed to remain mysterious. In 1956 Khrushchev visited Britain on board a new Soviet ship. It was anchored off Portsmouth and someone in MI6 or the Royal Navy felt it a good idea to have a diver examine the hull for new design features. Crabb, in diving terms now somewhat old, swam out to the ship. Two days later the Soviet ship departed and months later his headless and handless corpse was found washed up on the coast. Whether he was involved in an accident (being hit in a rather odd way by a ship's propeller, say) or was actually killed by the Soviets will never really be known, but the latter seems almost certain despite a rather desperate tradition that he got away and the corpse was a plant. The painfulness of the story lies in the terrible gap between the inspirational vigour of the Mediterranean in 1942 and the failure (or bad luck) of Portsmouth in 1956. But it also lies in the sinking feeling that this was what happened to plucky individual action in the Cold War: that remorseless, cold, ideological murderousness could in practice brush aside James Bond with scarcely a ripple.

ONE OF THE ways in which Fleming remains surprising is that despite the overwhelming weight of the Second World War on his and everyone else's shoulders, his books do not dwell on this too much. It is the essential backdrop, and indeed the books' entire purpose can be seen as carrying forward the certainties many felt about that war into the disorientating bitterness of an ever more impotent Britain. But Fleming's means are not specifically nostalgic—they remain at the outer edge of serious, but ultimately failing, attempts by Britain to remain aggressively relevant to the wider world. As the 1950s continue these attempts palsy and fall away under the sheer impact of that wider world's hostility. That hostility of course stoked British obsession with the glories of being one of 1945's "Big Three."

Fleming is aggressively contemporary in his storylines—the villains are atomic, Soviet-nurtured or (later on) in the pay of the ultimate mad multinational, SPECTRE. Superficially it seems somehow curious that he makes so little use of Nazis: after all, Europe was of course crammed with fit and quite young ex-Nazis and they would seem to lend themselves perfectly to a thriller writer's needs. Narratively, though, it is almost as though the advent of nuclear weapons and the Cold War suddenly made the whole, staggeringly savage Nazi realm, with its ridiculous philosophy based around the supremacy of a now blank, flattened little bit of Europe, seem antique and irrelevant. Other technology, from jet fighters to aqualungs, and other political events, from Indian independence to the triumph of Mao, buried the Germans with ruthless speed. If you wanted to write convincingly about the 1950s the Germans weren't really available for bookings. For Fleming, Germans feature merely in a couple of minor short stories—most memorably in "From a View to a Kill," with the ex-Nazi who Bond is sent to assassinate fulfilling everyone's hopes for what such a person should look like but with the detail of "hideous lips—thick and wet and crimson" and his chest and shoulder blades being covered in "a mat of black hair."

The one exception to this general lack of direct concern comes in the—in some ways—oddest of the novels, *Moonraker*, the third to be published (1955). Much of the book is taken up with a protracted and justly famous dinner and card game, but the plot itself plunges the reader into the murky world of almost straight pulp fiction—a story of weird implausibility about nuclear rockets under the South Downs being paid for by former Nazis who, having fooled everyone into putting them in charge, propose to fire one, the Moonraker, at London. This plan is foiled by fixing the firing instructions so that the rocket instead lands on top of the submarine in which the fiends are trying to escape. There are, naturally, idiotic moments in all the Bond books: Goldfinger's escape from Fort Knox on a train to the east coast, which could presumably have been stopped at any point by a quick phone call and a points change, for example. But *Moonraker* is daft in a helpless way, in its final pages putting the reader face to face with the sort of atomic-themed rubbish much loved in the thrillers of the period, but which has otherwise now fallen out of circulation. This feebleness also caused the filmmakers to back off using it until they had run out of other Bond novel titles.

The book is only really saved—club dinner aside—by its cheerful sadism, most strikingly the scene where Bond is strapped to a semi-nude policewoman and they are both squirted down with a industrial steam hose. It is also curious because it marks the point where Fleming decides to abandon Britain as a location: from here on out Britain is either incidental to the main action or is rendered in very constrained brackets (the health spa in *Thunderball*, the golf match in *Goldfinger*). It is as though Fleming realized while writing the book that his fantasies failed to ignite in such workaday surroundings. The long car chase down the A20 in *Moonraker* would merely make readers incredulous about the lack of traffic and the rocket silos under the South Downs would merely provoke thoughts about damage to an area of out-standing natural beauty. This was a lesson embraced by the filmmakers, who sensibly avoided Britain where at all possi-ble. Indeed, in some of the later films these locations provide the only interest: if Bangkok or Cairo were replaced by, say, Chester or Maidstone, audiences would have snorted with incredulity at plots which could seem plausible only in the cruel and licentious world of Foreignness.

Let's come back to the Nazis for a moment, though. They *are* fun and draw on the rich broth of British anti-Germanism, with every one of them cackling away and being sadistic at the drop of a hat, screeching "*Teufel*" and "*Wunderschön.*" When in the twenty-first century Germans complain about Britain's incredibly offensive jokes about them and our ever more dysfunctional failure to put the Second World War behind us it is impossible not to sympathize even when—after careful thought—laughing once again. The tired, automatic air with which huge numbers of jokes were dusted off and customized on the occasion of Cardinal Ratzinger being made Pope shows that there is not the remotest chance of Britain dropping its national obsession.

Fleming's invention of Sir Hugo Drax and his giggling torturer Krebs ("A masterstroke, *mein Kapitän*") is enjoy-able but minor. The class/country paranoia is really curious, though. The fantasy of *Moonraker* is about Drax's position as a seemingly blue-chip British millionaire at the heart of the establishment and a respected member of clubland. All the time he is in fact a secret, stay-behind, Nazi Werewolf agent bent on destroying Britain with a nuclear V2. Bond encounters Drax and ultimately defeats him and saves his country only because Drax quite needlessly cheats at cards at M's club. Without this tic (not being a gentleman, in other words) he would never have been found out. Fleming's fantasy cuts both ways—attractively it implies that the establishment is a farce and even a Nazi loony can get into it; unattractively, it implies an almost emetic loathing—a nightmare in which things that do not belong (and it could be humans like socialists or ghouls like inheritance tax) are secretly stalking even the inner sanctums of British life. I would like to think that Drax's story is a satire about the former, but fear it is more plausibly about the latter.

ANY DISCUSSION OF Fleming and Bond always rotates around those Siamese twins Sex and Violence. For Fleming himself they were intimately linked to his own enthusiasm for sexual self-punishment. This seems oddly linked into specific male English upper-class practices, originating in battalions of nannies alternately beating children with hair-brushes in a frenzy of rage then calming them down again by pressing them against their starchy, uniformed breasts. If you throw in for good measure the boiling, psychosexual Charybdis of the English boarding school then it is hardly surprising that the end product is impatient with the simple coital framework enjoyed, say, by Americans or Italians. Indeed, Britain's—until recently—overweening role in the world has perhaps often had the edge taken off it by the near universal belief in other countries that British sexual practices had a comic but also rather tacky flavour. Certainly the Bond books, with their ice cubes and lighted cigarette ends, stingray-tail whips and carpet beaters, have for many years offered cheerful ammunition to foreign well-wishers.

It is a recurrent motif in English ruling-class memoirs of a franker kind to dwell on the ultimate honourable scar in this area—the man who in the course of having sex with another man's wife gets his back lacerated by her long fingernails (the long nails of course being a symbol of leisure). Fleming's affair with Ann Rothermere is the seeming quintessence of this genre, with the ability to hurt each other high on their list of must-haves. This is an area in which I feel in equal measure rather sheltered and a bit puzzled. The idea of slashing toff fingernails just doesn't seem particularly appealing (the strange Labour peer Woodrow Wyatt boasted of similar wounds). These sorts of gashes could be replicated only by those an unfortunate Bolivian shepherd boy would receive if snatched from his lonely mountain pasture by a condor. The assumption that these wounds are provoked by some frantic orgasm too is perhaps over-flattering: the flaying nails could have been provoked by a frantic disgust. It certainly seems very culturally specific, conjuring up for me the chilly world of those red-brick apartments in Kensington where grim, beautiful, neglected wives, their nails immaculately honed for this kind of performance, stalk through enormous darkened rooms, proudly using the same art deco morphine syringes their mothers had used before them.

His complicated sex life and his and Ann Fleming's reported enthusiasms certainly pop up in the books at frequent intervals with the usual proviso that just because Fleming wrote about stingray-tail whips doesn't mean he necessarily used them—indeed they might have merely featured as a sort of early product placement for some Jamaica-based friend. Occasionally Fleming simply caves in, though, as with the splendid line in *Goldfinger* about Pussy Galore, who "in a black Dacron mackintosh with a black leather belt looked like some young SS guardsman." You can almost see Fleming collapsing against his typewriter.

The Bond books' sexual charge has of course drifted down to virtually nothing in our hyper-saturated environment. But at the time the books dragged sexual frankness into respectable literature. In one of the *Octopussy* short stories Bond passes the time while waiting to assassinate somebody by reading a piece of German pulp fiction, "prompted by a spectacular jacket of a half-naked girl strapped to a bed," called *Verderbt, Verdammt, Verraten* (*Ruined, Damned, Betrayed*), and Fleming had a key role in hauling this world into British living rooms. Peaks, groans, whimpers, jutting breasts, splayed legs, proud hillocks, snarls of desire now silently filled up household after household, corroding a space once reserved only for blameless gardening tips on the radio. Here we are at the absolute Genesis of the sexual revolution.

The films are badly flustered by sexual issues because they are desperate to arouse adult males a bit while not getting a certificate which would exclude a massive chunk of the audience, e.g., prepubescent dorks such as myself, clutching rapidly melting Old Jamaica chocolate bars. The books have no such problems beyond the usual one of simply not being able to represent different levels and kinds of arousal in anything other than an unintentionally comic way. My favourite example is in *Casino Royale*, where Bond, embracing the girl traitor, slips "his hands down to her swelling buttocks," giving readers the cheerful impression that her principal symptom of arousal is to inflate like a child's paddling pool.

THERE ARE MANY startling and good British war films — terse, unhysterical, thoughtful — and there are, of course, many completely awful ones. Watching now the ones made towards or just after the end of the War, particularly *The Way Ahead* and *The Way to the Stars*, is a striking lesson as to how clearly and carefully it was possible for serious artists to delimit Britain's wartime experience in a peculiarly moving and clever way. This genre was of course to become the dominant British one, alongside the brilliant Ealing Studios comedies (one of which, *Hue and Cry*, also managing to be a great memorial to the bombed-out East End). There were a steady stream of heroic, realistic and diffident films, effectively all variants on *The Way Ahead* and *The Way to the Stars*, from *The Cruel Sea* to *The Dam Busters* and *The Silent Enemy*. For me one of the very worst, however, is *Cockleshell Heroes*, made in 1955. Its pre-Bond antecedents are impeccable as it is an early movie on which Cubby Broccoli, the mastermind behind the Bond films, was executive producer with Irving Allen (not to be confused with Irwin Allen, the Rajah of Rubbish — *The Poseidon Adventure*, *The Swarm*!) and Richard Maibaum as writer, who went on to write most of the canonical Bond scripts. A considerable popular hit when it came out, this film now seems to have an almost avant-gardist disdain for its audience. It is based on the true and heroic story of how a small group of volunteers join a commando outfit headed by José Ferrer — an almost brilliantly lacklustre, uncharismatic actor — to go in canoes up the Gironde River and blow up some ships in Bordeaux. Even the generally reliable Trevor Howard is flattened by the sheer dullness of the narrative as all the usual training hoops are jumped through and, in due course, most of the volunteers are slaughtered by the Germans. The only survivors are Ferrer, a sort of Pillsbury doughboy in camouflage, and the grunt lucky enough to share his canoe. So dreary is everything that even Christopher Lee, as a submarine captain, is almost unrecognizable in the featureless gloom.

The whole odd film can best be seen as an exercise in the clever and malicious ruining of audience expectation. As Ferrer at the end marches away to a jaunty tune surrounded by the ghosts of his surely rather peeved recent comrades it can now only really be understood as one of the rather dead-end theatrical experiments of the period. And yet at the time everyone loved it and it was one of the films that really launched Broccoli. And this in the year of such wonders as *The Night of the Hunter*, *Bad Day at Black Rock*, *The Ladykillers* (Ealing's last great throw) and *Pather Panchali*. Why did British audiences appreciate this film so much? It can only really be because it is a parody of all the elements that were to go on to make the Bond films so successful, but without any of the interest value: it is an essay in amateurism, in being solitary, in the individual rather than the massed battalions making all the difference; it is also about expertise and voluntarism. It clearly mapped British self-image perfectly. It is at the very least curious that Broccoli should have detected the national mood in 1955 with such accuracy and would continue to do so from 1962 onwards. I do not know what Fleming thought of *Cockleshell Heroes* but surely its sentiments would have fitted him perfectly: as a sort of summa of everything he had done in the War and everything he wanted from Bond.

IT HAS BEEN a completely bizarre shorthand for Britain's decolonization experience to contrast it blandly to that of France, with its Vietnamese and Algerian horrors. This blandness has been an extremely important part of the decompression process by which Britain has mutated slowly and irritably into a medium-large European country. But the self-congratulation with which Britain has always painted its empire's end is very hard to sustain—most spectacularly and irredeemably of course in Britain's responsibility for the massacres surrounding the creation of India and Pakistan. It is somehow felt that with independence Britain was no longer involved, whereas of course Britain was profoundly implicated in the many years of rule and in decisions which ultimately generated such a disastrous result and so many deaths. Generally those who say that such a judgement is too harsh will tend then to castigate the French in Algeria—as though theirs was not just as historically thorny and nightmarish as Britain's own appallingly managed end of empire.

At the heart of all arguments about empire is of course "Suez"—in itself an evasive shorthand which ducks away from something more accurate, such as "the invasion of part of Egypt fuelled by hatred for Nasser, in secret collusion with France and Israel, and based on anti-democratic lying to the entire world." This extraordinary episode raises in one of its most pressing forms the degree to which we are either victims of history or can, through quarter-way intelligent statesmanship, move on. Anthony Eden, because he was so mired in his own myth of himself as one of the very slightly creditable figures in the late 1930s on the appeasement issue, thought that the charismatic General Nasser, Egypt's new leader, was the new Mussolini or even Hitler—a figure who through flirting with the Russians and through anti-British actions was tipping the world in a disturbing direction. In Eden's view it was the job of Britain, with its historic ties to Egypt, and its still vigorous role as America's proxy throughout much of the Middle East, to bring him down.

From our own perspective this seems mad—Nasser was part of an effectively global paroxysm or shudder against direct European control: certainly a legitimate nationalist with history in his sails. Watching film of Nasser at the time of the crisis I feel my entire sexual framework suddenly wobble like jelly—I'm just glad I wasn't living in Cairo in the mid-1950s to have my heart broken (to be honest he is the only nationalist leader it is possible to have vigorous sexual feelings about, setting aside of course Archbishop Makarios). Eden on the other hand oddly failed to succumb and appeared to have been in the grip of a sort of psychosis provoked by humiliation after British humiliation around the world and the sense that Egypt's actions in nationalizing the Suez Canal—Egypt the cradle of British self-esteem's rebuilding around the Battle of El Alamein, the Suez Canal the perfect symbol of Britain's continuing greatness—was the last straw. In this he had strong support.

Newspaper cartoons, particularly on the right, are a helpful shorthand for ideas that everyone can lazily agree to or laugh along with. Having spent too much time mired in the nasty world of *Daily Express* cartoons this is painfully clear: through the work of Leslie Illingworth the era's entire oddness is laid out. Illingworth's world of stupid black men,

brutish union members and excitable foreign crowds is a
very unattractive one: the Mau-Mau rebels are a black snake
wrapped around a white baby to be shot by a white settler's
pistol; the Iranians nationalizing Anglo-Iranian Oil (now BP)
are a deranged mob (this was another enormous imperial
humiliation I've failed to mention!); the Chinese are slit-eyed
nonhumans. Everyone gets a go in the world of the *Express*.
Nothing is worse, though, than the special cartoon published
on the occasion of Eden's becoming premier. He is shown as
a figure of frowning rectitude framed by all the people out to
get him—disgusting Cypriots, bald, vicious Khrushchev and
so on—and of course Khrushchev's stooge Nasser, invariably shown in cartoon after cartoon as an oily wog grinning
and snarling. During the crisis one Illingworth cartoon shows
"Suez" as a baby being held by the international community,
with its baby toy flung on the floor a little golliwog, clearly
Nasser. The *Express* was at the heart of popular support
for the Conservatives and, given that its readers were to be
disappointed over and over again (the terrorists, scroungers
and fifth-columnists basically won), it is in its way as useful a
shorthand as the Bond books for the rich stew that filled many
patriots' heads during this period.

And so, feeling backed by broad popular and Cabinet
support, Eden did a secret deal and then stoutly lied about
it—with France, who wished to shut down what she saw as
Egypt's role in promoting Algerian terrorism, and with Israel,
who wished to damage her most formidable enemy. The
trick—for Israel to invade and for France and Britain to then
follow to protect their interests in the canal and pretend to be
there to separate the warring parties—was pathetically trans-
parent, reminiscent of something from *Just William* rather

than from a specifically dangerous period in the Cold War with an American election in the offing and a wary and anxious new Soviet leadership looking for a rumble. In this one decision (and setting aside dozens of brutal, often crazily brutal, "police actions" around the world—and not least the vast system of camps and killings in the destruction of the Mau-Mau rebellion in Kenya), Britain disposed of any moral ascendancy it may have enjoyed for its role in the Second World War and tipped the equation between non-communism and democratic values into a pit of cynicism and weakness that boosted Soviet influence around the world.

Country after country drew the same conclusion: that for all the chit-chat about the United Nations, the Western powers were the same old ferocious, hypocritical shits who had crushed and humiliated their countries for centuries. The hopeless fresh twist, though, was that Britain was prevented from invading Egypt properly; American disapproval aborted the whole thing within days and Britain became not only a country synonymous with reckless militarism but also with pathetic weakness. The remainder of Britain's serious influence in the Middle East rapidly wound up shortly thereafter as even the most milk-and-water nationalism became incompatible with having anything to do with Britain. Surviving pro-British regimes were either violently terminated (most importantly in Iraq) or retooled so that Britain took on a weak and surreptitious advisory role, effectively at the level of providing bodyguards, pilots and factory managers for a range of minor and cranky despots around the Arabian Gulf.

It is impossible to exaggerate the damage done by Suez—an operation that had engaged a vast British armada of naval, RAF and army units. It was as though the U.S.-led invasion of Iraq had suddenly been brought to a halt by the UN in its opening week. For this book what really matters is what happened within Britain: the convulsion was completely extraordinary. Eden, an oddly admired figure since the 1930s and Churchill's only real protégé, was forced to resign, and the surprising beneficiary proved to be Harold Macmillan, who had first supported the invasion and then havered to a degree that made him seem very slightly less crooked than the rest. Whole areas of British society were left completely dazed (although a minority, who had protested throughout, were vindicated). Here was a country whose ideology had been based around telling much of the world what to do, whose raison d'être had been to flick through newspapers seeing who this week had been invaded and incorporated into the Empire, who now found itself after enduring a decade of steady humiliation being howled down by virtually every country, ally or enemy. The one remaining totem, the pound sterling, began to collapse again in the face of U.S. displeasure: the fundamental reason for the invasion being called off rather than a sudden belief in the values of the UN or in intelligent government. The lies told throughout by the British were particularly damaging because the crisis coincided with the Soviet crushing of the Hungarian rebellion and removed any moral ascendancy the West might usually have hoped to have. It was the end of Britain as an independent actor. Most of the world breathed a sigh of cheerful relief, but for a traditional patriot it was not an appealing time to be alive.

LOOKING TO the Suez crisis to explain why the James Bond books might have seemed pertinent and reassuring to their original, rather disorientated readers leads on to the point at which the political and the personal almost magically map each other. In the wake of the invasion, under immense pressure, hounded on all sides and feeling seriously ill, Eden decided to leave for a holiday. After discreet enquiries he settled on Fleming's Jamaican home and spent a happy time there recuperating, but also, if he had known it, frittering away any remaining political capital as even friendly newspapers suggested his behaviour was a bit odd. The idea that, having initiated the invasion as prime minister, Eden should, as troops continued to take casualties and American pressure mounted, fly off in a grim British autumn to lounge in the Caribbean, seems on the face of it almost as deranged as the decision to invade in the first place. Shortly after his return he resigned.

The only sad thing about Eden's weeks at Goldeneye was that Fleming himself was not there: otherwise here would be the perfect cross-over between the political world (which in Eden's case was substantially a mad fantasy) and the world of mad fantasy (which in Fleming's case said so much about real politics). Dramatically the trip would have been ideal— the baffled leader, veteran of dozens of British fiascos over two decades including one ongoing, at last brought low and finding solace with the shaman-like figure of James Bond's creator. It is *fairly* perfect even so: at the zenith of national incompetence, the architect of that incompetence stays at the very house in which the greatest reassurance and palliative, the Robin Hood of British imperialists' darkest hour, was created. Eden, humiliated, exhausted and finally ruined by Nasser and by Eisenhower, may have been one of the grandest beneficiaries of Fleming's troubadour role, but there were to be very many more. The next spring, *From Russia with Love* was published.

*

SEX WAS of course one of the books' first great selling points and Bond must be the single most influential figure, via both the novels and the films, in male British ideas about what a sex life should be like; a seismic figure then who must have caused in his way much unhappiness and considerable confusion and resentment within marriages.

Of course the books have, in half a century, taken a nose-dive in this area. Serious research is probably impossible now, but it is fair to claim that historical wear and tear have changed the book's sexual fabric from something that on publication was capable of arousing, say, a Hong Kong–based squaddie to something that can arouse almost nobody. The passing years though have added a real poignancy to the sexual aspect of the books. If in a sense they are a hymn to the purchase of com-modities then the women in them fall within that framework and profoundly reflect male attitudes both of the 1950s and— of course—the present, in ways which are both unpleasant and also painful.

Why Bond was so admirable to so many of his readers was that he seemed to bring to life in its purest and most extended form the male fantasy of a permanent, never-ageing present in which an infinity of girls from around the world could be sampled in the manner of cigars: sexual life as a frictionless, almost scientific series of encounters that build up an ever more convincing set of results allowing for the generaliza-tions about "what women are like" so dear to so many male hearts. The frustratingly partial, indeed almost infinitesimal, "knowledge" available to almost any British male in the 1950s (e.g., one or two women from Britain) could be supplemented by Bond's "learnings" and a whole range of discourses and assumptions happily chewed over in the pub forever.

Is this offensive? Well, of course at most levels it is offensive and depressing. Perhaps a more metaphysical case can be made in its favour. Perhaps the Bond books could in fact be seen as one giant riff on male sexual folly and the utter mysteriousness of our sexual existence. After all, Bond's sexual experience in practice is restricted either to romancing jaded international flotsam and jetsam or to rescuing girls who like sleeping with millionaire criminal psychopaths. Surely this latter tells us more about the values taught at girls' private schools in England than about women's sexuality more broadly understood? And even when Bond strays from this area his encounter is so specialized (a Japanese fisherwoman) that confident generalization becomes impossible. Bond, in practice, lives out his life scarcely touching the outer rim of sexual experience. The books thus become a disoriented, upsetting meditation on the transitory, unknowable nature of human life: threnodies of human failure and our inability to communicate. Well, I don't really believe it either.

The books are very cagey about what actually goes on in these encounters ("they were like two loving animals . . . they had no shame") and in practice it is true to say that the Bond of the books is, as you would expect, less promiscuous than the Bond of the films. In *Moonraker* he manages to sleep with nobody at all, despite being strapped to a policewoman and doused in steam (but perhaps I've mentioned that already?).

Bond also suffers traditional, almost overwhelming, anxiety about lesbians. His encounters with them in *Goldfinger* have the force of frozen horror and far too much of the narrative is spent with him mulling over the reasons (rooted in hormones and women voting) that have led to the contemporary efflorescence of lesbianism. Pussy Galore's Sapphism is tiptoed around in the film of *Goldfinger* and effectively available only for viewers who are happy with a very stifled set of code words. This is completely unstifled in the book, but the brunt of the discussion falls on the unhappy Tilly Masterson, who is eventually killed by Oddjob, the book implies, because she is too busy mooning after Pussy to pay attention. Bond eventually gives the definitive masculine pronouncement: "He was sorry for them, but he had no time for them."

Fleming's range of phrases for sexual activity is very broad and certainly he never repeats himself. Indeed, a close reading of the novels (possibly too close but I am writing this book and need to pronounce on such things) shows that he is remarkably rigorous about not returning to old ground— possibly Fleming's only real idée fixe on any subject is that steak is best when it can be cut with a fork, a harmless and minor stylistic tic. It also suggests that however acrid or hungover Fleming might have been, he kept the Bond universe complete in its ever more complex ramifications inside his head, never falling into the chaotic opportunism and self-contradiction that ruin serious study of, say, the Sherlock Holmes stories. Come what may, each sexual encounter is unique.

Many of us have little set phrases that knock around in our heads and pop up at odd moments. For example, whenever I see a crow—which is frequently—I find myself thinking the line from *Macbeth*, "The crow makes wing to the rooky wood." Another example is the phrase from the James Bond novel *You Only Live Twice*, "her exciting black triangle," describing an aspect of a nude Japanese fisherwoman. In my adult life this phrase has emerged unbidden in a number of social situations and seemed useful and valid. "Her exciting black triangle" became the title I wanted to give to an anthology I was preparing of quotes from the Bond novels (Penguin, 2000, incidentally). Against a thickening domestic backdrop of my wife's scorn and disbelief I dug in my heels. This was surely the ideal title for the book: *Her Exciting Black Triangle: From the Writings of Ian Fleming*.

As I reread *You Only Live Twice*, though, something awful happened. It emerged that Fleming never actually used this phrase and that for a quarter of a century I had lived a lie. I am not sure this puts me in a terrific light, to have misremembered such a tacky phrase. It was fine as long as I could call on ironic literary back-up, but it now had become painfully exposed. Nonetheless it can now enjoy a sort of ghoulish half-life in these paragraphs, standing in, in some tiny way, for the infinite confusion and ersatz with which our own sexual experiences are in fact crowded.

BEFORE ABANDONING SEX I have to slip in my personal contribution to the admittedly pretty uncontested area of textual variants and errors within Fleming's work. For many years *On Her Majesty's Secret Service* had the engaging but meaningless phrase "a succession of splendid, sweated young bosoms," to describe the girls working in Blofeld's Swiss lair. This has now been corrected to "sweatered," because of the Alpine context.

Chapter Five

"CHAMPAGNE AND BENZEDRINE! NEVER AGAIN"

THE SUBJECT OF Fleming's relationship with Jamaica is an almost crazily fecund one. As with so many aspects of this book there is a sense of a murky link between the collapse of Britain's international position and his private life: that somehow there *must* at some more or less cosmic level be links which show everything to be interrelated in a rational rather than happenstantial manner. It cannot be coincidence that two of the most influential and interesting apologists for traditional Britain, Fleming and Noël Coward, should have been close neighbours on Jamaica's north shore. Wandering around Coward's home, where he died and was buried in 1973, and seeing the table in the main room set as it was for a luncheon visit by Queen Elizabeth the Queen Mother in 1965, you have to blink to see if this is not made up by some mad symbolist. Is perhaps *all* post-war upper-class British social history not some fantastically patterned carpet of in-jokes designed to signal its despair to a later, baffled generation?

What is overwhelmingly obvious to visitors now to Jamaica

is the power and potency of the island's own myths of itself. In a hotly contested field it must lay claim to being one of the most terrifyingly violent, intolerably painful stretches of the planet: a country whose entire native population (the Tainos) have been exterminated (leaving behind a handful of heartbreakingly relaxed-sounding words—barbecue, canoe, savannah, hammock; words in which another race takes its ease), and which had then been populated by the Spanish and British entirely with people bought or stolen and then in effect crushed to make sugar for generation after generation. Even someone with a harshly irreligious, almost nihilistic view of human life and values would find himself feeling a bit wobbly.

When Fleming and his friends sat here, slurping their drinks in heavy cut-glass tumblers, Jamaica had stabilized as an almost entirely pointless place. Like the rest of the West Indies, its days of wealth and success (a wealth and success based of course on most of the population being treated as animals), when it had generated the great sugar boom, were gone more than a century ago, and it now found itself seemingly quite anomalous in the modern era. As a colony it had been run on a neglectful shoestring for years and people like Fleming could snap up substantial amounts of land for very little. Rescue of a provisional kind, though, was visible through the new mass tourism and through bauxite (the mines brilliantly used in the film of *Dr. No*).

Beyond the world of colonial economics, Jamaica was filled with very remarkable things. It is the one Caribbean island, aside from Cuba and Haiti, both much larger and with very different histories, to come up with a series of philosophies and counter-attacks against its atrocious fate. First there were the Maroons, the escaped slaves who fought the British to a standstill in the central hills and mountains and who maintained their independence. Then there were other serious, powerful and articulate rebellions against the British. Then there was the remarkable and charming figure of Marcus Garvey and his Universal Negro Improvement Association; an entire religion, Rastafarianism; and music, ska and reggae— all of which seem to imply that Jamaica is a big, not a small, country. Through vast effort, therefore, Jamaica made itself into something that, given its terrible history, it should not have been—an astonishing and impressive place, however much fate has rained down on it.

In Fleming's life there is little direct evidence that he understood this, and indeed his residence there each winter almost too easily coincides with this transition from old, battered Jamaica to new, internationally regarded independent Jamaica. What Fleming loved about Jamaica was its beauty, its remoteness from vexed, cold, socialist, dying England, and the sense it provided that he and his friends were still the cream on the milk.

This quest for status and ease convulsed Britain after the War, always a country of emigrants, but now a country too of part-timers such as Fleming who could jump on board the new transport technologies. Some of these post-war emigrants went in quest of lands where a fresh respect and glamour could be found and got it completely wrong (Egypt, Shanghai, Rhodesia) but for others leaving worked beautifully, as they exploited "kith and kin" links (much hailed in the media) even as the political links frayed. Not that these links frayed always that quickly. When the cantankerous, scarlet-faced former Australian prime minister Sir Robert Menzies—architect of White Australia and a man who viewed Asia as simply somewhere you flew over to get to Britain—was given the weird medieval British post of Warden of the Cinque Ports in 1966, this was the last hurrah for a particular form of total unpleasantness, sensibly forgotten about by many now and a reminder of how ghastly the whole British–Australian axis had been, based as it was on race, commodity shipping and arrogance. The struggles of the new, multi-ethnic, liberal Australia to shake off a Queen still venerated by unattractive recent British emigrants (of whom there were huge numbers into the 1960s) and various know-nothings is one of the epics of the early twenty-first century.

So in these senses, Fleming was merely one example among perhaps a million exiles (albeit in his case an intermittent one). This was fuelled not unimportantly by a yearning for sunshine—my own handful of days spent in Jamaica now seeming a mad fantasy of sea-grapes, bougainvillaea, hummingbirds and brown pelicans to offset against life back in London, stalking huddled with the children to school through the freezing rain and rotting, freaked-out pigeons of Wandsworth Park.

Beyond sunshine there was also a wish for respect, greater glamour, and a revulsion against what Britain seemed to be. To an extensive but less potent degree, this is true still now, as Britons scatter across sunny bits of the world whining. Some satellite could potentially be tuneable to pick up across broad swathes of the planet (a ghastly job to monitor this), from Bermuda to Malaga, from Antibes to Valletta, Perth to Vancouver, the insistent, specific, querulous pitch of British people sounding off about kith and kin, lowest common denominators, red tape, football hooligans, black criminality, the difficulty of buying Marmite locally and the Nazi origins of the European Union.

As usual with Fleming, however, he is both as disappointing as one would imagine and far more interesting. As a genuine and thoughtful Romantic he was drawn to Jamaica in a more than an anecdotal or nostalgic way—and indeed the anecdotes and nostalgia available in Jamaica, tending to rotate around whips, chains, burning plantation houses and mass misery, offered none of the superficially charming chit-chat available to people living in Sydney or Durban, say (although there are the odd pauses for thought in those cities, too). He also provided a very strange link between old Jamaica and new in his long-running affair with Blanche Blackwell, a white woman resident there who was both a fascinating figure in her own right and the mother of Chris Blackwell, whose Island Records was to turn Jamaican music global. I never tire of thinking about the strangeness of Fleming, perched in his house in the Caribbean tapping out the novels that were to have such a vast influence and which so beautifully articulated the pains of Britain's post-war predicament, sleeping with the woman who provided the fundamental link with the new ganja and dreadlock Jamaica—one that would have horrified and baffled Fleming. There is Fleming finishing up *Goldfinger* with Cecil Beaton and Noël Coward popping round for drinks, while just down the road the great musicians of the Skatalites and the Wailers are growing and tuning up. Indeed the Skatalites were to record one of the definitive versions of the James Bond theme (with, weirdly, an improvised section which uncannily anticipates John Barry's music for *On Her Majesty's Secret Service* four years before he wrote it). I've cut back as much as I can on this book's hobby-horses but if any reader has not encountered the Skatalites then they have not lived in the fullest sense of the term. One of the greatest of all instrumental bands, they recorded only over a brief period in the sixties but during that time performed dazzling numbers of virtuoso tunes—anyway, run out and get "Dragon Weapon," "Cleopatra," "Doctor Decker," "Guns of Navarone," "Christine Keeler." Immaculate.

Fleming would have had to live only into his late sixties to have seen Jamaica become to the rest of the world the country of Bob Marley, Rastas and pot—and an integral player in that vast surge of international jet tourism which Fleming anticipated and celebrated in his books, even as he would be stunned by the speed with which it enveloped his island.

It is perhaps just as well that he did not see the compelling elderly couple from Dortmund, both wearing only leopard-skin-pattern thongs and sailor hats, who placidly trotted back and forth along the beach day after day as I sat on my lounger slurping piña coladas during my own week in Jamaica. But then it is in moments like that where easy sneering at other people's grotesqueness can suddenly elide into a cosmic—if babyishly drunk and sunburnt—meditation on the pathetic frailty of all human fantasy and desire. Surely we are all so wretched, so *damaged* by our own moral failure that it is mere petulance even to suggest for an instant that there could be (spills rum on T-shirt) a God who can engage with our fates?

RACISM HAS ALWAYS been endemic in Britain, as it is in all other countries. Every country seems to have a penumbra of despised others who fringe it—shadings of language, colour, religion that throw up a range of stereotyped behaviour within which the picked-on group is obliged to writhe. Clearly it forms an important part of human identity in some depressing way—there is always another group more credulous, more lazy, more sexually debased, less fully functional than one-self. The only saving grace perhaps is that ultimately nobody escapes this net—that every nation or sub-nation that prides itself on its superiority (and which does not?) is uneasily aware that somewhere another nation or sub-nation finds them anaemic, impotent, locust-like, unimaginative, and so on.

British racism shares some of the same basis as Spanish racism in having come from a vast range of experience in twisting and manipulating the world. The roots of Hungarian racism, for example, are very different: necessarily restricted to views on the Slovaks, Jews, Croats, Germans, Italians and Transylvanians, who are all variously industrious, idle, feckless, superstitious, unmusical, grasping, lacking soul and so on. Hungarian racism is based on political control and social relationships (between Hungarian landlords, say, and Slovak peasants). Beyond this day-to-day racism are historic racist ideas about Turks and Russians based on their having at various points actually terrorized Hungary. But beyond this immediate circle everything else is mere exotica—Chinese or Africans or Aborigines or most of the world in fact were simply fun to read about for Hungarians as they had no political control over them.

Very narrowly within the geographical frame of the islands of Britain itself this latter context-free and "harmless" racism was absolutely dominant. Hungary is an interesting contrast because it is a country with a long imperial past based on the political control, until the early twentieth century, of all the countries immediately fringing it. Britain, aside from the important range of hatreds associated with feelings about the Irish, had no immediate political surroundings except salt water. An entirely homogenously white society could be racist without serious effect. My uncle had a gollywog (a cloth toy with cartoon black features) called Mr. Bustamante, after the then chief minister of Jamaica, and its offensiveness would I think genuinely just not have been seen in the 1950s. The 1950s though, of course, were the great changeover point, where an until then unimaginably uniform racial society began to embark on the multi-racial project which in half a century has made Britain effectively into a new kind of country. Racism as a series of fairy stories locked within a mono-racial society has no real implications; racism with lots of races around is obviously dangerous and unworkable.

There is a wonderful photo of a group of visiting Karen women (from what is now southeastern Myanmar) in Drayton Park, London, in the mid-1930s—the picture provides no context so it is impossible to work out why they were visiting. The tremendously elongated necks encased in brass rings, the jewellery, the great folds of fabric, could not offer a stronger contrast to the standard British "uniform" clothing of the baffled onlookers. These women were walking around in a society which simply had *no* other races in it beyond exotic visitors—a small old Jewish community, a small newer Eastern Europe Jewish community in the East End of London, very small groups of Africans and African descendants in dock areas, a few "Lascars" (Malays), Indians and Chinese in the same places, some Italians in particular trades but that was about it. These groups would have never been encountered face-to-face by most of the country.

The contrast between the British within Britain and the British once they were outside Britain of course could not have been stronger or more violent. And this, of course, is the vast area in which British racism has really kicked in—Britain's practical role as the main reorganizer of much of the planet, the depopulator and repopulator, the owner of countries in all climates, with all the world's religions and every conceivable colour. Someone living in Chad or Nepal will admire, despise or fear a specific range of immediate neighbours, while the British by contrast have—as reflected in our science and literature, and as shown in our colossal, and colossally vexed, legacy to the world—the entire human nightmare in their heads. When, in a little piece of despicable cowardice, the Labour government ordered the expulsion of the Palm Islanders from Diego Garcia in the Indian Ocean to make way for an American naval base in 1967, the only comfort can be now knowing that this was probably the *final* wretched example of an attitude which had profoundly tinkered with the world for at least three centuries.

As the reader will wearily anticipate, Fleming's novels are packed full of attitudes that are profoundly shaped by the British merchant, military and colonial exposure to the rest of the world: indeed at many levels Bond exists only as an expression of this—like a goitre or wen, he is merely a by-product of something much more fundamental to a body's ill health. As he continues in the twenty-first century to live out his busy life killing or sleeping with people all around the world in film after film, he is in effect all that is left of a British manner that is otherwise now *almost* defanged. A German or Egyptian Bond is unthinkable—he could be only a local policeman. An American Bond is equally implausible—all the great American thrillers have American settings. Bond is the natural, indeed unavoidable, expression of traditional British imperialism— there is no culture he cannot patronize, there is nothing he does not understand, nowhere he does not have access.

Whether he is in Las Vegas or Tokyo, Istanbul or Vera Cruz, he has a carte blanche denied to other nationalities.

This opens a rich if smelly vein in the Bond world. When the Caribbean islander Quarrel is reintroduced in the book *Dr. No*, Fleming gives an amazing little homily: "Bond took the warm dry calloused paw and looked into the dark grey eyes that showed descent from a Cromwellian soldier or a pirate of Morgan's time." This is almost too good to be true: race, class and conquest all swirling around in a mere handful of words. Quarrel's relationship with Bond is also compared to that between a ghillie and his Scottish laird. This relationship (Bond's "passport into the lower strata of coloured life") plunges us into a tightly meshed and imagined colonial world, although, interestingly, one that sees mixing of black and white as coming up with something admirable. The backdrop to Quarrel's ancestry, of Cromwell's soldiers or Morgan's pirates having sex with the slaves the Spanish had left behind to create dozens of generations later a proudly deferential imagined Scottish-style servant–master relationship is unbeatable. Indeed the two important black figures in the books—Quarrel and the Harlem-based gangster Mr. Big—are in effect "allowed" in by Fleming because of their mixed race, the latter being a Haitian with a "good dose of French blood." It can be said with some confidence that no other country could generate such a squirmy range of referents, with a history and a manner so densely strange.

Fleming's writings are full of this. The films too, of course, have a variety of racial assumptions which are fun, but too trivial on the whole to be very interesting: of course Egyptians are servile, Latin Americans hot-blooded, Japanese courteous yet self-sacrificingly violent. These are hardly surprises. In the later films often the only point of interest is discovering where Bond is flying to next and speculating on what racial tics we can expect to hop into view. The one film where race becomes central is *Live and Let Die*—made in part, hilariously, to cash in on the success of the blaxploitation movie *Shaft*—where Bond actually sleeps with a black woman. But the astonishingly feeble attempt to engage a little with race rapidly gives way to the crazily distasteful black-hands-on-white-flesh scenario for poor Jane Seymour which makes *Live and Let Die* such a shameful experience on each viewing.

There is no race in the books about which Bond does not have views: "So that was it! The old Hun again. Always at your feet or at your throat"; "He'd never liked being up against the Chinese. There were too many of them"; "They would soon be out of the damned Balkans and down into Italy. Then Switzerland, France—among friendly people, away from the furtive lands." And so on. Sometimes it is like being trapped by a maniac on a bus with unlimited race-based anecdotes. Bond is always being kissed demonstratively by Corsicans, offered encapsulated wisdom by Japanese, spat at and screamed at by Germans.

THERE WERE all kinds of abortive schemes to film the Bond books in the 1950s. None came to anything and it is interesting how this reflects Fleming's quite moderate prominence at the time, particularly in the United States. The one exception was *Casino Royale*, sold to CBS to make a one-off for American television in 1954.

In the case of *Casino Royale* it would have been a kindness if, like most television of the 1950s and 1960s, it had been wiped. The programme features an American "Jimmy" Bond, played by Barry Nelson. Nelson was a man with a bizarre head, an important percentage of which had been squeezed down into the neck, the effect being to make the head seem tiny and immobile as though supported on a flesh brace. This means that you are simply too aware he is a former athlete of some kind for him to seem acceptable as an actor: the athlete is always trumping the actual role being played. Pierce Brosnan has the same problem: no matter how long he may be on screen you are simply too aware that his much more core competency is to model risibly clunky, expensive watches of a kind that could appeal only to people who think of Monaco as glamorous. But I digress. Nelson's Bond wanders around a casino, fluffing his lines, and bizarrely and at great length explains the rules of the card game being played (presumably so that the audience does not feel left out). Particularly oddly he drinks only water, even having a little by-play with his opponent, Le Chiffre, about quaffing another glassful. It is a shambles. Everything about *Casino Royale* implies a dreadful alternative path for Bond—where he could have disappeared into the vast but ephemeral maw of fifties television, never to reemerge. The idea that Bond might have been chucked into the Dumpster in this way is truly upsetting: how contingent was Bond's film role in perking up British life!

The only eldritch note in *Casino Royale* is the astonishing appearance of the villain, Le Chiffre. Just when the laughter has worn off, and a general feeling of self-disgust is closing in, there, right in the middle of the screen, is the great Peter Lorre. This genuinely disturbing, miraculous actor of the 1930s is in poor shape here, but if Lorre was often doomed to parody himself it was still one of the great parodies. In a sense it is best not to think about this too much as Lorre would have been the perfect Blofeld. But the whole sequence was wrong: Lorre died in 1964 and came from a much earlier generation, doomed to pick up whatever work he could by the 1950s — such as parts in rubbish CBS shows. But, but . . . Perhaps the same computer modelling breakthroughs of the future which might allow Sean Connery to be spliced into *On Her Majesty's Secret Service* could also allow Peter Lorre of circa 1940 to appear as Blofeld in *You Only Live Twice*?

This footnote has itself a footnote: the alienation of the rights to *Casino Royale* meant that they were passed on outside anyone else's control to the makers of the Swinging Sixties movie disaster *Casino Royale*. This David Niven/Woody Allen horror is rarely seen and effectively has nothing to do with Bond — or with anything. It is cruel that Bond should be played by David Niven — one of the essential British actors of the forties who somehow went completely wrong and spent the rest of his career pimping to some deep-seated American wish to see British twerpy ineffectuality in action. Thinking further about this film is pointless, though — it's not even a mad cousin locked in the attic.

The news that after endless negotiation *Casino Royale* will be the name of the Bond film due for release in late 2006 may be good news. For years fans have dreamt of the book being turned into a faithfully adapted film as it could be a brooding, noirish, rather despairing mood piece. I fear however that the reality will consist of John Cleese as Q campily unveiling some follow-up to *Die Another Day*'s invisible car.

IF THERE IS one thing around which we can all unite in making fun of poor James Bond, it must be his smoking. He smokes immense amounts. As Fleming never tires of telling us, Morlands of Grosvenor Street makes him a "fragrant but powerful" Macedonian blend, each cigarette bonded with three gold rings. Bond "let the smoke come out between his teeth in a luxurious hiss." Spectacular. Bond has no specific leg-up in popular consciousness based around smoking—the movies were jammed with appealing smokers and Bond merely fits in with the crowd. The tobacco artisans at Morlands had to work pretty hard, though—"then he lit his seventieth cigarette of the day" is an unimprovable line. Fleming carefully maps Bond's tastes—his attempts to get fit in *Thunderball* result in switching to the weak, beautifully named Duke of Durham brand and he toys with Royal Blend, Laurens jaune and Shinsei at different times. Mercifully, he never affects Fleming's own absurd cigarette-holder—another inexplicable habit of yesteryear.

Of course, we all see the drawbacks of Bond's habit—the world's least-in-demand sniper, driven mad by a mere half-hour of nicotine deprivation, hacking and rasping and, with tears pouring down his cheeks, giving away his position to the enemy, then wildly and inaccurately firing off his rifle as his gorge fills with another glob of blackened, spongy material. By the time, pathetically, that he is let into M's office in *The Man with the Golden Gun* in his hopeless, brainwashed attempt to assassinate him, it is hard to tell whether the hard knocks or the cigarettes have brought him so low—a wheezing, shuffling figure reduced to fantasies about sleeping with the new departmental secretary.

In the films, the smoking gives out fairly rapidly—although Roger Moore once has an ill-judged Havana—but back at the beginning with *Dr. No*, the whole film legend had been launched as Connery is first introduced at the baccarat table with huge, carnal jets of smoke pouring from his mouth and nostrils, a dinner-jacketed dragon. As smoking becomes more or less extinct will this image become ever more weird, ever more disgusting, or ever more alluring?

The drinking is pretty continuous, too. Bond's drinks include martini, sake, bourbon and branch water, vodka (pre-war Wolfschmidt from Riga), Algerian red, Stingers, Americanos ("a musical comedy drink"), Calvados, Marsala, gin and tonic and lashings of champagne. As himself one of the great drinkers of the fifties, Fleming wrote marvellously on the grandeurs and miseries of alcohol and a little book of permanent value, in a lavish binding, could be made simply from his comments. Drink is also the binding agent for many other concerns: drinking while flying, drinking while enjoying (or not) a new country, drinking while trying to sleep with a girl. In *Moonraker*, he comes up with the ultimate wisdom: "Champagne and benzedrine! Never again." And for anyone hypnotized at once by alcohol, by travel and by geography, as some of us are, Fleming comes up, in *You Only Live Twice*, with the last word:

> When the aircraft flattened out of 30,000 feet, [Bond] ordered the first of the chain of brandies and ginger ales that was to sustain him over the Channel, a leg of the North Sea, the Kattegat, the Arctic Ocean, the Beaufort Sea, the Bering Sea and the North Pacific Ocean . . .

FLEMING'S VILLAINS are immeasurably aided by a distinguished succession of sidekicks. Some of these have almost become more part of the language than their masters. They also find strong support from the animal kingdom—but these (scorpions, giant centipedes, tarantulas) are the usual rigmarole, contemptuously familiar to Dr. Fu Manchu and many others. The human sidekicks are really remarkable though, and here is a thoughtful table:

Book	Name	Nationality	Characteristic
Casino Royale	none	Corsican	Thick body hair
Live and Let Die	Whisper	Black American	Missing lung
Moonraker	Krebs	German	Says "Wunderschön"
Diamonds Are Forever	Wint & Kidd	White American	Gay
From Russia with Love	Grant	Irish	Enormous
Dr. No	n/a—a weakness	n/a	n/a
Goldfinger	Oddjob	Korean	Eats cats
Thunderball	Largo	Italian	Uses scent freely
The Spy Who Loved Me	Sluggsy	White American	Devoid of body hair
On Her Majesty's Secret Service	Bunt	Swiss	Lesbian
You Only Live Twice	Bunt	ditto	ditto
The Man with the Golden Gun	Hendriks	Dutch	Cheap teeth crowns

There is no question of course that Oddjob in *Goldfinger* is the most totemic of these figures—both in the film, perfectly played by Hawaiian weightlifter Harold Sakata, and in the book. In the book he is far more mad and more horrible. It is still undoubtedly true that the way books, or good, well-imagined books, project onto the brain allows far more instability and strangeness than can be managed in film's relatively realist framework. In *The Old Curiosity Shop* the dreadful dwarf Quilp mutates as the book goes on into something genuinely dredged up from a nightmare: drinking boiling alcohol, screaming at and hitting an abandoned ship's figurehead, turning up at places and times where it is physically impossible for him to be. As the book progresses, there is a stifling sense of dread and disorientation for the reader which could in no way be reproduced in a film. The idea of drinking boiling alcohol and laughing maniacally while doing so is wonderful: seeing it on screen would be less so.

This absolutely applies to Oddjob. However enjoyable he may be in the film, Oddjob dominates the book in insidious disturbing ways. There is an extraordinary set piece of lunatic inventiveness where Goldfinger, at his country mansion, gets Oddjob to use his karate skills to smash up his dining room. What is unleashed is clearly a demon rather than a human being, doing impossible violence (and Goldfinger rewards him with a cat to eat: no reader searching for racial stereotypes goes unrewarded). When Bond later struggles with his satanic adversary, this elicits Fleming's marvellous line "The sickly zoo-smell of Oddjob enveloped him."

Fleming manages the same trick repeatedly. When, in *Diamonds Are Forever*, the gay killers, Wint and Kidd, turn up in the ship taking Bond back to England, it is wholly implausible:

how would they be there and why would they bother—except, except that they are forces of pure malice and are not motivated by logic. The hoodlums in *The Spy Who Loved Me* should be dead but they lurch to life ("a big, glittering turnip-face, pale and shiny under the moon, was looking through the glass slats!") in an appealingly zombie-movie sort of way.

The other sidekicks all have their exclusively literary pleasures: body hair, lizard eyes, hunchbacks, and so on. Even passing minor villains such as the Mexican would-be assassin in *Goldfinger*, with his single, immortal line, "You like pretty girl—go jig-a-jig" (managing to convey in six words an entire squalid personality), have a truly Dickensian air.

If I had to nominate a favourite, it would be the evil Floridian bait-and-fish guy in *Live and Let Die*—an entirely marginal figure who participates in Felix Leiter's mutilation: "His complexion was the colour of tobacco dust, a sort of yellowy-beige. He looked cruel and cold, like the bad man in a film about poker-players and gold mines." The whole aquarium fight between Bond and this man, blasting away at each other with bullets smashing exotic fish tanks, is one of the most delirious set pieces in all the books, and proof of why Fleming was so often far, far more than a hack.

When Bond first encounters this loathsome figure his loathsomeness is signalled by his completely pointless murder of a brown pelican with his gun. Who can ask for more? Note the very British angle: he must be evil because he has shot a bird; millions of members of the Royal Society for the Protection of Birds, having felt, on the whole, bored or indifferent to the earlier killing of humans in the book, will now stomach any level of violence from Bond in the destruction of this man.

*

WHAT SHOULD we make of Bond's chief, the remarkable M? He is a figure in the Bond mythology on a par with Blofeld and retains an astonishing potency. If post-war Britain had expressed its debt to Bond in a landscape dotted with temples then M would undoubtedly get a substantial building to himself (this is an easy and enjoyable game with any number of temple layouts—at its best played with a more Asian sense of duality, forces of evil or violence also getting their place: it is easy to imagine a slightly disturbing folk cult growing up around Oddjob, say, and a lovely alcove for Pussy Galore). In a sense, M is more of a religious focus than Bond himself—a Jupiter to Bond's Mercury; Wotan to Bond's Loge. The books in effect make him the father of the nation, the figure who is always awake and alert and who, through silent coup after silent coup (delivered via the figure of Bond), keeps us all safe. He therefore incarnates in its perfect form the Conservative ideal: of patrician omnicompetence over a silent, uncomprehending, safe, passive flock.

Bernard Lee's beautiful impersonation of M in the films makes it impossible to re-create what Fleming imagined when M existed only in his novels: Lee superimposes himself too strongly. In the *Daily Express* cartoon-strip version of the novels M is shown simply as a shadowed face. In many ways this is truer to the spirit of M and the sense in which newspapers have used the idea ever since—"The New M," "Who was the Real M?"—as more than just a fictional character but also almost more than a mere human being. His power and meaning are such that we should think of M in the same manner that a small group of Hindus thought of Gandhi, trying to persuade Richard Attenborough that for his film Gandhi should be played not by Ben Kingsley but by a pure point of light—a dramatically dubious but surely interesting, or even preferable, suggestion.

Bond himself is devoted to M: "the tranquil, lined sailor's face that he loved, honoured and obeyed," "the cold voice that Bond loved and obeyed" and so on. In the books, as in the films, M in every case initiates a sequence of events which will result in the saving of the West in some form, with a sort of lunatic prescience about Bond's needs and locations that again argues for his being a deity rather than a human. Indeed, if he is a god, then the books certainly come up fresh and with a sort of redemptive flavour à la *The Lion, the Witch and the Wardrobe*.

The difficulty that readers of the books have with M is that clearly at some level Fleming thinks he is absurd, and just to entertain himself gives M short speeches—on how the Swiss manage their beatnik problem or how homosexuals cannot whistle—that imply he is mad. He is also given a faintly (or not faintly) ridiculous hobby of painting watercolours exclusively of English wild orchids. That the security of the democratic world should be in the hands of such a limited man makes M's role in effect savagely satirical—it was such figures who had presided over all the disasters of the era and who so singularly failed to see that British intelligence's most crucial role had in practice been the unhappy one of siphoning off Anglo-American secrets straight to the Russians.

M is also exactly the sort of imperturbable philistine boor, zanily digging away at ripe bits of Stilton at his private club or lecturing Bond on the evils of pasteurized milk, that for generations of foreigners has personified everything hateful about this country. He *is* "perfidious Albion," the patriot who will screw over anyone viewed, by some narrow judgement, as a threat or inconvenience. As any but the least reflective readers of the books must have felt (and indeed had rammed down their throats by events reported in newspapers almost every day of the fifties), M's days were over and the long century of British steamrollering humbug had gone. When, in one extraordinary scene in *You Only Live Twice*, M sends Bond to Tokyo to be a guest of the Japanese secret service but cannot remember what it is called, "some unpronounceable Japanese rubbish," it is hard not to feel that England's future is in somewhat palsied hands, particularly as Bond himself cannot speak a word of Japanese. Wittingly or unwittingly, Fleming, in his creation of M, exposed an entire aspect of Britain's elite which in every imaginable field was to cause havoc for decades and may well still be doing so. The serio-comic involvement of MI6 in the run-up to the 2003 war in Iraq and the growing sense that they did not have any idea at all what was going on in a country we had been closely mon-itoring or actively fighting for the previous fifteen years, seems to indicate that M, perhaps simply as a brain in a tank, is still in charge. On the frequent occasions I take my own children on the train through South London that trundles past MI6's ziggurat-like headquarters, I feel a sense of shame as the boys scream with excitement and try to spot spies and assassins walking in and out of the building—when in practice the ziggurat's inmates are probably just drunkenly photocopying each other's bottoms or staring at CNN broadcasts. Here is an area where Fleming's influence remains enormous—where the secret becomes public (Burgess, Philby, Maclean, Blunt and so on; the failure to predict the end of the Cold War; the failure to brief anyone intelligently on Iraq), the result is dangerous and depressing farce. But thanks to Fleming, and it can only be thanks to Fleming rather than to any observable reality, we all feel that secretly, secretly M's "frosty, damnably clear, grey eyes" are still keeping watch.

IT IS HARD when thinking about M not also to think about Harold Macmillan, the debonair, moustachioed figure who took over as prime minister after Eden resigned in early 1957, crushed flat by the Suez disaster. Like M, Macmillan was for many a reassuring figure. He had a sort of patrician unflappability which reduced the entire population to the status of panicked yet loyal estate workers, reassured by the Master's self-control even if it was clear to everyone that the farm animals all had some foam-flecked, rolling-eyed illness and that the manor house was burning down. He stood for an attempt at real if watery political consensus, an agreement to support Attlee's welfare inheritance in return for social peace: a stance which in due course made Macmillan such an overwhelming hate figure for Thatcher and her associates.

Like M, too, there must be a strong suspicion that Macmillan was at some level stark mad. Seriously wounded in the First World War, a life-long and prominent cuckold (or more strictly a wittol—Macmillan connived at his wife's three-decades-long affair with another Conservative MP), a relatively minor figure in the Conservative Party until his late fifties, Macmillan spent his life in thrall to colossal forces of social, global and technological change. The gap between his schooldays at the top-dog planet of Eton in the reign of Edward VII and the threatened atomic wastelands of the 1950s seems unbridgeable. It is hardly surprising that he should have spent his evenings reading the soothing novels of Anthony Trollope. As prime minister at the most genuinely terrifying point in the Cold War, Macmillan had the sole, zany responsibility, once Britain's hydrogen bombs were functional in the late 1950s, of authorizing their use: a decision which would have killed an estimated eight million Russians at around the same time that an agreeable, leather-bound copy of *The Last Chronicle of Barset* along with its moustachioed reader and the whole of London were reduced to radioactive ash.

It was perhaps his personal sexual humiliation that prepared him quite well for the political humiliations of the time. Hardly a month seemed to go by without something else going wrong for Britain, and if the Bond novels provide literary reassurance to the fevered patriot then Macmillan, with his amiable bedside manner, did a similar job politically. Macmillan agreed to full-scale decolonization, but the motives of his government were drawn from financial realism and cynicism rather than a happy embrace of Third World nationalism. The Suez invasion had been a serious attempt to crush colonial insubordination, just as the hanging of more than 1,000 Kenyans had also been serious, but the trauma of Suez was so great that it generated a sort of peevish helplessness which gave most of the British Empire its freedom within four or five years. What had been called the "Scramble for Africa" in the 1870s had become, in the appealing phrase of a Kenyan politician, the African desire for Europeans to "Scram from Africa." At the time there were cries of anger from the traditional right and their friends at the *Express* and *Mail*, but also some more sceptical voices suggesting that countries with tiny professional classes and no governmental traditions at all since Britain's often annihilatory raids generations before might be poorly placed to rule themselves with less planning time than a single British electoral cycle.

This was of no interest to Macmillan's government, who simply wanted to be shot of everything. In the light of what was to happen, for example, to the Algerians, Angolans and Vietnamese in the coming years at the hands of the French, Portuguese and Americans, Britain's decision simply to dump its empire (generally with some ceremony involving a calculatedly offensive marginal member of the royal family) seems a brilliant one. The anarchy, civil war and despair that unfolded in countries such as Nigeria—while fuelled in part by British weapons, advice, finance and oil interests—had magically been transformed into a problem for the UN rather than the UK. Any commentary on the end of the Empire under Macmillan has somehow to balance a sense of provisional relief at the end result with a frantic attempt not to suggest that Macmillan should get any credit at all. There should also be relief that Macmillan refused to send British troops into Vietnam—a critical decision, followed up by Wilson, and one which has had incalculable effects: implying an alternative and *far far worse* sixties.

As the mature (well, fairly mature) Bond novels were published, Britain itself began to enjoy some modest growth, and this was a necessary background to decolonization: a sense that although Britain was being stripped down to a small overcrowded island with a murky future, people were at least better off. This now, of course, seems a cruel hoax as Britain over the longer term seems almost alone among countries on Earth in not having seriously ridden the period's great wave of general prosperity. The sense of gradual rebuilding that gives Macmillan's rule such a happy air had become a sad fantasy even before the Cuban missile crisis of 1962, with a mounting sense of panic that, despite hacking away a mountain of imperial commitments, Britain simply was not functioning properly as an economy, that there was something deeply broken. For Macmillan the twin disasters were Britain's exclusion from the Kennedy–Khrushchev meeting of 1961, the point at which any thin pretence evaporated of there being a "Big Three" rather than simply a "Big Two," and de Gaulle's refusal of British entry into the European Community (the "Common Market") in 1963. Macmillan may have avoided repeating the crushing disaster of Suez and he may also, through cunning American brinkmanship, have avoided giving the order to incinerate eight million Russians during the Cuban missile crisis, but, as he wearily resigned in 1963 with *From Russia with Love* playing in the cinemas and a very unwell Fleming flying to Japan to research *You Only Live Twice*, Britain's future seemed absolutely grim—a grimness that was to be played out over the next two decades.

THERE IS NOW no choice but to get to the heart of the matter, the three books which genuinely justify Fleming's reputation and which carry intact (or intactish) into the present his claim to being more than a lucky toff thriller writer: *From Russia with Love* (1957), *Dr. No* (1958) and *Goldfinger* (1959). Each book is very different and all have their flaws, indeed often almost disappear under their flaws, but how attractive they are! Even agreeing that they are formulaic, dated, snobbish and so on, they have a vigour and pleasure in themselves that makes them exceptional. None is a complete work of art, because Fleming was too slapdash and Bond himself too weak a character to carry a complete book, but when he hits his stride Fleming can offer unique pleasures. Just when he appears to be merely filling space, he will rescue everything, with one of his villain's timeless deranged speeches ("You are right, Mister Bond. That is just what I am, a maniac"), a beautifully observed meal or fish or act of violence. It would be mad to say that Fleming was a better writer than, say, contemporaries such as William Golding or Kingsley Amis, but it *would* be possible to say that in many ways, from where we now stand, he appears at least as interesting. I can think of no writer—and it doesn't matter if it is accidentally or deliberately that Fleming does this—who comes close to bringing to life the neuroses, panics, highs, dreams and disappointments of a Britain that has now vanished and whose death throes he romanced.

It is not a coincidence that it was these three books that were the first to be filmed, as their plots are so rich and fascinating. It *is* a coincidence, although I would say not much of one, that these are the books that were written, published and hugely read during the final implosion of the old British imperial state with Macmillan's post-Suez decision simply to bail out, at all costs, from empire.

Whereas the first four Bond books were in their different ways simply above average ways of passing the time, Fleming seems to have realized after *Diamonds Are Forever* that he was confronting something much better, that he could write books which could permanently implant Bond on the cultural landscape. First he needed to make Bond into a mythical figure, which he did in *From Russia with Love*, then he needed to make the most of Jamaica, which he did in *Dr. No*, and then he needed to create the perfect criminal megalomaniac and perfect deranged sidekick, which he achieved with Goldfinger and Oddjob.

What is really striking about these books is their closeness to fairy tale: the most startling figures in them—the Russian spy-killing chief Rosa Klebb, the freakish, metal-handed Dr. No in his island lair, the unhinged gold-bullion obsessive Auric Goldfinger and the speechless bowler-hatted murderer Oddjob—have no claim to being real at all and are not treated as such. There is a little of this in the earlier books, but even the most convincing figures, such as Mr. Big in *Live and Let Die*, are, in effect, slightly too realistic to be plausible—you are aware of Fleming operating merely within a set of pulp conventions, albeit with appealing gleams of excellence. There is something authentically nightmarish about these new inventions—partly pantomime, partly myth. They are Expressionist in the sense that they can only make grand gestures. There is a strong air of *The Cabinet of Dr. Caligari* about them or, very strongly in the case of Dr. No, of Conrad at his most Expressionist in the emaciated maniac Mr. Jones, the terrible villain of *Victory*, with his skull-like head and claw-like hands. Wrapped in an "old but gorgeous blue silk dressing-gown . . . he resembled a painted pole leaning against the edge of the desk, with a dried head of dubious distinction stuck on top of it." Mr. Jones' eventual corpse is like "a heap of bones in a blue silk bag, with only the head and the feet sticking out." Fleming describes No, his Chinese-German villain (a wonderful combination), in closely related terms: "It was odd to see a forehead as smooth as the top of the polished skull"; the emaciated doctor was "like a giant venomous worm wrapped in grey tin-foil." Bond is so revolted by No that he expects to see a slime trail behind him on the carpet and the reader happily feels the same. Giving him steel pincers instead of hands is a beguiling touch, too.

From Russia with Love marks the rather belated centre-staging of the Soviet Union, a shadowy presence in the earlier books beyond the Soviet representative who, unwisely, saves Bond's life at the end of *Casino Royale*. I will keep to my rule about no plot summaries here but *From Russia with Love* makes vast and explicit claims for Bond which he has earned in *Moonraker* (by saving London from destruction by Nazi maniacs) but for which, in the pulp tradition, he gained no discernible reward—either from his superiors in MI6 or from his readers. In his other adventures he had been a small-time operator: humiliating and then indirectly destroying a French agent of the KGB and then tangling with black and Italian-American hoodlums of some grandiloquence but no global importance. The Russians had lurked in the background in all these cases, but there is no sense that Bond himself is very important.

In *From Russia with Love* everything changes. In Fleming's single happiest decision he removes Bond from the book for the whole of the first section—the entire opening consisting of discussions in Moscow and elsewhere by SMERSH (the spy-killing wing of the KGB) about how to bring him down. When the plot cooked up by SMERSH and its fiendish operatives Rosa Klebb and Kronsteen unfolds it is on the Orient Express and owes something to Eric Ambler and something to Graham Greene. It also, sad to say, features the despairingly weak intervention of a metal cigarette case stopping a bullet (shouldn't there be some world body that stops plot devices like this?). Nonetheless, the cigarette case cannot damage in the end a marvellously realized set of inventions. By objectifying Bond, by reproducing his KGB file ("Signs of plastic surgery on back of right hand [see Appendix A]" and so on), by showing Bond as a man alone against a vast, fiendish bureaucracy bent on his destruction, Fleming vaults way over his genre to create the figure who has lasted, albeit in diminishing form, until the present. When there is a chance he might be dead at the end of *From Russia with Love* this is a cause for anxiety — just as his return, only a little shaky, in *Dr. No* is cause for relief.

When Fleming describes Rosa Klebb, clutching a blood-spattered apron, rushing so as not to be late for a torture session inside KGB headquarters, where "she breathed in the victim's screams like perfume," there is something far more going on than mere thriller writing. Oddjob too is clearly not meant to be human — with his snout-like upper lip, blackish teeth, hairless body and hands and feet reduced to mere nerveless implements for performing karate he is like something terrible from the *Arabian Nights*. Oddjob is not someone who can be killed — it would of course be very easy to shoot someone with Oddjob's skills, his freaky bowler-hat weapon notwithstanding, but that is never an issue. He is, like Klebb and No, a demon and beyond normal human action until the plot eventually has no further use for him. Goldfinger himself is a lesser man, a hint at the dull, later figure of Blofeld, but he is rescued by the grandeur of his plan to steal the Fort Knox gold, by the supporting gang of mobsters, by Pussy Galore and the sad English sisters killed by Oddjob in spectacular ways, and by himself having some of the best set-piece speeches, of which one cannot have too many.

HOW BOOKS disseminate and become successful is one of the unsolvable mysteries of publishing, if not of culture. I have worked for ages in the book business and feel none the wiser. Almost no books come out with the expectation of failure, and yet vast numbers do fail. Only rarely can something be published with total confidence in its success and the bestseller charts remain studded with books which have been embraced by the reading public totally to the surprise of both publisher and author.

Fleming's success was quite gradual. There was always something slightly aloof and grand about the books, which were published by the distinguished literary imprint of Jonathan Cape and could never be confused with run-of-the-mill pulp. Fleming took enormous pains over his jackets and from *From Russia with Love* onwards commissioned Richard Chopping to produce strange, beautiful paintings to very precise specifications, the pictures becoming ever more tangential to the texts and culminating in the marvellously freaky *You Only Live Twice* cover of a toad gripping a dead dragonfly. Fleming had no control at all, though, over the paperbacks and these *were* initially published as straightforward hard-boiled fiction. The 1960s Pan paperback covers were carefully abstract or allusive (a bullet hole, a playing card), never showed Bond's face, except on the current film tie-in, and have been worshipped by cover designers ever since. They have therefore always preserved an independent life, albeit one on which millions of readers superimposed Connery's face. The 1950s paperbacks, however, are far distant from the 1960s minimalism. These all make the huge error of showing Bond, generally in ripped clothing and with a woman clinging to him. The artists are terrible and the designs spring from the same rich soil that make so much of British fifties paperback design such a mixed bag. Bond's features wobble about but seem to be a blend of Biggles, Dan Dare and Marvel Comic clean-cut. It is hard to recapture any real sense of whether or not these were effective covers and Fleming never commented on them, seeing them presumably as a necessary evil.

The books' success accumulated steadily as the series unfolded—by 1961 or so they were very famous, and President Kennedy's public enthusiasm for *From Russia with Love* put them into a unique orbit in the United States (his endorsement in a list of his favourite books was in fact rather odd, as the list included quite a bit of fruity "carriage trade" publishing of a kind quite at odds with Kennedy's tough public image). So who read them? Even now, with endless market research, nobody really knows who reads anything. As anyone thinking about their own reading habits has to concede, book choice is very odd and fluky. Books move through space, time and price. Their trajectories are like the great wave created by the explosion of Krakatoa—with a sufficient initial impact the ripple can reach around the world. Because of the way the media works, the dissemination of books around the planet, except to quite remote communities, is fairly instantaneous but it is fun to imagine some chartable, delayed reaction through the English-speaking world. Most famously, of course, this had happened with the fabled early Victorian crowds waiting in New York Harbor for the final, cliff-hung episode of *The Old Curiosity Shop* to arrive by ship, but it occurs in all kinds of small and hidden ways even today. I like the idea that as a book is becoming unfashionable in London and New York it is becoming all the rage in Droitwich and Duluth before moving on eventually, many months later, to Pitcairn and Tierra del Fuego. Could there be communities off New Guinea who are only now wrestling with the moral implications of *The Water Babies*?

In any event Fleming's books had, within his lifetime, become an enormous cult in many languages. By the present day he is reckoned to have sold in total some hundred million books. I have my own ideas about his British readers and they are implied in what has been written in this book—they are undoubtedly too narrow though because the millions of copies sold imply all types of readers. The reader I think about is the reader most upset by the changes around them, economic, social, imperial, for whom Bond must have been immensely comforting, but many others were attracted by the adventure, the sex, the potent sense of a sequence of adventures, making each new novel build on the ones before. By the time of the first film there was a frenzy of expectation, a frenzy which, when satisfied by *Dr. No*, in turn impacted on the books' sales. Fleming's last year of life was spent in a great swamp of money with the promise of vastly more.

THE ATOMIC nightmare which unfolded for much of the world in the late forties and fifties and which so crushed Macmillan unfolded for Britain in a very odd way. Fleming turns twice to atomic weapons for his plots: in a simple and uninteresting sort of way in *Moonraker* and more threateningly, or at least more plausibly, in *Thunderball* (1961) as a source of what has now routinely become described as "nuclear blackmail"—indeed contemporary terrors are still quite adequately fed by *Thunderball*'s storyline.

British scientists were involved from the beginning in the development of the atomic bomb and Britain poured scarce resources after the War into the creation of its independent Bomb. Given what was involved and that the Cold War played out in ways that made the existence of that independent Bomb completely irrelevant, it now looks as though this is yet another of those areas in which Britain's rulers seem to have behaved in a pathetic and half-mad way, irradiating chunks of Australian desert and wasting the careers of thousands of people fruitlessly engaged in creating, coaxing and improving a weapon that could never be used and which was in any event unnoticeable in the face of the American and Soviet arsenals. But perhaps this is one of those areas of modernity where a certain amount of empathy is really needed—a culture cannot be desperate and backward-looking in most respects and yet also be castigated when it is at the cutting edge in some area using quite different criteria. Perhaps the Bomb was an inevitable aspect of staying current and valuable in the immediate aftermath of the Second World War—and therefore took on a momentum which whatever its irrelevance to Britain's true position by, say, the early 1960s, meant it was unstoppable.

The absolutely strange aspect of Britain's Bomb, however, was the almost insouciant way in which it implied that most British people would die in the event of a war without any gesture even to protect them. I may have been to a series of schools peculiarly wedded to a form of mad fatalism, but in the 1970s I remember no mention of any kind of what would be expected of us in the event of war. At least in America there was the low comedy of duck-and-cover and, when living in New York, I remember seeing countless signs pointing to fallout shelters (albeit to shelters either to which the keys had long been lost or which had been turned into clubs). France had since the 1960s invested in huge numbers of deep underground car parks all of which were convertible into fallout shelters. Indeed it would have been possible to survive in these quite well for a bit as the nuclear winter raged outside, existing on cans of choucroute and those individually wrapped sponge cakes that seem to have no sell-by date—survive at least until fingers and jaws falling off made it an unequal battle with the packaging. Presumably too, in practice, all spaces in these French shelters would have been reserved for those working in local government on parking-control issues, each enjoying some secret code allowing the little entrance barrier to lift up and let them in as the missiles zoomed overhead. What had at one point appeared as a harmless perk would then become a genetic disaster, as the handful of French survivors, their guts ravaged by choucroute vinegar, hauled themselves to the surface to mate and leave mankind's future in the hands of a new generation combining personal cowardice, narrowness and pedantic failure.

At least the French and Americans had plans. The British secrecy culture means that much remains hidden about the 1950s, but what has been revealed is a handful of Cotswold fallout shelters for senior civil servants and a deranged plan to whisk the Queen to safety on a special little train, neither aspect exactly making survival for anyone else seem specifically tempting. It would have been interesting to know how far the Queen's little train would have got: an object of burning speculation to twenty-third-century treasure-hunters from Patagonia, picking through heaps of jagged wreckage with their foil-wrapped tentacles, looking for the diamonds. After the Cuban missile crisis the Home Office issued the advice to potential survivors of a nuclear strike that they should wear "stout shoes" and not forget a "travelling rug" to keep them warm. Perhaps, more seriously, the options available to policy-makers seemed so grim that—with the growth of the American and Soviet missile systems simply ensuring Britain's extermination as more or less collateral damage—it was futile to bother with real survival strategies. From what we know of the governments of the fifties and sixties this does not seem to be the case, though. The nuclear threat seems so foul and so immobilizing that it is hard to imagine cabinet meetings that did not consist of everyone simply staring around in wordless horror waiting for the end. But reading about such meetings it is clear that this was not how they worked—indeed huge amounts of time seem to have been spent happily chatting about tiny affairs. That people nonetheless airily enjoyed themselves, became better off, went on holidays, raised families and happily read Fleming's fantasies about London's destruction by nuclear rocket is perhaps yet another example of how complicated the past is, how hard it is to fathom reactions to it and how hard it is to imagine the future. Were they all meditating the meaning of Armageddon or were they all just looking forward to lunch?

THERE ARE MANY reasons of course for James Bond's survival in our culture but a crucial one must be the whole world of "man talk." There must be other novels that do this equally well (or badly) but Fleming had a brilliant gift for creating situations where Bond has to hang out for a few pages with another guy (Felix Leiter quite frequently, the Turkish secret agent Darko Kerim in *From Russia with Love*, the drunken Australian Dikko Henderson in *You Only Live Twice*) and sound off about cars, politics and women. These conversations now have the value of creatures caught in amber—perfectly preserved sentiments from a bygone age which, however, remains visible to us today. There are some amazing scenes: the best (or perhaps that's not the right word—the most startling) is Darko Kerim's magnificent account of winning a "Bessarabian hell-cat" in a fight with some gypsies, whom he knocks out and then keeps chained naked under his table, feeding her scraps at mealtimes. With amusement he recounts how his mother found out about this and came to rescue the girl—"'but when the time came, she refused to leave me.' Darko Kerim laughed hugely. 'An interesting lesson in female psychology, my dear friend.'"

Time to move on. For all that Bond is meant to be a loner, this could make for quite dull books, so Fleming is always trying to pep things up by giving him either internal monologues, in which he can sound off about British Rail or the welfare state, or a friend to chat to about race issues or the end of the Empire. Helpful tips are also passed on: about what to wear in bed, about why the Japanese are always killing themselves, about how black Americans are now so sensitive about the word "nigger" that instead of asking a barman for "a jigger of rum" you have to ask for "a jegro," and so on. Man jokes, bitter commentaries on the state of the world, many of them presumably lifted from Fleming's own conversations in Jamaica and elsewhere.

As Bond remains the patron saint of contemporary male-interest magazines a case could be made for this being his most lasting legacy, given that most other novels of the 1950s seem so strangled and anaemic. The Bond novels could be read, as they can still be today, as a sort of distilled ancient wisdom on how to fix up a car, sleep with a girl and so on. They lay out a whole world of kicked-back, drink-fuelled camaraderie which is, well, completely nauseating. Bond's every action and thought may have helped both crystallize and reassure male distress at the collapse of Britain in the world, but his more lasting legacy is perhaps Bond's laughing reminiscence in *You Only Live Twice* of how his friend Dikko smacked a girl's bottom so hard that she fell over.

*

WE CAN ARGUE almost indefinitely about which Bond film is the worst—but in the end it is an argument that sullies us all. The very fact of having to recall, say, Roger Moore dressed as a clown in *Octopussy* or Blofeld in a wheelchair being tipped down an industrial chimney in *For Your Eyes Only* makes everyone feel uncomfortable. With the books, though, it is easy: *The Spy Who Loved Me* (1962) is dreadful. *The Man with the Golden Gun* (1965) is not very good, a sad work by a dying writer, but *The Spy Who Loved Me* is a potent weapon in the hands of those who claim that Fleming was in practice just a terrible novelist, written when Fleming was in reasonable health and no excuses could be made. Fleming himself realized his mistake, even before the overwhelmingly bad reviews, and refused to allow a paperback to be issued. After his death—with the ethical thoughtfulness of publishers the world over—it was decided that Fleming had not meant this and a massively successful paperback duly appeared.

It has to be said that all this is a bit painful for me because I myself have happy memories of *The Spy Who Loved Me*. Age twelve and staying in a Welsh holiday cottage near Barmouth I enjoyed two nirvanas: the wholly unexpected naturalist's one of seeing a killer whale's fin carving along out at sea, matte black and terrifying, and the sexual one of tucking into *The Spy Who Loved Me*, the only Bond I had not read and which was merrily sitting on the cottage's little bookcase.

Essentially, as the holiday progressed, I became a sort of poster child for Victorian ideas on self-abuse, a palsied, drooling, whey-faced figure reluctantly prised from his bedroom to attend meals before disappearing once more to leaf through an ever less resellable copy of *The Spy Who Loved Me*. Rereading it some five years ago for the first time since then I found I had finished it without even noticing the sexual passages that had so ravaged my much younger self—which was both mournful and rather a relief.

The chief offences at the heart of this novel are two: that it has no ambition for Bond—he simply encounters and kills two small-time hoodlums in a Vermont motel—and that it has the deranged ambition for Fleming, driven at least in part by boredom with his creation and with himself, of writing a novel as a first-person female narrative. Nothing can redeem this latter decision beyond the happy realization that by writing it Fleming is in effect trying himself to be seduced by Bond, an entirely plausible quirk at this point in their relationship. Not once in the narrative is it faintly plausible that the "I" is a beautiful young Canadian woman trapped catastrophically in a deserted motel and then rescued and romanced by Bond. The "I" is always a turtly old novelist in a bow tie disturbingly working himself off under his clean-limbed hero in front of the watching world. It is a surreal performance, even crowding out the fact that the book must be seen as offensive to even the most brutalized and reactionary male reader ("the sweet tang of rape"). (It even raises disturbing questions about what happened in that Welsh holiday cottage.) But, let's move on. *The Spy Who Loved Me* is one of those odd books, such as Gustave Flaubert's *Salammbô* or Beatrix Potter's *Little Pig Robinson*, that mark an absolute wrong turn in a writer's career. These wrong turns no doubt have a value and create their own, often very small and perverse, sect (I certainly belong to the one for the sweltering *Salammbô*). Those in the sect will defend them unrealistically and raise them insistently in conversations about wholly other subjects, rolling about in the hopelessness of their cause and almost dreading the idea of anyone agreeing with them. But this is the world which values only B-sides or cover versions or soundtrack albums. It's a strange faith, and writers who attract it can endure in odd ways denied to those with an altogether cleaner slate.

BOND LOVES smoked salmon. He eats loads of it and is always commenting on it. Like Bond's, Fleming's daily cigarette consumption was such that all his food must have tasted as though it had been first rolled about in a clinker-littered grate. Because they had no taste buds Bond and Fleming have very clear takes on food: each mouthful is a pure signifier of prestige and class rather than of genuine connoisseurship.

At the distance of half a century a strange gap has opened up. As inlets all over the Scottish Highlands fill with thousands of tons of farmed-salmon excrement and smoked salmon has become associated as much with parasites that send sperm counts crashing through the floor as with tastiness, nothing seems to be going right for the concept of luxury. The reader of the Bond books now is reminded almost constantly of how the genuinely closed circle of traditional British luxury has mutated in the face of ever greater prosperity and relentless market pressure—and that the Bond books themselves were an important conduit for making middle-class audiences understand what was expected of them and what they could copy once some money got into circulation. Indeed an argument could be made that the early Bond books portrayed simply *too* great a gulf between their luxury worlds (even the straitened luxury of *Casino Royale*) and the paucity of day-to-day British life. Only with the modest uplift of the Macmillan period could people afford to enjoy reading about special yogurts or lovely suitcases.

Fleming is trapped looking both ways: he wishes to show off (and, to be fair to him, also to mock) his class values as though from a great height—but by doing so and by writing sensationally successful books he was in effect blabbing Masonic secrets. While this lies behind all the books, it is never clearer than in Fleming's obsession with food. There are many fine meals in the books, from a loving account of Turkish breakfast in *From Russia with Love* to a Florida crab feast in *Goldfinger*. The biggest set piece of greedy elitism, however, must be the blow-out Blades Club dinner in *Moonraker*, a meal so long and so lovingly described that it almost makes the entire plot topple over. This sensational binge, crammed with lore about vodka, champagne and steak, is Conservative Britain laughing at its enemies: we have the luxuries, the knowledge, the deference and you have *nothing*. But the writing itself destroys genuine elitism: it is as though Bond and M are munching away with thousands of readers pressed up around the table, knocking over the club furniture and soiling the carpet. If for much of its life the British Empire led its existence away from prying eyes, as I have suggested earlier, the same was true of its rulers. Fleming blows this principle completely and so, through his very success, becomes an unwitting agent for the sort of democratization he himself loathed. *Moonraker* becomes the Book of Genesis for brand-name consumerism that now dominates our world, with each chapter constituting a wilderness of eating, drinking and behavioural tips, albeit often of an arcane kind—such as how to remove poisonous residual oils from traditional Russian vodka: it's all there in *Moonraker*!

Fleming hands out the whole works in the course of the books: there is no meal, no social ritual, no personal tic that does not wind up in the reader's hands. It would be possible, pretty much, to walk into a casino and go through the entire rigmarole with complete confidence thanks to Fleming's information: not least because so many people who go into a casino now do so only because of having read about or watched Bond in the act. It must be a reasonable bet that almost all the men in casinos who are not actively infirm must imitate Bond's tension-sprung gait. I tried it once in Las Vegas and nobody laughed: but that was possibly because my audience consisted of a heap of deranged oldsters propped against the one-armed bandits and two very bored black bodybuilders dressed as Ancient Egyptian temple guards.

Fleming's trick of giving away the whole show was perfectly synchronized with the folding up of the Britain he was so entangled with. It is absolutely impossible to prove, but Fleming delivered the private, elite world of the traditional upper classes into the hands of a mass readership exactly in lockstep with the final implosion of that world's rationale—that it was legitimate because it was the reward due to a successful military and political cadre.

As the fifties progressed, and as Bond's popularity escalated, so this rationale became ever more threadbare. It had taken a kicking from Attlee's government but had survived in many areas until relief of a kind was found in the new "Elizabethan Age." As upper-class life came under ever greater pressure from taxation, economic collapse and changing customs so its world and its rituals began to cave in, too, and the National Trust scampered in to take over its houses. The oak-panelled insiderish world so loved by Fleming came to be associated not just with the "Victorian" British Empire (its dress and attitudes one of the great butts of sixties jokes) but also with such totally discredited figures as John Profumo (in the scandal that most damaged Macmillan), Kim Philby and, later, Lord Lucan. This great democratic shift occurred with the 1964 Labour victory but also with such epochal changes as the *Lady Chatterley* case. Britain was increasingly a society simply *not* built around deference and history, but around consumer rights, open access, self-improvement. It is hard to imagine two more violently opposed worlds than the Blades Club and the Open University.

By the 1970s, Fleming's world is hard to see—both for positive reasons (it had been discredited) and negative (nobody had any money left). It all reflates, as Thatcher's grip exerted itself, but in a new and more consumeristic form, a form which it is still very hard to encapsulate with any confidence as we so much live in its shadow.

If Fleming had been cryogenically frozen and could now be brought back to life (which would have been unusually hard, given the damage all the toxins in his system would have done to the equipment) he would be amazed by Central London: how sleek and self-satisfied Clubland remains and how prosperous the luxury trades around Jermyn Street have become again. But he would be absolutely astounded to see enormous supermarkets loaded with foie gras, caviar, salmon, luxury chocolates, Moët, rare teas, grouse; and the streets filled with very odd people dressed in Burberry and carrying Louis Vuitton bags. He would have been stunned too to find that British cuisine had mutated so violently, the roast-and-boiled country he inhabited, buried forever under a Vesuvial slurry of nam pla, crème fraîche, garam masala and crispy wontons.

He would not have lasted long though in the early twenty-first century. He would have either had a seizure within minutes on noticing how since his death women had decided to dress to display rather than conceal their bodies or, more cruelly, he would have made the mistake of asking someone to show him how a DVD player worked and settled down to enjoy Roger Moore in *The Man with the Golden Gun*.

Chapter Six

THE BEATLES WITH EARMUFFS

I HAVE ALWAYS loved movies and cinemas. I have never shaken off the sheer wonder of what can be seen as vastly enlarged figures walk around an endless variety of landscapes, shaped and framed into an appealing flat oblong, coupled to the rich sense of communal experience.

If I had to chose one building I revere more than any other I would have to plump for function over form by nominating the National Film Theatre in London. It has been prettified now but for many years its architecture was a sort of poorly realized *hommage* to the Mao-era Chinese communal toilet, but like its inspiration it combines the ideological and practical to impressive effect.

Going to school in London, living in London, it was always for me the focus of the city. Living in other British cities or living in the United States always meant an irritable hunt for something even faintly comparable. The NFT's great charm is its struggle within a sprawling, immense cornucopia of a programme between frozen austerity and camp self-indulgence: between wanting to show cinema as profound art and wanting to wallow in cinema as brash, corny blow-out.

Over the years this has developed into a highly cerebral game with its audiences, who know and love every twist and turn. The hundreds of films I have seen there (whole *months* of life must have gone by) have had an effect akin to being flung along in a fairground ghost-train ride, with marvels and terrors pressing in on every side—and the not infrequent realization that the spooky spiderwebs are merely bits of dirty string.

A chief pleasure of the NFT is the programme note handed out before each film. The authors of these are doomed, in some contemporary variant of the fate of Sisyphus, to begin each evening back at the bottom of the hill, trying to convince a fresh audience (sometimes achingly tiny) of the merits of some often preposterous film. Connoisseurs of these notes must surely have kept them immaculately filed away. Once a film has been chosen for a season (*all* of Barbara Stanwyck's movies, say, *everything* directed by Ken Russell, movies united by some sexual or racial theme) then the game is on. The programme-note writer *must* validate that film for someone who has, after all, paid to come and see it. The sadism of the programme makers forms a happy alliance with the masochism of the audiences, with the programme-note writers trapped in the middle trying desperately to come up with rationales for the convulsively inept *She Was Bad*, or for *A bientôt, Monsieur Trictrac*, a justly shunned 1950s thick-ear *policier*.

One favourite piece of code is to say, for example, that *She Was Bad* "holds up within the star's early work remarkably well," which means it is a complete dog. Or "the film's failure at the time now seems all the more inexplicable given Barbara Stanwyck's firecracker—if brief—role in the hospital scene," another serious alarm bell. Another ploy is to say that "it has moments of real feeling in the ensemble work," meaning that the star himself/herself is visibly drunk, ailing, ashamed, in deep financial difficulties.

Like a hamster in some lab experiment—always taking the wrong turn in the maze and getting happily electrocuted by the biscuit every time—I have been tricked by these notes into seeing so many dozens of poor films that I have learned important lessons. Most people see films from idle curiosity, from boredom or from a wish to accompany someone they intend to have sex with. I go because I adore films and am energized rather than depressed by the idea of the thousands still unseen. Years of sitting through great drifts of stuff at the NFT has made me realize that I have barely engaged yet with the subject (Myrna Loy retrospective next month!) and that in practice there are almost no *entirely* rubbish films: that there really are pleasures of design, dialogue, atmosphere, narrative that are unconquerable—and that these pleasures mutate and mature over time in unexpected ways. A worthless 1950s American comedy becomes a dazzling parade of clothing, slang, sexual expectations, sofa colours, cocktail choices and glimpses of city streets, all virtually invisible both to its makers and to its first audiences. A banal, production-line Weimar Republic slice-of-life drama teems with buildings, faces, aspirations, worries, pleasures all preserved effectively by magic, sheltered forever from any knowledge of Hitler's rise to power.

I describe how much my life has been twisted and ruined by films only to make some simple points: that I have been tricked into seeing so many atrocious movies that I really *know* that *Die Another Day*, for example, is a disgrace; that it was while watching *Dr. No* yet again at the NFT that I realized the opening twenty or so seconds are the most important in British cinema; and that through spending so much time at the NFT I met the great, now late, Leslie Halliwell, creator of the indispensable *Halliwell's Film Guide*.

Halliwell was responsible for many years for picking the films shown on a British television network. Rather than letting the cumulative effect of watching an infinity of awful films go to waste, he developed a film guide with a ruthless asterisking system (four asterisks very, very good, no asterisks abysmal). While quite often wrong, his enormous film guide was suffused with a romantic attitude towards the major Hollywood studios, a resolute refusal to mark films down because, say, their special effects no longer looked good to a modern audience, and a very inclusive attitude towards world cinema. His film guide was the necessary corrective to the NFT's full-on, mad enthusiasm for everything and a happy time could be had comparing the one ("a coarse-toned and uninteresting drama") with the other ("delectable ensemble playing and Technicolor to die for"). I still went to every piece of tat regardless but it was a stimulant both to have this wise voice in the background and also to know that even the worst films could provoke quite different responses for different reasons—with Halliwell focusing more on drama and acting and the NFT more on semiotics and culture.

In the early 1980s I went to interview Halliwell for a magazine, so stuffed to the gills with NFT-going that this seemed the only rational thing left to do. Waiting outside his office I felt ravaged by conflicting feelings. Part of me was like a novice from some bleak, yak-filled, eerily distant part of Tibet astonishingly being ushered into the presence of the Dalai

Lama. The other part, however, was like the ice-pick assassin waiting to see Trotsky in his Mexican fortress. Once in Halliwell's surprisingly dull office, face to face with the Master—himself perhaps slightly dull, having of course like one of the Mole People spent most of his life in the dark—I half wanted to thank him, tears soaking into my ill-judged floral-pattern tie, and half wanted to pin his hand to the desk with a knife and hiss, with all the violence of the confused and frightened fan down the ages: "Why do you give *Diamonds Are Forever* only one star and call it 'campy' and 'rather vicious'?"

HOW CAN popular culture have such delicate tendrils that it seems sometimes to taste history with almost perfect timing and grace? The year 1962 saw the developments that were to wind up the rest of Britain's African Empire, leaving it only with a handful of unresolved anomalies and problems. It also saw Ian Fleming writing the last of the "megalomaniac world peril" Bond books, *On Her Majesty's Secret Service*, almost as though, with Britain's major international position now at last finishing, these potent fantasies of secret greatness were no longer needed. The same year saw the overwhelming success of *Lawrence of Arabia*, whose great final scene, a scene of mute grief and inarticulacy, shows Lawrence been driven away from the desert and the Arabs. Few moments in art can better convey the sense that both the fantasy and the reality of imperial power was over for Britain and that an "adventure" (however defined) for millions of individuals during some three and a half centuries was now finished. The winter of 1962 also saw another global epic, the banging and crashing *The Longest Day*, neatly enshrining among other things Britain's final great outing at D-Day as a global power. It also featured, quite lost in tiny roles amid the welter of genuine scenery-chewing American stars, Sean Connery as an Irish squaddie (a truly horrible performance), Gert Fröbe (soon to be Goldfinger, but here briefly glimpsed as a joke fat Nazi provisioning sergeant on a tiny horse) and Curt Jürgens (web-fingered fish-mad super-criminal in *The Spy Who Loved Me*, but here playing a parodic elegant Nazi officer).

Entangled with these two monster-truck movies *Dr. No* opened in Britain, cinematically unveiling the fresh fantasy (but no reality this time) of Britain as the planet's secret saviour. If the Bond books were a reaction to a genuine crisis in Britain's ruling and imperial classes, then the films project onto a post-imperial country the assumptions and attitudes that came from that empire. In the year 1962, this transition was made—from real power to secret power. How could everyone, working from such different scripts and with such a range of motives, have known *exactly* where to stand on the stage?

AFTER YEARS OF impatient and unsuccessful negotiation (*Casino Royale* in CBS's series *Climax!* not really being followed up on), Fleming at last sold the *Dr. No* film rights. The movie went into production with a mixture of international financial sources (the Bond films' investors were only ever quite loosely "British") put together by Harry Salzman and Cubby Broccoli (whose family had *indeed* originally been Italian market gardeners and had perfected the strain of brassica that has ruined so many young children's lives across the Western world ever since). While *Dr. No* was not a very cheaply made film, corners were definitely cut and it is now quite hard to enjoy, having a slightly made-for-TV atmosphere. As the makers of the film realized, it is not possible to have international grand guignol on a shoestring, but *Dr. No* was a risky project which would have sunk its investors without a healthy international box office. Now it seems incomprehensible, for example, that Stanley Kubrick should have been so impressed by Ken Adam's sets that he hired him to do his spectacular work on *Dr. Strangelove*. Adam's *Dr. No* sets now look put together from old cereal packets with a few flashing lights glued to them. And yet . . . and yet. Much of the formula's success *is* in place and can be found in the film's quieter moments. Not least of course, there is Sean Connery himself: a former Mr. Universe competitor who had knocked about minor films for years, including the horrible *Darby O'Gill and the Little People* and *Tarzan's Greatest Adventure*, where he is excellent and very Bond-like as a mercenary jungle gunman (or at least I remember his being excellent some twenty-five years ago, but I am too scared that he isn't actually to be willing to fact-check). Fleming himself was horrified by Connery's getting the job, referring to him as "a Glaswegian truck driver," but as with John Barry's music or Bernard Lee's "M" it is one of those founding elements without which the whole enterprise might have caved in.

In any event *Dr. No* was a significant success and held out the magic prospect for Fleming, Salzman, Broccoli, Connery and everyone else involved of an effectively indefinite, hugely lucrative set of films based on the now substantial backlog of books and Fleming's ability to write more. The delays in getting Bond transferred from books to films which had so vexed Fleming in the 1950s therefore seemed to have worked to everyone's advantage. *From Russia with Love* followed a year later in 1963 and became a vast international success, *Goldfinger* (1964) was at that time the fastest-grossing film in cinema history and *Thunderball* (1965) made even more money for everybody. *Thunderball* proved to be a hysterical climax to the Bond experience, breaking all kinds of records and almost disappearing under a welter of associated merchandise, action dolls and media frenzy. After that, the project started to wobble around. *You Only Live Twice* (1967), an orgy of cheerful nonsense, proved too much for Connery, who retired for a mixture of financial and personal reasons. He is a visibly bored and rather graceless presence in the film. *You Only Live Twice* also marked the start of the bloat-then-purge cycle that has been so characteristic of Bond films ever since—that absolute excess could not then trump itself further. This had to be countered by an almost Calvinist attempt to return to the text and pure basics, in this case with *On Her Majesty's Secret Service*, gadgetless, plot-driven, realistic (well, somewhat realistic) and very close to the book. But the attempt was a failure—it contains many marvellous things, but it was too long, the new Bond—an Australian model who had featured in a chocolate biscuit advert—was not liked and the ending (Bond's new wife being killed) was a downer.

The Bond films were the dominant British movies of the 1960s and exported an image of Britain that was globally enjoyed—as all-pervasive as the Beatles (also a product of 1962)—and strangely at odds with the grim status Britain otherwise had, as the 1960s unfolded, as a sort of economic leper colony.

THE 1963 PREMIERE of *From Russia with Love* was an ecstatic occasion: the people who had been riskily involved in financing and boosting *Dr. No* were about to get their reward. There can be few headier environments than those where a gang of individuals are teetering on the verge of massive wealth—and wealth with a longevity that, as it turned out, was to last beyond their lifetimes.

For Fleming himself however it was all much less happy. He hosted a lavish Russian-themed party with endless supplies of caviar and vodka, but was clearly dying. He wandered in a spectral fashion among his guests for a while and then disappeared. It seems almost too banal to be feasible that the quintessential forties and fifties figure was to die at just the moment when Bond took on a level of global fame beyond his creator's most extreme fantasies and came to define the sixties (a decade which, like all decades, fails to find its definition properly within its numerical frame). In photos of Fleming posing with Connery there is a disturbing contrast between the wan weariness of the one and the high-tension wire of the other.

Fleming's death at fifty-six seems terribly premature, but the habits of a lifetime had prepared him for such an end and it was a tribute to his frame that it had withstood such prolonged battering by so many thousands of cigarettes and gallons of spirits. It would be difficult to claim that Fleming had been a very admirable person, but I have tried to show that he was at least interesting. Like many better or worse writers his actual success was something almost incidental, handed to him by a world aligning itself belatedly with what he had written. It was as though the luxury, cruelty and excess he celebrated had been too rich a dish for Britain in the early fifties and as ordinary readers recovered from extreme austerity they began too to warm to the books—with sixties consumerism opening the floodgates (which Fleming and Bond spoke to almost perfectly). It was too late for Fleming, though. Creatively the timing was just right—he had seen his vindication in *From Russia with Love*'s cinematic success—but he had nothing more to contribute himself. He had been bored with Bond for years and killed off Blofeld in *You Only Live Twice*. He wrote the anaemic, small-scale *The Man with the Golden Gun* as a farewell to Jamaica but more simply to keep himself alive. The book ends with Bond successfully killing a petty assassin in a swamp and—fulfilling all manner of civil-servant fantasies—having sex with the beautiful office secretary on a paradise island.

FROM RUSSIA WITH LOVE stands for strange things in my mind. I have almost no sense of what my mother's life was like before she met my father in the early sixties—the more than ten years during which almost her only activities seemed to be to walk through the Great London Smog and be upset by the book of *From Russia with Love*. This lack of information changes in the winter of 1963 with a perverse interlocking of events. On 10 October the film of *From Russia with Love* was released. Six weeks later, on 22 November, President Kennedy was killed, an act that horrified and disorientated people almost as much in Britain as it did in America. Kennedy had not been president long enough for anyone to judge one way or another whether he would have proved a good one, but in Britain it was impossible not to compare his apparent energy, youth and decisiveness with our own prime minister, the desiccated, skull-like antique, Lord Home of the Hirsel, lurking in the twilit final patch of Conservative rule. One of Kennedy's smaller claims to fame was his endorsement of

From Russia with Love, with the result that the Bond novels became huge business and Fleming—again, really too late—became the bestselling thriller writer in America.

A mere three days after the assassination there was another event. My future parents went to see *From Russia with Love* in a West London cinema. The combination of fighting gypsy girls, panicked rats and exploding helicopters was so potent that my mother went into labour early and I was born prematurely at home the following day.

I have wasted a lot of time wondering if there might be some hidden, Hermetic pattern that links *From Russia with Love*, Kennedy's assassination and my birth. Perhaps in some later century this will become childishly obvious—but for now it seems hard to make out, indeed invisible.

ONE OF THE great humiliations Britain suffered in the sixties was France's decision in early 1963 to veto its attempt to enter the European Community. Having spent years deriding and ignoring everything European and with eyes firmly focused on the imperial relationships which were in practice falling apart like wet sugar lumps, British policy-makers in the early sixties realized their terrible mistake and made a panicked attempt to refit. Correctly spotting the bad faith, scrounging and chronic weakness of Britain and savouring a personal revenge for years of snobbish and perfidious behaviour from the likes of Eden and Macmillan, Charles de Gaulle gleefully said, "Non."

Watching the opening scene of the film of *Thunderball* it is hard not to enjoy the feelings of its original audience. Here is a Britain without an Empire, but also a Britain shut out from its economically booming neighbours, and it is only

Thunderball that can provide catharsis. In one of the most enjoyable of all the films' fight sequences, Bond struggles with a French assassin in a beautifully rendered room in a château, crammed with the sort of French furnishings so derided by the English, all spindly little chairs and effete panelling. The Frenchman is further humiliated by being disguised as a heavily lipsticked woman in tights, high heels and a black dress. He is eventually throttled by a poker and left dead in the ornate, baronial, perhaps rather draughty fireplace, covered in flowers contemptuously tossed onto him by Bond. How *Thunderball*'s first audience must have cheered. That's what you can do with your European Community! Indeed—with history and fiction madly intertwining—could de Gaulle's renewed 1967 veto of British membership have been provoked by his having sat through— rocked by a patriot's disgust and shame—a special presidential showing of *Opération Tonnerre*?

As the 1960s progressed, Bond's ability to maim and kill foreigners became a great consolation to millions of embittered and confused people whose traditional world picture had changed with alarming speed. Bond in fact became in the 1960s pretty much the only British national capable of damaging anybody at all.

If the 1950s could be summed up as a humiliating disaster for patriots, imperialists and concerned right-wing citizens— a perhaps mainly middle-class disaster—then the 1960s were the working-class disaster. As the world's countries moved into fresh relationships with each other, within the European Community, within the Eastern Bloc, within the startling new framework of Japan's trade, none of these in a central way included Britain. Over an alarmingly short period of time the complex framework which had Britain at its apex and which sustained a great range of industries simply folded up and vanished. Full employment continued a little longer, but enormous, horrible problems were stoking up uncontrollably.

There will always be arguments about the government's role in the catastrophe unleashed by the end of the 1960s. Lulled by war-winning triumphalism and by full employment in the 1950s, there seems to have been no sense that a fundamental change was coming and that the political battles around the Empire winding up would be followed by an economic disaster. The aura of decaying twerpiness around Eden and Macmillan adds to a general sense that here was an island with a large population, entrusted to the palsied hands of a gang of exhausted, querulous, upper-class cynics.

Harold Wilson's new Labour government, which came to power in 1964 at the height of Bondmania, inherited a nightmare. Someone in their teens in the 1950s would have enjoyed a whole gamut of long-established routes into productive, lifelong work—and with no inkling that by the time he was in his thirties most of these huge industries would have fallen to pieces. Governments could only look on in impotent horror as long-term structural change crushed Britain flat. For much of the world there was a piquancy in the idea that the country that had done more than any other over centuries to create a global trade framework that had pauperized, devastated and colonized so many formerly wealthy and autonomous parts of the world should now be caught in the crossfire. This piquancy was not appreciated very widely in Britain itself. As enormous audiences sat dreamily through *Goldfinger*, *Thunderball* and *You Only Live Twice*, a devastating new cycle of post-imperial trauma was well on the move.

I have tried to avoid statistics, but the pace of change can best be shown by them. In a generation nine hundred thousand cotton textile workers were reduced to two hundred thousand, leaving the once busy and prosperous county of Lancashire almost without a point. Three hundred thousand steelworkers became fifty thousand. In the early 1950s Britain had accounted for about a quarter of all manufacturing exports in the world—by the 1970s this had collapsed to insignificance. Employment in the army and navy, always an important outlet for working-class life, dried up with the general lack of things to defend. The shipbuilding that had fed the enormous British merchant marine, which made the Empire work and which had allowed the country's physical survival in the war, simply fell to pieces. In only forty years Britain went from supplying 40 per cent of the world's shipping to less than 1 per cent and whole cities (Belfast, Glasgow, Newcastle) that had been for many years a form of shorthand for national pride and strength became synonymous instead with desperation, crime and urban dereliction, while the great commodity ports (London, Cardiff, Liverpool) became equally spectral.

There is a prolonged, hard-to-watch scene in *You Only Live Twice* which has no real bearing on the—admittedly incoherent—storyline. Bond is chased through a Japanese shipyard by unarmed Japanese dockhands whom he proceeds to shoot one by one while John Barry's marvellous score blares away on the soundtrack. As with the Frenchman-slaughtering moment in *Thunderball* it has a strange, bitter resonance that must have given some satisfaction to its original audience. The Japanese were a particular focus of hatred both because of the recent and—with the disappearance of empire—completely futile experience of fighting them and because of

their principal role in destroying Britain's shipbuilding industry. Their sinking of "Force Z" in 1941 had marked the
beginning of the end of Britain's naval domination of the
modern world and their crushing of Britain's shipyards did a
similar job for merchant shipping in the 1960s.

Japan was hardly unique, however—essentially every
country had a go, each year of the sixties revealing some fresh
enormity as somebody somewhere trumped yet another suddenly vulnerable British business. The number of incredulous,
sweaty board meetings can only be imagined—with lots of
nervous fingering of silk ties and unfortunate graphs. Wave
upon wave of despairing strikes dominated the period: viewed
so often at the time as the work of subversive wreckers who
had created the crisis, but now far more clearly understood as
just a desperate symptom. Within a few years almost nobody
was to work in a coalmine, very few people built aeroplanes,
the car industry (which in 1950 had supplied half the world's
exports, incredibly) had become an international joke and
the engineering firms which had designed and built much
of the world for generations had almost all packed up.

From this safe distance Wilson's government seems to in-
habit a peculiar, whistling-in-the-dark doldrums—supervising
a country which had been torn from its hundreds of imperial
connections but which had not yet been plugged into mainland Europe. The generational switch marked in the 1964
election from rulers defined by the First World War to rulers
defined by the Second made little difference in practice. Both
generations were obsessed with state planning of a kind that
now seems baffling. The early Wilson governments (Wilson
went on to run a further, utterly demoralized government in
the mid-seventies) seem quite jaunty because of their valuable

social legislation on homosexuality, "the age of consent" and abortion. But it is hard not to feel that these could have been put through on a wet Wednesday afternoon and that otherwise years were spent simply staring at things getting worse with no plan for the future. The contrast with the sheer zippiness of Germany, France, the United States or Japan, for example (or the USSR, for that matter), is a baffling one.

Aside from the government's generational shift a huge amount of energy has traditionally been spent celebrating the sixties as a watershed in British life, with the shorthand for this being the Beatles and the James Bond films. Clearly a sort of nascent super-consumerism did peep shyly about in the sixties but it is amazing how few people it affected and how heavily qualified it has to be. My father, for example, was the same age as John Lennon but beyond the occasional swirly tie seemed entirely unaffected by the sixties. I have an almost limitless ability to sit watching old *Ready, Steady, Go!* tapes but it is impossible not to notice as the studio audiences jive around a clumsily lip-synching Lulu that they all come from an incredibly small age and class bracket. What is odd about the sixties in the shape of "the sixties" was that virtually the entire population were in practice left out—too old, too young, too poor, too busy. This is clearly the case with the James Bond films. These are the fantasies of older men—fantasies of the War, of British greatness, of military service, of class distinctions. What has "the sixties" to do with exclusive golf clubs, knowing what wine to drink with fish, Venetian hotel suites? The answer of course is a great deal for an older, wealthy generation who felt the whole country was going to the dogs. When in *Goldfinger* Connery says that drinking unchilled champagne is like listening to the Beatles without earmuffs the entire swinging sixties collapses into pieces. These are films for all those executives about to be fired from their manufacturing companies, for the millions of ex-servicemen, still only in their forties, for whom the economic and social changes were personally deeply threatening and who found themselves stranded, like the government, on a planet that didn't have much to say about them. The Bond films provided a profound, wistful reassurance that for at least one British male, things were still going well.

IN THE RICH and various tapestry that is my mishandling of our children's upbringing, one of the most elegant panels has concerned gender—and gender (or rather one of the genders) of course lies at the heart of the Bond experience. I had imagined it might be possible with two boys and a girl to raise them in a way which did not pander to stereotyping, which allowed them to flourish as complete human beings not as merely females or males, and so on. In practice this meant a ban on toy guns and suspicion about dolls. As each child hit about four the whole thing went clearly and disastrously wrong, with every faintly feasible long object (bits of wood, bits of cardboard roll) being turned into machine-guns and anything dainty or brightly coloured being suborned into interminable tea parties.

Believing wholeheartedly in the power of film, I dreamed that there might be some way of correcting these trends, while sticking only to old films, because they are not too brutal or rude. Perhaps getting the boys to watch *Meet Me in St. Louis* or *Top Hat* or *Mary Poppins* would bring out a nicer side— or perhaps something a little grittier with Barbara Stanwyck? Or would it be feasible to sit patiently with the six-year-old

THE MAN WHO SAVED BRITAIN

girl taking in *Pork Chop Hill* or *They Died with Their Boots On* or *For a Few Dollars More*? This complex, doomed project never really came to fruition. *Fists of Fury* or, loosely, any movie featuring Lee Marvin stood no chance against carefully burping Baby Friendship or making sure her hat was on properly in the winter. Equally, *Please Don't Eat the Daisies* or *Fried Green Tomatoes* was never going to fly with the boys.

If we had been more wholehearted or leaned more on mind-controlling substances we could have got further (or perhaps I just chose the wrong movies) but instead the house echoes to gunfire in some corners and tea parties in others. The final capitulation was over a decision to buy our daughter a massive Playmobil doll's house. Playmobil is a German firm which specializes in turning out immensely detailed plastic materials with little people and props of deranged complexity (their research and development offices must be some of the most disturbing places in Western Europe). Our sons, for example, have—and this is not made up—a Spanish colonial prison complete with brutalized, unshaven guards, bottles of rum, cutlasses and playing cards and a cramped barred fetid cell, the whole implying a uniquely Spanish moral and religious squalor which British or American toymakers could not have dared to create for decades.

In any event, the Playmobil doll's house, unveiled one Christmas, is a little girl's Shangri-la—a traditional *haut bourgeois* home with massive windows, a balcony, imposing mansard roof with paned windows and heirloom furniture (or at least as heirloom as is feasible in three-centimetre-high plastic), heaps of plates, paintings, a parrot on its perch and a strict but fair-looking nanny with her hair in a bun and a sensible apron.

There is a point to all this. Of course within moments of this domestic wonder being unveiled our sons (who are older) took it over, promptly sweeping out all the painstakingly assembled bits and bobs—the tea trolley, the candelabra—and moving in the Spanish colonial prison guys and a miscellany of U.S. cavalry troopers and Caribbean pirates. In a very small period of time the sedate, Bismarck-era lawyer's home had been turned into a 1970s West German nightmare—a sort of Baader–Meinhof squat with clear fields of fire, massive stocks of weapons and a mixed bag of middle-class teen radicals despoiling the furnishings.

This sort of irreducible male response—so hardwired that nothing can deflect it—has to lie at the heart of the male–female split over everything to do with James Bond. A world which turns a doll's house into a terror headquarters, which will imagine that a toilet roll could be a sniper-scope or a fir cone a hand grenade, is a world in love with James Bond. A world in which a doll's house is a doll's house will find Bond nauseating and absurd; fair enough. As my sons and I loaf on the sofa in a sort of piggish idyll watching *Thunderball* ("Jesus—the harpoon went straight through him!" . . . "Cool!") it is impossible not to sense, in restless moments, a silent critique being offered by other elements within the house. Nothing can be done about it and I fully realize that those critiquers will not have got anywhere near this point in the book.

ANY FREE-ASSOCIATION exercise initiated by the words "James Bond" will promptly elicit "cars." Cars are one of the features which fill both the books and the films and which are always a source of comment. There was a painfully stupid moment a few films back where Bond switched to a BMW from a British brand: on the face of it a bare minimum sort of decision to stay alive, but enjoyably stoked (as the film's makers knew it would be) as a "Bond betrays Britain" issue (has anyone ever looked at the films' financing sources?). Cars as a key element in international ideas of masculinity are of course strangely poignant, and nowhere more so than in Britain, where a colossal battery of regulations, limits, "traffic-calming" gadgets, police cameras, etc., create a sort of unbreakable Vulcan's net over the poor would-be knight of the road. However growlingly powerful the engine, however sleek the lines, cars in Britain can never do anything much— mostly just noodle around shopping centres or occasionally be allowed out onto the world's least erotic motorway system.

Bond at the wheel therefore offers a powerful, effectively sexual charge for those individuals who choose to identify themselves with a wheeled, industrially generated arrangement of metals, fabrics and plastics. Fleming phrases such as "the quiet bubble of the twin exhausts" or the car "was painted in rough, not gloss, battleship grey and the upholstery was black morocco" clearly put a specific audience onto a higher plane. Tires scream, exhausts growl, "Bond drove it hard and well and with an almost sensual pleasure."

Car chases (and, of course, the only point of a car is to chase in it) are frequent and vivid. The most absurd is undoubtedly the one through north Kent in *Moonraker* where somehow Bond is able to drive in his Bentley from Belgravia to Charing at various insane speeds in pursuit of the evil Drax and Krebs in their white Mercedes (a sure sign of criminality). During the entire fifty-mile chase they encounter only a single car (an Alfa Romeo) and a truck—surely an odd outcome even in the thinner-traffic world of the fifties. In practice they would have been trapped in heavy congestion around Vauxhall and rarely got above 20 m.p.h. before Rochester, crashing ignominiously shortly thereafter as they rashly tried to gain a little speed.

Fleming is great at the sounds of crunching glass, groaning metal and frantic cries for help. He loves different makers and marks, funny specifications, concealed compartments. The banality of real cars (you buy them in a shop) is rescued by the creation of fun hybrids: a Studebaker with a Cadillac engine (a Studillac), a Mark II Continental Bentley with a Mark IV engine and so on. The word-to-the-wise knowledge that Bond claims about women, food and travel also applies to cars, but with the same heartbreaking proviso about the limits of experience available to him in practice—most models, most engines, most roads, most places being in fact a complete blank to him.

This becomes more painfully clear in the films where scene after scene can occur only in the light of both immaculate road knowledge and there being no other vehicles. This combines to disastrous effect with crude back-projection and obvious speeding up of the film in chase after chase. Nobody would thank the makers for creating a film that ended within minutes in multiple internal injuries and a long spell in hospital (possibly filmed à la Warhol in real time over months of painful reconstructive surgery). But there is something poignant about the wishfulness of the chases and an audience shackled by fines and proscriptions at 55 or 60 m.p.h. The one exception is perhaps the car chase around Goldfinger's Swiss factory that benefits hugely from being in both a restricted space and a space that it is reasonable to think of as clear of traffic. All the other film car chases leave the viewer simply too aware of the awkward upcoming junction, the nasty bend or the parked milk float.

Owning a genuinely powerful car must be akin to being a prisoner in one of those possibly legendary castle cells which are too low to permit standing upright and too narrow to permit lying down. How must it feel, outside the maniacal planet of the Autobahn or some long, dusty stretch in Texas, to have all this power and not the faintest chance to use it? As Bond's car careens through clouds of mud and water or blazes through the streets of Las Vegas, do watching Lamborghini owners feel empowered or merely gelded? These chases offer one of the purest examples of how films—all films—replay on an eternal loop a vision of power and pleasure which will always remain immaculate while we ourselves collapse into senile, aphasic malfunction. We become like the much-cited decrepit old spaniel which, lying dozing in its basket, yaps and convulses as in its dream it closes in on a rabbit. Incidentally, the owners always claim it is a rabbit Fido is dreaming about, when—as with the owners of powerful cars—the dream prey is almost sure not to be a living creature at all but a can of meaty chunks or a dish of pellets moistened with water.

A STATUE IN a public park does not really change over any given fifty-year period—it is designed so that with minimal cleaning it gives a strong impression of being imperishable, which of course is why it was raised in the first place. What makes such a statue so poignant though is the gap between the intentions of the people who commissioned it and the ferocious corrosion of passing time. For such a big, heavy thing a statue is in practice tossed about outrageously, even if it remains physically robust, as once-great legislators become wholly unknown or once-revered poets dissolve under a flood of sarcasm. After a while most statues, like most graveyards, lose their specific features and take on the far more powerful symbol of everything transitory and futile. If it were only possible to measure through time the impact of informed, contemptuous, indifferent or moved glances striking statues, what an upsetting process it would be.

But at least, unlike James Bond, they have kept their basic shape. It is one of the crueller things about film that it not only suffers the inevitable abuse or neglect of time for its sentiments or manners but that it also deteriorates in absolute ways—through changes both in technology and in film processes. What was absolutely cutting edge (and therefore, in effect, invisible to viewers of the period) becomes painfully and irredeemably dated in a matter of years. Black-and-white film, once it has reached a reasonable level of sophistication, is much more proof against this process than colour—it simply gives everything a beautiful sheen. Colour can look horrible, and it could be that in the end the disaster of Bond in the 1970s stems as much from the kind of film used as anything else, with colours often so lurid and grainy that breasts look like cheap bath sponges and Bond's clothing can induce a migraine. This is a problem, of course, for all films of the period, but most do not define themselves by their being at the cutting edge, and the colour process's frantic awfulness could not advertise more clearly just how untrue this now is. Conversely the early Bond films benefit from their lovely colour qualities—particularly *From Russia with Love* and *Goldfinger*, which have a sort of muted tastiness that carries them through even so-so scenes.

The curse of passing time has particularly affected the famous opening credits. I once went to a depressingly underpowered exhibition at the Victoria & Albert Museum on British design in the sixties. This featured the opening credits of *From Russia with Love* on a tiny television screen with a patronizing label saying how influential they had been but how dated they now were. I remember bridling at this injustice: *of course* projecting the words *STARRING SEAN CONNERY AS 007* in coloured letters on a belly-dancer's stomach looks dated on a tiny screen: but it looks fabulous when blown up to about sixty feet across. More broadly, though, the point is probably true: most of the famous opening credits do look pretty awful now. The one exception is *Goldfinger*, which still seems to me a sort of imperishable wonder—the linking of film, music, image, text magically done (like *From Russia with Love*) by the great Robert Brownjohn, an American designer who had been taught by the legendary László Moholy-Nagy. There is one staggering moment in the credits where a gold-painted girl's face has a car number-plate replacing her mouth which (by accident, of course—but that's fine) seems far more frightening, nihilistic, Sadean, fetishistic than anything else in conceptual art. It is just on the screen for a moment, but it is a true nightmare, choking the viewer, but crystallizing something nasty at the heart of the whole Bond project.

The opening credits, however, are most closely associated with the very odd Maurice Binder, who had designed *Dr. No*, including the gun-barrel opening shot—a stroke of genius which, with the contrast between the strange, radio-frequency plink-plunk music that then erupts into the very first hearing of the Bond theme, is one of cinema's greatest pieces of theatre. He took over permanently on *Thunderball*, inaugurating a long era of witless enjoyment. In photos he looks exactly as you would hope, indeed too good to be true—a tiny little American bloke, very dapper, surrounded by vast, leggy models. Around the world an entire generation of young men were damaged by his nude silhouettes of girls licking guns, being shot with harpoons and so on, all with the kind of unintentionally hilarious technology that dates so cruelly. Perhaps the least battered of his works is the credit sequence for *Diamonds Are Forever*, which makes beautiful use of Blofeld's white cat with a diamond collar. It is also a perfect example of the problems cinema faces: on the big screen it is a sensuous marvel, all fur and flashing eyes plus piles of nude silhouettes, of course—but on the small screen it transmutes alarmingly into a sort of zany cat-food commercial.

The makers of the films to the present day have never really come up with an answer to the overwhelming influence of Binder's suffocating legacy—a tradition which still blights the films years after Binder's death, where ever less plausible theme songs have to be whooped and hollered while nude girls fill up with flames or—*really* oddly—get covered in crude oil. The crude-oil disaster long postdated Binder himself, who bowed out with a final titillating masterpiece for *License to Kill*. He was one of those richly enjoyable figures from a different world whose very specialized skills in manipulating buttocks against coloured backgrounds earned him a unique niche in film history.

IT'S A SMALL THING, but I've always been grateful for not being one of those hiccupping, spider-eating film fans who know the entire cast list for every John Mills movie or silently mouth all the words to *Brief Encounter* as they watch it for the twentieth time, wearing their special sweaters. I've seen an incredibly indiscriminate pile of films but in a happy, non-completist spirit, having long resisted, at least in part, the more rigorous aspects of the National Film Theatre.

It is hardly fair to deride such people, though, as they are the backbone of the DVD business, the big-plasma-screen business and indeed the whole ineffable land of fandom. That they have entire secret rooms wallpapered with signed photos of Bernard Cribbins or Joan Collins is merely one symptom, alongside others, such as genuinely caring about, collecting, renovating and loving film, always waiting outside premieres, sending disturbing drawings in the post and being detained in Beverly Hills by security operatives. The fandom can stop at any point on this curve even if it remains true that they are all linked in ways that actors both acknowledge and rightly fear: today's autograph-hunter being tomorrow's stalker.

My interest in James Bond simply does not match up to any part of that scale. I admire Ken Adam and John Barry and the early films' writers, editors and directors. But even on the central, indeed sacral, issue of Sean Connery himself it is hard to develop specifically devotional feelings. He is just right in the first four Bond films but there is almost no wider interest that can be generated by his films. In truth he is rather a horrible actor outside the narrowest of ranges. Perhaps any temptation to hero-worship was struck on the head by watching *Zardoz*, a John Boorman science-fiction disaster from the early seventies where Connery stomps about with a bizarre moustache and top-knot and orange cut-away clothing. Indeed it is probably fair to say that Connery has made no other good films—or at least no films that are good because of him, except perhaps *Robin and Marian*, where he stars alongside an equally battered Audrey Hepburn, a heartrending movie of which I have such fond memories that I daren't see it again in case it is in fact completely terrible.

Ultimately it is fair to say that the Bond films are not really major films in a world-historical sort of way. Their intricacies and by-ways are essentially minor, however aggressively commercial they set out to be. One can read interesting things into them and their success but not because of any discernible greatness. They are too British, a bit too silly and a bit too derisive of themselves. *Ben-Hur* or *From Here to Eternity* or *El Cid* may dare you at various points not to laugh, but they believe in themselves and their giant stars in a heroic way: Charlton Heston or Burt Lancaster may look, just for the sake of argument, a little camp and dotty, but they are *gods on earth* just the same. Sean Connery, let alone Honor Blackman or Telly Savalas, for goodness' sake, would be, in such company, mere spear-carriers in tiny type in the closing credits. Even typing such truth-telling makes me feel like Judas—but a Judas with a reasonably clear conscience.

BECAUSE OF his role in the films and because he has been so widely parodied, the Bond villain everyone recognizes is Ernst Stavro Blofeld. This is a pity in many ways as he is an almost featureless invention—an old-fashioned villain of a type John Buchan, say, would have been familiar with, but beefed up for the atomic age. In the books there is effectively nothing to remember about him—he has no visual presence, beyond the weird, extended discussions in *On Her Majesty's Secret Service*, as to whether or not he has earlobes. He never remotely takes on the mad, independent kinetic joy-in-evil of Dr. No or Goldfinger, and his sidekick Irma Bunt is a mere shadow of Rosa Klebb. There is a happy madness about the earlier Bond villains, a sense that they are in the midst of the deepest English pantomime tradition, that makes them marvellous. That is sadly just not true with Blofeld, who was always intended as a cinema figure (*Thunderball*, the book in which he first appears, began as a film script) and one with a minor role (as the hidden mastermind) rather than as principal villain. He remains completely uncompelling in Fleming's attempt to write a realistic novel, *On Her Majesty's Secret Service*, and only really becomes enjoyable in the last full Bond book, *You Only Live Twice*, where he is propped up by such a vast range of Japanese costumes, customs and torture instruments that he takes on a sort of winged, armoured and lacquered life while remaining a blank inside—a sort of samurai Mr. Punch. However, towards the end of the book Blofeld becomes the victim of Fleming's own serious illness and ennui. When he declares to his minions, "Prepare the blowlamp and the electrical machine," you know Fleming has lost interest. The blowlamp and the electrical machine never appear, because they were never really imagined, and Blofeld dies almost casually as his castle collapses around him.

The Blofeld of the films is quite different, beginning with the inspired if entirely unscriptural decision to give him a white cat in *From Russia with Love*. The actor who plays the faceless Blofeld, the camera focusing only on his hands caressing that cat, does as much to launch the myth of James Bond as anyone, each of his lines—whether talking about Siamese fighting fish or the working time of venoms—to be treasured until the end of human history. It is probably a sign of the series' increasingly imaginative bankruptcy that, having kept Blofeld again beautifully anonymous for the boardroom electrocution scene in *Thunderball*, the filmmakers stumble in *You Only Live Twice* by revealing that Blofeld is the dreary jobbing actor Donald Pleasence with a prominent scar and a beige sort of Nehru jacket. From that point on Blofeld is wholeheartedly passed to the parodists and takes on an enjoyable non-Fleming life of his own. Within the films themselves, however, Telly Savalas as Blofeld in *On Her Majesty's Secret Service* is at least able to seem plausible as someone whose body double might ski, whereas Pleasance would have collapsed, squealing. Charles Gray in *Diamonds Are Forever* is a bit of a camp disaster—but it is a measure of the Bond films' wobbliness by this point that the original plan had been for the villain to be Goldfinger's twin brother. The difficulty lay in the extremely narrow range of behaviour available to Blofeld's character and indeed to criminal masterminds in general. Effectively the genre was used up by the fifth Bond film, but the films kept on being made, with ever weaker variations on the same theme, the blighted actor involved forever doomed to wave around implausible additional features (webbed hands, a little beard, additional nipples) or no features at all (Christopher "Sleep" Walken) in a wholly vain attempt to appear un-Blofeldy.

The problem in the end is that none of Blofeld's schemes for world domination seem even faintly interesting or worth anyone's time and effort, compared to the far more vigorous and mad plans of Fleming's earlier inventions. There are untold thousands of minions in the films, the security men, drivers, assassins and so on, who die futilely in his service, leaping from burning boats, getting skewered by ninjas, being impaled on modern sculptures, and not once does their loyalty seem plausible or their cause inspiring. There is none of the pantomime madness in Blofeld's heart that makes

Mr. Big or Rosa Klebb so unbounded and admirable. It is a shame therefore that of all Fleming's villains it is Blofeld who has become the shorthand, the common currency. It could not be more absurd and offensive, for example, that Blofeld should be the man to whom Pope Benedict XVI should immediately be compared on his election, when it is obvious to any thinking person that Pope Benedict is far more closely akin to *Moonraker*'s Sir Hugo Drax.

FLEMING'S DEATH, a month before the premiere of *Goldfinger*, posed a serious problem for the industry he had generated. By 1964 he had sold millions of books, and both fans and publishers around the world were, in their different ways, devastated. The fans could only sit in attitudes of mute appeal, but the publishers wiped their eyes and rolled up their sleeves to see what could be hauled out of the corpse. The first major result was *The Man with the Golden Gun*, a full-length Bond novel which was not much good but still became a vast, nostalgic bestseller. This was followed by the bits and bobs scraped together as *Octopussy*. There is a completely horrible-sounding dish from the southern United States which, in a mock medieval way, stuffs a boned chicken inside a boned duck inside a boned turkey. The resulting Dr. Moreau–style horror is called a turducken—almost unbelievably this is also available as a pet-food flavour, where I first encountered it (alongside other cans of "Cowboy Relish," "Barbecue Cookout," etc.). Anyway, *Octopussy* is a turducken, but it sold brilliantly anyway.

Beyond this publishers faced huge problems. There was an attempt simply to commission brand-new material— Kingsley Amis in 1968 wrote the Bond book *Colonel Sun* under the pseudonym of Robert Markham. This has a couple of passages of nicely handled sub-Fleming sadism but does not for a moment approach a convincing texture and Amis seems to have done it for a laugh and as an act of piety towards a writer he admired very much. He would never himself have claimed that it was one of his major novels or even minor major ones (the latter an important and hugely enjoyable element in his output). The book's Greek setting is so outside Fleming's own frame of reference that it merely becomes peculiar to imagine that the main character has anything much to do with Fleming's Bond. Why is he in Greece? Who are all these people? Why am I reading this rubbishy spy novel? If the magniloquent zany castles built by Fleming in *Goldfinger* and *You Only Live Twice* were undermined and crumbling in *The Man with the Golden Gun*, then they were a dead turducken by the time Amis was finished.

Just to finish up this sad issue, there were three ways in which Bond's life continued beyond the frame of the books. The first was the obvious one of commissioning yet more sequels in the 1980s from John Gardner and others. The hope had been that these might feed into the films in some way and that once Broccoli had finished filming all the Fleming titles he might gratefully turn to *Brokenclaw* or *License Renewed* as source material. This never happened and hardly anyone read the new books anyway and so the much admired Gardner found himself spending years as the high priest of a temple that nobody was worshipping at.

The second and most heartbreaking area was in the *Daily Express*, which had been running its adorable little Bond cartoon strip since 1958, thereby perfectly matching up one of the "woe-is-Britain" newspapers with the greatest palliative for that woe. I myself cannot quite be sure that I was not reading this strip even before seeing *Live and Let Die* at the cinema: the strips from that period, *Die With My Boots On* and *The Girl Machine*, ring a bell. In any event it was a tiny strip, like the daily version of *Peanuts* only with guns and tits. It must have run out of actual Bond stories in around 1968 and kept going at its incredibly slow pace (about a novel every half a year, the strip was so small) for some years. It eventually got shunted to the *Sunday Express*, then, after a break, to the *Daily Star*, where it finally expired in 1983. A lot of the drawings had a happy pulp immediacy (it had to be pretty immediate with only three or four drawings a day). I remember one ludicrous adventure where Bond's secret weapon was a pair of "Harlem hotshots" — single-shot guns built into his shoes fired by stamping in some specific way. It still rankles that these would have (i) needed Bond to wear stack boots for them to function; (ii) been impossible to aim; and (iii) blown off his feet — but then, here I am frowning with righteousness about a defunct strip in a semi-moribund newspaper!

The real headache, though, of course lay with the film-makers. Fleming's death was followed by the overwhelmingly vast success of *Goldfinger* and years of money lay ahead. The films increasingly diverged from the books but the book titles all made marvellous movie titles and provided a crucial imprimatur, with strange almost fetishistic little nods within many of the later films towards their distant source (the Fabergé egg in *Octopussy*, the female would-be assassin in *For Your Eyes Only*). The total bin-end of the Bond experience came with the using of short-story titles (*The Living Daylights*) as though more than an infinitesimal fraction of the audience could care. The final twinge was calling *The*

World Is Not Enough after Bond's ancestral family motto in
On Her Majesty's Secret Service before finally handing over to
marketing brand-concept people (in the manner of Accenture
or Consignia) to generate such despairing gestures as *Die
Another Day.*

WHY SHOULD we care about James Bond films? This is
one of those terrible faith-based issues. It is clear, I think,
that we can really care about only the first four films—*Dr. No*,
From Russia with Love, *Goldfinger*, *Thunderball* (although
the sense of caring is sagging fast in the last's interminable
underwater scenes), and cannot care much about *You Only
Live Twice* before caring somewhat, in a vexed, tortured,
stabbing-to-death-the-one-we-most-love sort of way, about
On Her Majesty's Secret Service. After that, childish infatua-
tions aside, it's just a blank stare and a sense that it's late
and there are other things to do. The films continue to say
fascinating things about Britain, but they are simply not good.

How then do we care about these four films? Well, we crop
them further by not caring in fact a great deal about *Dr. No*,
which has aged in ways it is hard to like—it is too cheaply
made, too many scenes are too feeble, the air is thick with
special pleading, it looks like *Hawaii Five-0* in more ways than
just having Jack Lord as Leiter. *Dr. No* is symbolically wonderful—it has the music, the girl, Connery, some lively
moments: the opening twenty seconds are impeccable, but it
doesn't live.

So in the end it is three and three-quarter films which
really matter and, whatever small moments they may have
where you are forced to turn away or file a quick mental
reservation (the Yugoslav scenes in *From Russia with Love*

so clearly being filmed in Scotland, for example), these substantial fragments are a slightly ruined wonder—a monument to a particular moment in British life which can be wandered around and admired for generations. Conservatively I must have seen *From Russia with Love* and *Goldfinger* at least forty times each and they still give the same pleasure as when I first saw them at age perhaps eleven. Of course *Goldfinger* is not major art by most kinds of definition, but it scores by some. However trivially intended by its makers it is fair to call it a sort of total artwork (a *Gesamtkunstwerk* indeed): an integration of design, music, technology, script and scenery of immense beauty and complexity. Its nature, values, appearance, scope could not have existed a decade earlier or a decade later—it is perfectly poised within its time. It screams volumes about that time. It is very boring to give examples in a written text of something so essentially visual, but I was struck as much on the forty-sixth as on the third viewing by its immense subtlety, its great visual allure, and the sense of love and relish that has gone into its making. It is an artefact of post-war life in Britain—and what mattered to people—of immense power—as complex and interesting in its way as the Post Office Tower or Jodrell Bank. Works of art need to be more than merely alluring, of course—all kinds of objects can plunge the observer into the armpit smell of a specific time or place, but some do it very well. Many of the paintings we now most value or the pieces of music we most enjoy listening to were first produced as by-the-yard palace-corridor decoration or to be heard in the background at levees, as the most casual, disposable tat, entirely secondary to the prince or bishop it was meant to glorify or indeed merely very slightly divert. All those courts and all that power have long vanished and we are left with the bits and bobs. We are too close to our own culture to know anything much about what will last (and of course it doesn't matter—the future will sort that out) but we *can* be sure that at different times some very surprising things will be of value and others derided. In Anthony Powell's *Dance to the Music of Time* (a good example of a great cultural artefact of the fifties and sixties which now seems in difficulties—perhaps it will reemerge with a new audience in the next decades), the narrator in old age talks with bemused exasperation about how a novelist he had read back in the 1920s who was specifically *known* to be a talentless and absurd fraud had become by the 1960s, many years after his death, one of the towering, much studied figures of English literature. I find it hard not to think that something similar will happen to some of Fleming's work and to the first Bond films. Or, of course, they could just as readily evaporate completely.

Chapter Seven

SWEAT AND POLYESTER

FOR REASONS THAT NEED NOT detain my handful of remaining readers, I once found myself driving on my own all the way round Lake Huron. I had been living in America for some years and would often set out on palpably absurd road trips—partly, it has to be said, to be annoying but mostly because I could not get enough of the country's endless landscapes and oddities and found that the least promising areas would throw up fascinating surprises—the Cornish miners of Michigan's Upper Peninsula (with their degenerate, horrifying Cornish pasties), the Finns of Sudbury, Ontario (recruited en masse for the nickel mines there because they could not speak English and so could not interact with other workers and unionize), the devastated strangeness of Detroit and so on.

I mention this only because I have such clear memories of one specific moment. I was driving along the freeway by the magically named Fort Michilimackinac. I hardly ever thought about James Bond, had a girl and a regular job, and was generally a clean-living figure. The roadside, I remember, was littered with the corpses of huge numbers of possums, raccoons, skunks—a sort of furry friends' *via dolorosa*—and I was just fiddling, slightly mournfully, with the radio when suddenly the theme tune to *On Her Majesty's Secret Service* came on—just as a fragment and used as the backing in a local radio advertisement. Now I have always loved this music—John Barry's most haunting tune, a strange piece with growling brass and a bass line of happy simplicity. Suddenly, within a bar or two, it was as though my normal adult life had collapsed completely—how ecstatic to be washed once again in Barry's music. That moment in Michigan put me back on track—the picturesque local features becoming a blur as I impatiently waited to return to New York and a high-quality local video store.

John Barry is an almost perfect example of someone who became tangled in the Bond films and, like many of the actors and directors, wound up doing his best work for them. Somehow in other contexts (his scores for *Zulu*, for example, or *Born Free*, for goodness' sake) he just became workaday, albeit proficient and Oscar-winning. Something in James Bond changed him. Exactly the sort of pleased-with-himself sports-car-driving smirky 1960s ladies' man whom Fleming would have loathed, Barry had turned out good but forgettable material (not least a 1960 cover version of "Walk Don't Run" which could be seen as the idiot theme tune to Macmillan's Britain) before becoming involved in orchestrating some of Monty Norman's music for *Dr. No*. Norman, a successful composer of musicals, had been commissioned to write some genially synthetic calypso tunes in Jamaica.

Did you know that the Bond theme began life as a sitar-backed song from an abortive Norman musical based on V. S. Naipaul's *A House for Mr. Biswas*? I certainly didn't and in some ways would prefer not to. Norman's tunes infuse *Dr. No*—most famously "Underneath the Mango Tree"—but there was anxiety that something more vigorous was needed as a main theme. Eventually Norman came up with this tune, which Barry orchestrated with great aplomb, thereby creating one of the most famous melodies in the consumerist world, propelled along by the immortal Vic Flick on guitar. What is it about this music? It can no longer be heard for what it is—an orchestral showpiece in the spirit of Bernard Hermann's scores such as *North by Northwest* or something by Perez Prado's orchestra—or a grander version of the Shadows' *Edgar Wallace* theme or Duane Eddy's *Peter Gunn*. I have always particularly liked the drumming—it has a sort of mad seriousness essential to successful pop. As usual with large professional orchestras there is a happy tension between imagining that the drummer is some stubble-headed, sweat-drenched, purple-heart-reliant maniac with two burly psychiatric nurses hovering just off stage, or—just as probable—a heavily spectacled, tiny, cross-word obsessive who gets the same train back out from London to Dorking every evening and never does overtime.

After *Dr. No*, Barry came to dominate the films. For *From Russia with Love* he took Lionel Bart's slightly cheesy theme song and converted it into a series of frisson-inducing variations for a dementedly varied orchestra, becoming as structurally important to the film's beauty and coherence as the city of Istanbul itself. Everything works perfectly in *From Russia with Love*—the creepy harp music whenever Blofeld is speaking, the crazy sort of giant church bell clanged in the scene in Hagia Sofia and so on. He then perfected his art over the following films—summing up in *Goldfinger* particularly a specific flavour of the sixties which, of course, existed only in Barry's head but which now seems to stand as a short-hand for excitement, exotic travel and British fantasies about America, a vision painfully remote from most people's experience of the period but which populated many dreams.

I have always lived by a few simple rules—perhaps the most fundamental being: don't buy soundtrack albums. This is so important that I feel obliged to pass it on to readers in case they should ever fall into temptation. The one exception, though, has to be Barry's music for *On Her Majesty's Secret Service*, which, with a couple of embarrassing indignities characteristic of the genre, is otherwise immaculate. It seems, to me at any rate, stupefying that Barry should have got a Grammy for the lugubrious *Midnight Cowboy* score while in the following year this work of genius was shunned by the same body.

If *On Her Majesty's Secret Service* provides beautiful sound pictures of mountains and ski chases, Barry's fine, creepy score for *Diamonds Are Forever* has a sweat-and-polyester air equally matching that film's atmosphere. Indeed, so excellent are Barry's scores, particularly for *You Only Live Twice*, *On Her Majesty's Secret Service* and *Diamonds Are Forever*, that it is possible at many points to enjoy them fully without even watching the screen: indeed, quite often this enhances the entire experience. But after *Diamonds Are Forever*, it is all downhill. Barry missed the first Roger Moore film, *Live and Let Die*, which was handed to a flailing post-Beatles Paul McCartney and George Martin. Something clearly went wrong for Barry now—quite possibly he himself realized how dreadful the films were becoming and was simply responding as an artist to their general, leaden helplessness. *The Man with the Golden Gun* has the score it deserves and, after taking a further break from *The Spy Who Loved Me* (which gave Carly Simon a strange sort of opportunity), he shut down all further interest in his career with his *Moonraker* score. Perhaps his really was a more active decision—a score, perhaps delivered at the last moment so it could not be changed, so dull that it might heave the entire, ailing Bond phenomenon into oblivion. Certainly the film and its music are as one. Except, except—for one marvellous Barry moment. Towards the end, the secret space station comes into view and Barry gives it music of incredible grandeur and menace—a few moments of Mahlerian, hair-raising brilliance—suggesting some vast, bat-winged manifestation of Evil stirring at the back of its cave. But this music is used for what? For a scene featuring a visibly puffy Roger Moore *in outer space*, dressed in tin foil and looking like the manager of some failing firm about to be sacked for fiddling his expenses. Barry goes down with the ship, which is honourable, but it is impossible to have a view on his later Bond scores—for *Octopussy* or for *The Living Daylights*—because they are almost feature-less. Something happened to him or to the zeitgeist or to the films, but in any event John Barry stopped being John Barry after *Diamonds Are Forever*. But so what—nobody else has written seven extraordinary scores and orchestrated one of the most famous tunes of the twentieth century. There is an argument that John Barry's music is in fact the reason more than anything for the Bond films' success. It is very strange music, a melodic gift that has not been copied successfully by anyone else and scene after scene, often quite incidental (walk-ing through a hotel lobby, driving a car along, flying through the Alps), becomes magical through Barry. That he could pro-duce such galumphing horrors as the score for *Zulu* (which almost sinks the film) while also writing *Goldfinger*, with its spare, sinister, icy little melodies that have been plundered, sampled and parodied ever since, illustrates almost perfectly the vagaries of human inspiration.

*

THERE IS A disastrous moment in Jean-Jacques Rousseau's *Confessions* when, having spent many pages convincing his readers that he is a heart-on-sleeve, impetuous, head-in-the-clouds kind of guy, he almost in passing admits to having had five children all of whom, over the mother's protests, he placed in an orphanage and none of whom he ever saw again. He announces this in a way that implies he has built up enough trust to have his excuses heard out, but it is all quite hopeless: the guests drift away with fixed smiles, the book drops from the duped reader's hand. I feel in a similar position when I confess that in all honesty, and unlike the books, I do not and have never found the Bond films even remotely erotic. Bracing myself to be denounced as some spermless milquetoast I will not only stick by my inner conscience, but more aggressively suggest that you would have to be very odd indeed to find them even faintly alluring.

The vapour trail of sex left in my ten-year-old brain by first seeing *Live and Let Die* was not an erotic response, but a realization that sex might exist, beyond the realms of toy soldiers and the fairly cock-free brands of derring-do available in *Biggles Defies the Swastika* or *Gorilla Adventure*. Actually seeing the gormless British beauty Jane Seymour playing with tarot cards and saying, "Oh, James," was really *not* erotic.

This is surely one of the odder conundrums at the heart of the films: that they need to imply to their audiences that theirs is a world of roaming male adulthood but without for a moment jeopardizing their general-admission certificate. As one perceptive film critic said of the *Thunderball* screenplay, it "stands on tiptoe at the outermost edge of the suggestive and gazes yearningly down into the obscene." For all the discussion of how sexy the women are in Bond films, in practice they are not. Honor Blackman in *Goldfinger* may be a fine actress and a smart person but she teeters on the verge of being a sort of headmaster's wife or head nurse. She is the worst, but surely breezy head girl Diana Rigg or school prefect Jane Seymour cannot be viewed as actively desirable on screen. Of course, this is partly to do with passing time and fashion—in casual photos Luciana Paluzzi, the female villainess in *Thunderball*, was incandescently sultry and one of the great *ocelots d'amour* of the sixties, but in her daft dresses, shellacked, stacked-up hair and depressing make-up she becomes a near blank.

The problem of the "Bond girl" is also of course that she shares the curse of virtually everyone else in the films of never becoming famous for anything else—going on to live out lives of perhaps fifty or sixty years without further impinging on any pop-culture consciousness. This may be lucky for them, but it is odd: whatever happened to Claudine Auger or Daniela Bianchi or Shirley Eaton—or dozens of girls in the later films? Maryam d'Abo? Lois Chiles? Some, like Barbara Bach or Britt Ekland (can anyone forget Britt's sheer helplessness in *The Man with the Golden Gun*?), married someone who kept them in the public eye. One, Jane Seymour, would invite magazines to photograph her beautiful garden in the West Country somewhere and scratched a living in the daft *Dr. Quinn, Medicine Woman*. One, Diana Rigg, became a great and famous actress but she was the only one who specifically recoiled from the whole experience, and had been famous anyway for *The Avengers* (an intermittently magical Bond knock-off in itself) before becoming entangled in *On Her Majesty's Secret Service*.

The main exception of course was the woman who started the trouble: Ursula Andress. Despite wearing a saggy, sand-khaki bikini in *Dr. No* she is without doubt a striking presence when she emerges from the sea—although a great deal less striking than she would have been if the filmmakers had followed the book more closely and had her emerge entirely nude except for a knife belt. In a sense she launches the Bond films more effectively than Connery does in her iconic moment—although she is thrown away thereafter, merely mucking around in the shower and weedily running around. Again, the book is more striking here. Dr. No straps Andress's character nude to a rock and talks in some detail about how she will be pulled apart alive by thousands of land crabs, but once again—and perhaps justifiably—Fleming's private concerns got the cold shoulder from the filmmakers.

Just to round off the "Bond girl" issue: recently there was an evening-newspaper headline announcing BOND GIRL IN BUST UP WITH EUROSTAR MANAGER. Which Bond girl could this be? And what strange spell do the films still weave with a sick, backward British readership that an argument on a train can be interesting if it has a Bond element? In any event— excitedly buying the paper with shaking hands—I found that the "Bond girl" was not some long-forgotten victim of exploitation, but the formidable Grace Jones, who appeared to little effect as a subsidiary villain in *A View to a Kill*. For a time in the late seventies she had been absolutely everywhere: photographed nude in an animal cage, given fangs, wrapped in leather, her cruel face and amazingly blue-black skin a sort of riot of post-colonial sexual chaos. Based in Paris, she turned out bizarre pictures and terrible dance albums, a living embodiment of Continental European failure to engage seriously with American music. For uncountable numbers of buffalo-shouldered, coconut-oiled jet-skiing men of the Côte d'Azur she had provided both masturbation material and disco anthems for years. Surely we owe it to these men, as they now, many years on, disconsolately violate their family's trust with ever younger female relatives and anxiously examine their crumbling hairlines and plummeting sperm counts, not to dismiss Grace Jones as a mere "Bond girl"?

AN INTRIGUING minor note to the Bond films is the role of clothing—and particularly men's hats. The early films are now decisively dated in their opening seconds by Bond's appearing within the white circle of the gun rifling in a very fetching hat. One of the defining pieces of irritating continuity in the early films are the variants around Bond tossing his hat onto a hat-stand in Miss Moneypenny's office (another figure who may have seemed more straightforwardly charming at the time, but who now seems passive in a rather macabre way). We never see Bond actually wearing a bowler, because he would have looked catastrophically unassassin-like even in 1963, but hats both civilian and military float around the early films. Indeed, the moment in *From Russia with Love* when Bond leaves Moneypenny's office clutching his hat and muttering, "Ciao," his torso and hat filling the screen as the theme-tune plays is one of those almost meaningless yet magic pieces of business that made Bond so emblematic—the texture that sets the films quite apart from normal thrillers.

Of course the 1960s are famous for the collapse of the male hat. Somehow everyone is wearing bowlers, homburgs, derbies and caps in 1960 and they have mostly gone by 1970. There are at least two interesting theories. One is that it reflected a generational switch between those who had been in the military, and who therefore naturally wore something on their heads, and those who did not. The other is related to Kennedy's inauguration as president and his breaking with precedent by not wearing a hat. As Kennedy had served in the Pacific theatre during the War, however, this messes up theory A. Perhaps it was so warm there he didn't wear a naval cap much? In any event, by the mid-sixties hatters were in free fall, carrying with them a whole world of hat-stands and hat-check girls. Setting aside the *Sgt.-Pepper*-Victoriana-related male hats circa 1967 and the occasional loosely *Cat-in-the-Hat*-oriented psychedelic hat, the industry vanished but—unlike many industries—without a more modern replacement: male heads just stayed bare. Flat caps have clung on in a limited way, but were devastated by the closure of the industries associated with them; bowler hats, once almost compulsory for many grades of financial worker in the city of London, vanished with such speed that by the 1970s only those actively wishing to appear backward and eccentric in a dazed way could be seen in them. It is strange to think that Oddjob's famous murder weapon of a steel-rimmed bowler would have, had he not been electrocuted in 1964, made him a perhaps unacceptably over-conspicuous assassin within only a few short years.

For the Bond films these fashion changes have more generally been a disaster, but an interesting one and one which feeds into far wider issues. The early films have complete confidence in male couture, carried over from the books and their world of semi-uniform dressing. What could be more adorable than a black knitted-wool narrow tie and tailored suit? The spectacular collapse of traditional male dress—which had been fairly stable since the 1920s—is charted in ugly and chaotic ways by James Bond himself. The world which had set up the books and the films, a world based on order, deference, nostalgia and hierarchy, had to retool feverishly in the face of uncontrollable spasms of democratic waywardness. We turn our eyes away from the humiliations of Connery's notionally Japanese fishing clothing in *You Only Live Twice* because of the far greater humiliation of his "Japanese" special toupee and plucked eyebrows. (Is this little scene in fact the nadir of the films' catastrophic wish to ape elements in the plots of the books? Why, having jettisoned much of the original story, did they keep this one demeaning, ludicrous notion, that Bond could be disguised as a Japanese fisherman? No wonder Connery left at this point.) By the time of *On Her Majesty's Secret Service* in 1969 the audience's face is being stuffed into some unredeemable clothing disasters—Bond's white dress shirt decorated in freakish curls and flounces, an offensive kilt, a weird plaid jacket. And from then on it is all unstoppable—a short pink tie in *Diamonds Are Forever*, a safari suit in *Live and Let Die*—but by now we are plunging into the world of Roger Moore's dress sense, which may or may not be reflecting wider societal changes, but is in every important way a personal disaster.

The hat itself clings on in the opening sequence until *Live and Let Die*. It had been an antique before then but in *On Her Majesty's Secret Service* it had at least implied continuity and trust at a tricky time for the series, but then it disappears forever, a victim both of changing times and, possibly, Moore's odd box-shape head.

*

> Edelweiss, Edelweiss
> My favourite James Bond film's *You Only Live Twice*
> Edelweiss, Edelweiss
> It's good to see Bond eat some rice

THIS FAMILY RHYME has so coloured my feelings about *You Only Live Twice* that it is almost the only way I can now think about it. It was not always so—for years I spent random moments mentally putting together what I intended to be a definitive article for the *New York Review of Books* to be called "Some Notes on Rewatching *You Only Live Twice*," which would have shown in an unanswerably brilliant way how this was a film that both defined the 1960s and that said profound things about the nature of film and of history. I no longer believe this—it turns out that I had just carried over my teenage infatuation with Nancy Sinatra's voice in the title song, soaring, ethereal and incredibly sexy.

The most curious thing about *You Only Live Twice* is the overwhelming role in the film of two figures with immaculate Second World War records: Roald Dahl, who wrote the script, and Ken Adam, whose astounding sets dominate the film. These two ex-RAF fighter pilots are the most direct evidence that what really mattered in the films as it did in the books was the War and its legacy—that these were not even tangentially "swinging" movies at all but artefacts of an older generation whose interests were far removed from those of the sixties as we understand them. I rather overlarded this idea in my matchless, if now lost, notes for my "Notes"—both men were equally just having a laugh. But there is something about *You Only Live Twice* which is simply so wistful—that Bond, the solitary Englishman, should be trying to save the world in such a relentlessly, exclusively American-dominated part of the planet just cannot be believed for an instant. Fleming had used Japan in his novel as a beguiling frame for the Gothic mishmash of Blofeld's final, rather low-rent incarnation as a supervisor of a garden for suicides. The filmmakers wisely dropped this but the plot that they substituted was too silly to be believed—and showed how intensely vulnerable Britain had become. A fantasy in which Soviet, American and SPECTRE space interests and world war could be trumped by a Scottish actor dressed up as a Japanese fisherman is a fantasy that is a cry for help. The film also offers a perhaps even more perfect example than *Dr. No* of the poignant spectacle of a megalomaniac genius pouring billions of dollars into a criminal project that could be wound up in minutes by a squad car of reasonably motivated beat coppers.

You Only Live Twice is the perfect showcase for any discussion of one of the most widely parodied elements in the Bond films: the boiler-suited minions who are gunned down in tremendous numbers in the finale of each film. We have already seen glimpses of these people—the rather charismatic hard-hatted bauxite-mine security guards in *Dr. No*, the Chinese troops in *Goldfinger* wackily attacking Fort Knox and Largo's scuba-diving chums in *Thunderball*, but they at least exist as part of a wider, albeit dotty, storyline. *You Only Live Twice* introduces something new: a wholly zombie duty-bound phalanx who combine atrocious marksmanship and a selfless wish to be shot, blown up or eviscerated without for one second flinching. In reality this is just the sort of mercenary army who would, when faced with hundreds of government-backed ninja abseiling into their volcano lair, hastily change out of their distinctive costumes and claim to be blameless sanitary workers. Blofeld would in practice have been betrayed by a thousand accusing fingers (followed probably by a class action for personal trauma) but instead his men fight to the death. This is in effect a sort of pinnacle of right-wing obedience fantasy where two sides grind each to powder while the single strong man steps in and through guile (Bond's tiny rocket hidden inside a cigarette, for God's sake) turns the balance. These showers of boiler-suited figures are one of the features that make the later films intolerable, but at least in *You Only Live Twice* they have a comic novelty value.

IT MUST in many ways have been a very happy life being involved in making the Bond films. There was clearly a family atmosphere generated by Broccoli and the same gang appear and reappear. It must also have been quite sheltering, as some of the talents involved were pretty feeble. Even admitting that British directors had very little work in the 1960s there is something embarrassing for the true fan in the total failure of directors or scriptwriters or, indeed, actors on the whole to shine in any other context. How could Guy Hamilton, who had made *Goldfinger* so effortlessly beautiful, create the humiliating *Battle of Britain*? Why did Terence Young, who so completely shaped the Bond ethos as director of *Dr. No* and *From Russia with Love*, have such a dead hand on other projects—his filmography (*Bloodline!*, *The Klansman!*), like that of other Bond directors such as John Glen and Lewis Gilbert, is really just awful.

The many smaller roles also had their pleasures for those involved—a regular source of work for heavies and stuntmen, not to mention legions of stagehands, carpenters, dressers, property managers, location scouts and so on. Many of the same names recur and plunge us into the strange world of film-as-craft and of the enormous group of actors who are not at all successful but who have garnered a sort of respect and private glamour. It is appealing to think of the sheer numbers of villas in southern Spain built over the years with Bond money, each with its sunken bar area decorated with brass divers' helmets and ships' wheels; to think of the opportunities individuals must have had to go on to sell motorboats or to buy a pub in Dubai. Many of those in the "family" involved in technical or advisory roles must have relished the whole thing, gaining local celebrity, cash and a pile of enjoyable anecdotes.

Among the crucial minor Bond figures I always think of Bob Simmons. Pure fans should probably look away (more jaded fans will know this already) but it is not Connery whom you see stalking along in the gun-barrel circle at the beginning of the first three films, but Bob! When I first discovered this I found I had unconsciously gripped the table until my knuckles were milk-white—this was a blow on a par with knowing Connery had a toupee or that Gert Fröbe's lines in *Goldfinger* were dubbed. (At what point would the whole Bond edifice just fall apart like some gunned-down pantomime horse? How much artifice can we withstand?) Simmons appears unobtrusively here and there in various roles, often as a body double throughout the early films, and was a sort of Master of Stunts. His great claim, though (aside from now ruining one's enjoyment of the opening of the first three films), is as the French assassin in drag at the beginning of *Thunderball*. In a weird way, given that Simmons rather than Connery is—as it turns out—the actual iconic Bond, this fight between the two of them is therefore a lurid moment of E. T. A. Hoffmann–style *Doppelgänger* violence as Connery at last kills the genuine Bond—both the Bond of the opening credits, and also the genuine stuntman rather than the pampered Scots superstar with a limited acting range. In *Thunderball* this strange anomaly ended and thereafter the actor playing Bond is also the figure in the gun rifling at the beginning.

The stuntmen and fight arrangers who became so lucratively entangled in Bond over the years all had to face the cold reality of the main problem facing the filmmakers. Each film *had* to up the ante on the previous one (setting aside the occasional "unplugged" Bond films such as *On Her Majesty's Secret Service*). This has proved over forty years very hard to sustain. Dozens of soldiers blasting away at each other in *Goldfinger* had to be capped by making them fight underwater in *Thunderball* and then in a hollow volcano, filled with space rockets, in ninja clothing in *You Only Live Twice*. Each of these films required ever more complex and terrifying stunts.

Traditionally the approach for movie stunts had always been to strap some boss-eyed amphetamine-packed cockney misfit into a car seat and urge him to go off a cliff, into a river or whatever with fingers crossed. It is a very odd effect that with passing time these stunts, which however staged were real enough, now look fake, whereas contemporary computer-generated or computer-enhanced stunts, which are substantially false, look plausible. Children now laugh cruelly at Bond film stunts which at the time involved real danger—and it is impossible in the end not to join them. It is weird that the rocket-pack at the beginning of *Thunderball*, which was a genuine, if hilarious, U.S. military experiment, should look so hopelessly unconvincing. Here is a real test pilot risking his life for some daft film, while a comparable result could have been obtained by strapping an Action Man doll to a bottle-rocket.

One final member of the early Bond troupe has to be mentioned: the German-born actor Walter Gotell. In the 1950s and early 1960s no Second World War movie is complete without his almost benignly fiendish presence. Gotell made a good living from playing Nazis to beautiful effect in, to name but a handful, *Ice-Cold in Alex*, *I Was Monty's Double* and *The Guns of Navarone*. He was able to wear assorted Wehrmacht uniforms and sand-goggles and say, "For you the war is over," with such style that you can almost sense the laughter that will break out among the cast the moment the cameras are switched off. So close to omnipresent is he in the dramas of the period that it is almost normal at some point for viewers to think: Oh good, here's Walter Gotell. Gotell had the small (his parts were always small) yet exquisite role in *From Russia with Love* of the head of the SPECTRE training complex. He has the honour to walk away from the camera holding the rubber James Bond mask at the end of the opening sequence, he guides Rosa Klebb around the training camp, he kills the criminal masterbrain Kronsteen and he is incinerated in his boat during the rather feeble-minded boat chase at the end (are boat chases simply *always* feeble-minded?). He is also lucky enough to have my favourite line in any of the films—he has the *privilege*, a privilege he seizes with gusto, to say to Rosa Klebb, as he waves the cardboard document file on the assassin Grant: "Homicidal maniac—superb material." His existence in the 1980s Bond films, as the entirely boring General Gogol, can in no sense stand in the way of his immortal moment.

MY FIRST REAL JOB was working as a sales rep in Africa, the Middle East and South Asia. I was selling books of all kinds and managed to do this for about two years before an amazing range of mutually supportive illnesses made available to me by shuttling to all points between Sierra Leone and Bengal caused my entire system to implode.

I mention this only because before it all went wrong and—a gaunt, eructating figure—I moved on, so much of the adaptive behaviour hardwired into me derived from James Bond. The whole business of travelling around the world, clearing customs, checking into hotels, ordering room service, taking taxis and tipping is so beautifully laid out in the books and films that I don't remember having to think for myself for a moment.

This began with the clothing. Driven by instinct rather than advice, I had hardly been offered the job before I rushed to Tropiccadilly, gentlemen's outfitters, for the right kit. This shop has long vanished but was a cornucopia of late-imperial nonsense: special high-sided boots, bewildering hats, mould-proof bags and, of course, devastating tropical-weight sand-drill suits. The few surviving photos I have from the period invariably show me lolling in cane chairs from Monrovia to Riyadh to Bangalore in these suits, allied to a pair of heavy Italian sunglasses. I had seen the Bond movies and I knew how to dress. Thinking back of course a tiny voice says, "You looked like a moron," and there were those who I worked with who have since suggested that any book orders I received were provoked by the customer's intense sense of pity. In the often rather dazzling hotels I stayed in (which absorbed most of the profits of each trip) I could never understand the general air of sourness and irritability that I would generate — porters and waiters always seemed outraged, however suave my tipping and backchat. The twenty years that have passed since then have been spent in gradually realizing that they all thought: Why am I doing something for a twenty-two-year-old dick in a very peculiar suit? My very existence served to destabilize their sense of dignity and left a trail of radicalizing bitterness that plagues several regions to this day. But at the time I felt great and hardly noticed the gap between Bond's own sex-and-murder-themed foreign travels and my own mission to sell disturbingly out-of-date computer textbooks to Cameroon schools.

This sense of "knowledge," of always knowing where to go, whom to tip, how to behave is central to Bond's success. I genuinely cannot think of another source for my behaviour as a sales rep. I had never been anywhere even faintly exotic before accepting this job — and yet I felt no twitch of self-doubt as I hailed airport taxis, stalked into lobbies, inspected hotel suites, erratically tipped ("It will do very well — keep this"), ordered drinks. Sex was a bit of a disaster — indeed I don't remember meeting anyone anywhere at any point who could have been a candidate. I guess the worlds of bookselling, librarianship and teaching are fairly settled ones, but equally it could be true to say that I didn't look an overwhelmingly obvious candidate for some carnal free-for-all myself, either in or out of my increasingly odd-smelling suit. The one hot tip I had received — a Jordanian librarian —

proved to be a matronly, cake-nibbling scarf-swathed figure millions of miles from the pantherine operator I had been alerted to. I will never fully resolve in my mind whether I was the victim of a joke or whether—on seeing me sweating and stumbling towards my appointment—the scarves and cakes had been hastily flung on top of her more habitual fine-mesh body-stocking studded with gold coins.

Aside from embarrassing hotel and dress tips have I felt myself to be influenced by Bond in any way behaviourally? For many people this is undoubtedly one of the saddest aspects of the whole business. In any given month one or another male-interest magazine will have a "you can be like James Bond" feature: a sexual technique, a line in ruthless quips, a new, hopeless gadget. It is hard to be quite certain, but I really would like to feel that I enjoy Bond while not being like him. I might have propped myself up in bed next to a girl, smirking post-coitally à la Connery, but I am a bit too conscious of my general flabbiness and lack of serious, crackling body hair—I certainly don't have Connery's spectacular chest matting, which must have given women having sex with him the sensation that their breasts were rubbing against a wolverine.

I have never been in a position to kill anyone, or even mildly hurt them; I am a slow, readily panicked driver; two martinis are enough to make me strike my head on the bar. But as my younger self folded his dark glasses and stalked with feral grace across the lobby of the Riyadh Hilton, oblivious to the staff's incredulous titters, I *knew* who I was modelling myself on.

THE SHEER lack of money is one of the most startling facts in 1960s British political life, with so many of Harold Wilson's decisions based on simply not being able to pay for anything anymore. Devaluations and currency crises gave Britain a sort of constant financial diarrhoea and the late sixties saw a final, parodic round of imperial collapse, generally on the grounds of cost rather than nationalist pressure. Reading the minutes of, for example, the meetings in Washington, DC, in 1965 between the United States and Britain, there is a squirmy horror to the British position: the Americans, in a firmly friendly, i.e., not at all friendly way, offer to fix up Britain's financial nightmares, but only in return for x, y and z military concessions. What is strange now is seeing how even in the notionally "post-colonial" world of the sixties Britain continued to be tangled in endless, unsustainable Great-Power gestures of a kind that now look crazy.

Denis Healey, the minister of defence in the Labour government, fascinatingly sums up Britain's headaches both in his life and in his decisions. After a very successful career fighting in North Africa and Italy, Healey, a thoroughly compelling and interesting figure, found himself having to carry through policies after 1964 which effectively ended Britain's Great Power status, not specifically in the face of national-ism (many of the countries involved had small populations or specific reasons for wanting British help—for example the Malaysians in the face of Indonesian aggression in Borneo), but simply because the money had all gone. He was much hated at the time but now seems to have been entirely sensible. As the money ran out he killed off the most symbolic project of all: the TSR-2, the brainchild of Barnes Wallis, inventor of the Wellington bomber and the "Dambuster" bomb among many others, and a quintessential British hero. The TSR-2 was the last major independent strike aircraft to be developed in

Britain, but its costs were deranged and its scrapping caused endless bitterness—not least because it marked the end of Britain as a serious aircraft designer, choking off yet another area of national self-definition. Healey also grandly proclaimed—as though it were a strategy rather than an enforced fiasco—a military pull-back "East of Suez": the winding up of a variety of treaty arrangements in Southeast Asia and the Gulf micro-states, creating new countries such as the United Arab Emirates just at the point when they were about to become enormously wealthy. Given the military complexity of what unfolded in the Gulf since the seventies this was inadvertently a good move, but shows how recently British rule, however indirect, had continued there, and why the inhabitants might be sceptical of British intentions when Britain turned up vigorously again in the area with the Americans from the 1990s onwards.

In other moves, a peculiarly cynical and repulsive deal was done with the United States to expel all the people who lived in the remaining islands owned by Britain in the Indian Ocean to give the United States a completely "sterile" military base. Decolonization also took on the weird characteristic, driven by a desperate need to save money, of effectively forcing microstates in the Pacific and Caribbean to become independent simply to save tiny sums: leading to the ultimate absurdity of paratroopers being sent to Anguilla in the Caribbean, whose citizens were insisting on *not* becoming independent. A regular feature of the right-wing newspapers too became agonized discussions about the shrinking Royal Navy as frantic attempts were made to balance the budget by closing yet more bases, disposing of ships and shrinking personnel numbers. This navy discussion became a sort of wearying idée fixe on the right for decades with, characteristically, the implication that there was some plan fomented by treachery to destroy our magnificent old naval traditions. As each country and each base slipped from British control, the navy's diminishing size became the surrogate for all the self-loathing and embarrassment generated by Britain's plight. Every government took turns to cut the navy and paid no attention to a vocal lobby who would in any event only have felt satisfied had the entire British population been crewing thousands of battleships and been given orders by whistle in the manner of the von Trapp family.

An extremely brutal (and almost pathologically backwards-looking) war was fought in what is now southern Yemen to maintain Aden—the last dusty little bit of a very recent supremacy—as a completely isolated and vulnerable British base, with countries as diverse as Nasser's Egypt and Saudi Arabia all merrily throwing in resources to get the British out. In scenes eerily previewing of the 2003 war in Iraq, British troops blasted away, killed stacks of terrorists and found their only supporters to be a handful of feudal chiefs, who were summarily killed by radical Yemenis the moment the British, having declared a rocklike surety of purpose—yet again—fled in 1967.

At the same time, in a final fantasy, the RAF proposed a base on Aldabra—an uninhabited island off East Africa, home only to some 15,000 giant tortoises. This idea was scrapped on both finance and common-sense grounds. I love the brief Aldabra debate as it now stands so beautifully as a summary of the last, flickering gleams of an imperial mindset that had seemed utterly solid only twenty years previously. It was a dream of an absolutely pointless airstrip on a tropical island with no human inhabitants and therefore—at last—no troublesome nationalists, but unfortunately useable only for bombing runs against some putative Madagascan or Antarctic enemy. Presumably a substantial ground crew would have been needed just to keep the airstrip tortoise-free.

Looming over all these humiliations was the "unilateral declaration of independence" by white settlers in Rhodesia. All of Britain's other major African colonies (aside from some southern African trusteeships) being made independent by 1964, the tiny white elite in Rhodesia realized they were next and, correctly guessing that Britain would respond by doing nothing, simply ignored any further orders from London. The tide of history was flowing so hard against the settlers that it is impossible to imagine that a small paratroop drop would not have resulted in immediate capitulation. The settlers after all were in many cases recent arrivals and could define their roles only in relation to the framework provided by the British Empire: without that they were a group of opportunistic jokers of a kind that in this period was being expelled from country after country. The fuss that was caused by the Rhodesia issue and its polarizing effect now seem thoroughly bizarre. The *Express* and the *Mail* saw it as a nostalgic fantasy of supporting "kith and kin." Desultory attempts were made to solve the problem, despite sanctions which, bizarrely, simply resulted in Rhodesia getting its supplies from South Africa. Wilson did nothing and Rhodesia remained throughout the seventies as a startling metaphor for British turpitude, cynicism and exhaustion.

IT IS A CURIOUS feature of films that different elements within individual movies will mature, like bottles of wine, at quite different rates. A particular kind of masculine beauty, for example, may suddenly become risible, or specific racial assumptions just too nasty to watch, leaving high and dry other entirely appealing aspects.

This is very markedly true with the Bond films. The sexual politics bottles never tasted great, but have by this point exploded, leaving a suppurating mess all over the cellar floor. More unfairly, many of the special effects, which at the time looked gleaming, now taste pretty sour—the revolutions in CGI make the exploding toy helicopters and matte-screen rockets often look hopeless. But there is one area where the drinkability just gets ever better—the sets. Ken Adam (and Syd Cain, who designed *From Russia with Love* and *On Her Majesty's Secret Service*) may for future generations, uninterested in imperial hang-ups, prove to be the whole point: a major artist given the resources by these daft films to do something genuinely brilliant.

Indeed, watching even a not very good film like *Diamonds Are Forever* there are countless pleasures to be had from the Adam sets which only show how frustratingly narrow our definitions of art really are. Surely any account of the aesthetics of the sixties should centrally include many of Adam's designs: not simply the famous big set pieces such as his Fort Knox fantasy in *Goldfinger* or the volcano in *You Only Live Twice*, but in a sense far more suggestively the numerous modernist interiors—impossible fantasies of power and grandeur, such as Blofeld's penthouse in *Diamonds Are Forever* (with its gorgeous steel lift) or the Japanese industrialist's office in *You Only Live Twice*. They are as specific to their era as any account of music or painting and as suggestive and strange.

These sets also feed into interesting contemporary ideas about conceptual art and video/performance art. The sets can be seen as meditations on insubstantiality—they appear to be so arrogant, almost unspeakably aggressive and yet they were mainly painted chipboard, had at most only three walls (because of the cameras) and generally lacked ceilings (the film lighting went there)—these last being painted in and filmed later. So not only did these marvellous rooms never exist as they are seen on the film, but they were dismantled at Pinewood Studios the moment they'd been shot. So Adam's designs exist only as complex artifices projected onto a flat screen and only as something glimpsed behind the actors. How plangent is that! They also have the strange side effect of making everything which is filmed in actual, unfake locations—the casinos in *Diamonds Are Forever*, say, or the external shots of the stud farm in *Goldfinger*—appear less real than the artifice, as they are so compromised, so unfilmic, compared to Adam's unified vision.

Perhaps it is really only now that we can fully engage with the sets —with freeze-framing as a happy spin-off from digitization. If freeze-framing is done on a conventional projector there is of course a disaster. I remember once watching Hitchcock's *Family Plot*, which was immeasurably improved when the film stuck and, in a frisson accidentally worthy of the Master, in a few moments the characters were paralysed, drained of colour and then melted. Of course on videos freeze-frame was a disaster, with the action hiding behind a blizzard, but with DVDs Ken Adam's sets become entirely savourable. The astonishing fantasy Chinese bedroom at the beginning of *You Only Live Twice* (seen only for a minute or two): its colour, beauty and scale are incomparable. Or, surely one of the great visual coups, Syd Cain's grandmaster chess palazzo at the beginning of *From Russia with Love*—a Venetian interior that trumps all genuine Venetian interiors but that existed only for a few weeks, on a sound stage at Pinewood, would have stunk of paint and sawdust, had wires everywhere, lacked the magnificent ceiling seen in the film, and would not have seemed even faintly real to the actors wobbling about on it.

AS THE SIXTIES ended, Bond's fate became increasingly unclear. Was he doomed, like the girl trapped in the red shoes, dancing herself to death, to kill, smirk and fornicate forever? How could a series built on excess continue to exceed? Given the very restricted range of behaviour available to Bond was there anything that could be done to surprise audiences? This straitjacket meant that—at its most extreme—Bond could never suddenly give the audience some tremendous shock: the scriptwriters could never propose, for example, that he incompetently crash his car, throw up after his fifth martini, have a leg suddenly sheared off by a crocodile or come all over the bedside lamp. But it also meant—more sensibly—that he could never express any surprising emotions or extend his range: a problem tackled to nobody's satisfaction in the two later Bond movies starring Timothy Dalton. This issue bedevilled the film's producers and, as already discussed, regular attempts were made to fix it, by stripping the films back and making them more realistic. With the passing of time these attempts seem strangely honourable. Following the bloat-out fiasco of *Moonraker* (1979) came the back-to-basics *For Your Eyes Only*—a film which at the time seemed like a wretched holiday-camp exercise but which now, in relation to the horrors that followed it, has a grimy integrity that makes it look as though it was directed by Andrej Wajda. This in turn makes the first back-to-basics, *On Her Majesty's Secret Service* (1969), seem akin to something put together by some austere, Amsterdam-based revolutionary collective.

I have a rather vexed relationship with this last film—it has astonishing, almost Warholian longueurs, a savage piece of brilliance in filling the main role with someone who cannot act (an anticipation perhaps of some of Werner Herzog's experiments with hypnotized actors) and the humiliation of the great Diana Rigg. This is cinema of a very strange kind. It is very long and can boast in patches (the bullfighting scenes, the wedding) some of the most boring cinema of the entire decade. Having the film climax with Rigg's murder by an unpunished Blofeld was a downer, too, and the film's unfortunate box-office failure led to panic—Bondmania was definitely over. Here was the point where Fleming and the cult of Fleming had become a liability: the attempt faithfully to follow a novel in the manner of *From Russia with Love* no longer worked. From now on the filmmakers were simply to loot Fleming's titles, take the odd feature of the book (often quite incidental and included in the film only in the manner of some battered cult object long torn from its proper setting) and make the rest up as they went along. They also went on bended knee back to Connery, showering him with money (which he passed on to an educational charity) until he agreed to make the nonsensical *Diamonds Are Forever*. And yet, and yet, is *On Her Majesty's Secret Service* perhaps a great film?

The obvious and impossible problem is George Lazenby's playing Bond, at which he is terrible. There is a sort of consensus that if at some point a time machine were invented, the first order of business would be to whisk an emissary back to

1914 and suggest Franz Ferdinand visit some more inno-
cently folkloric part of the Habsburg Empire than Sarajevo
that summer. But what if it were better employed going
back to 1968 to send an emissary to plead with Connery to
stay on for one more film and make *On Her Majesty's Secret
Service*, perhaps taking along some production shots of
George Lazenby in a kilt to make clear what was at stake—
and in due course, as a further plea, not to bother to sign up
for *Diamonds Are Forever*? Time-machine issues offer the
usual complications—by definition, of course, there is all
the time in the world to choose which order things would
be rearranged once such a machine existed. And, of course,
there is always the possibility, the strong possibility, because
it is the only rational explanation, that it was some other time
expedition that got Lazenby the job—because in the future
they knew that Connery would have in fact been killed in
one of the skiing sequences. Indeed, so many embassies
from the future may have cluttered this period with their
Bond-related manoeuvrings that they may have accidentally
generated the Summer of Love or a host of other innovations.
In any event.

For me, *On Her Majesty's Secret Service* has always been
an anomaly because I never saw it until I was an adult and so
never fell under its spell, beyond sometimes hearing the hypnotic music (which was played in the cinema as mood music
before any Bond feature began). I have a pathetic memory of
myself on a train station at age eleven being packed off to my
boarding school for a month and staring in despair at the
huge poster for *On Her Majesty's Secret Service*, advertising
its rerelease (with *Diamonds Are Forever*) at our local cinema
the following, utterly unattainable weekend.

When I eventually got round to seeing it in my late teens everything about it seemed tiresome: George Lazenby, of course, but the film's whole existence seemed a weird affront, with its odd, choppy editing, its slow pace—and the fact that it was not a natural element in my own childhood. The film was therefore both itself an illegitimate intruder and I an illegitimate intruder on it. Since then, though, after numerous arguments, I have come through to a hard-won understanding of my error and in a spirit of contrition and remorse have reached the other side. The whole point of hundreds of visits to the National Film Theatre was to understand that a few moments of greatness in a film can redeem us all. Orson Welles' *The Lady from Shanghai*, for example, may be pretty awful, but the shoot-out in the Hall of Mirrors (which occupies only a few seconds) converts it all into gold. Similarly, long patches of *On Her Majesty's Secret Service* (can anyone sit through the safe-cracking scene without feeling that his or her life has taken a wrong turn?) may be unspeakable, but it doesn't matter. Bring together Fleming's atmosphere and story, his hero, one of the great film scores and a brilliant editor/director (Peter Hunt—who had contributed so much to the earlier films), and sometimes things go right. One short scene I can replay over and over: Diana Rigg distracting Telly Savalas by quoting poetry at him intercutting with helicopters flying over the Alps at dawn, and a wondrous, glacial variation on the main theme tune playing. No matter how often I see it, this seems to me everything that film is for: mood, colour, sound, light, a weirdly imagined complete world that for perhaps thirty seconds suspends everything in the pleasures of a great medium at full stretch, attaining something which almost no films ever reach: a Higher Nonsense.

Chapter Eight

AN ACCEPTABLE
LEVEL OF VIOLENCE

WELL, THERE MAY have been more enjoyable years than 1972 to be a child in Britain but I would be hard pressed to come up with one. If you were an adult, or even a faintly politically sentient teenager, it was part of an unfolding House of Horrors, but for my nine-year-old self, happily flicking over miniature plastic soldiers in simulacra of the Dieppe Raid or the storming of Monte Cassino, it was the immortal year of the three-day week and the electricity cuts. An era experienced by adults as one of multiple nadirs meant for me that my father was more frequently at home and that at seemingly random intervals all the power went off to be replaced by beautiful candlelight. The wooden, implausible Conservative prime minister of the period, Edward Heath, has always had an affectionate glow for me because his mishandling of the crisis gave me the pleasures of candles on the mantelpiece and an oil-burning storm lantern. There was probably no right way to handle it—effectively the entire country was flying to pieces with a million unemployed, grinding, terrible inflation and despairing demands for wage increases of in some cases almost 50 per cent, both because so many people were so poor and to keep some sort of pace with inflation. It is surprising in a way that politicians did not simply throw in the towel, and it is a striking comment on the stability of Britain's institutions that in the following few years there was no military coup.

This magical, fairyland atmosphere enjoyed by children had a pretty limited non-infant circle of fans, as 1972 was also the year when it became quite clear that Northern Ireland was out of control. Any attempt to explain the fighting in Ulster will come unstuck, with some idle assumption betraying a distorting prejudice of one kind or another. What now seems very clear however is that Ulster was in effect the last phase of Britain's imperial dismemberment. The settlement of Ireland by the Protestant Scottish and English had been the first and one of the most wholeheartedly brutal epics of the Empire and it was therefore both appropriate and inevitable that it would also end there. The contemporary horrors of Rhodesia and its tightening civil war were always resolvable by the patently idiotic status of the white community, many of whom had only recently arrived and all of whom were in effect just squatters with guns: the withdrawal of British imperial power, money and philosophy left them completely beached, albeit many miles inland. The horrors of Uganda in the same year, when some 27,000 Asians living there were forcibly expelled to Britain by the terrible Idi Amin, were more painful as so many of those Asians, two or three generations back, had been semi-forcibly moved there by Britain as indentured labour: their plight was the same as that of the white Rhodesians but with far more of a sense of absolute post-imperial tragedy. The situation in South Africa, however much it had been stoked by imperial policy, had at least, through cunning and cowardice, been "indigenized" by Britain and was no longer Britain's responsibility (except, ummm, in moral and historical terms).

Ulster, though, was completely intractable: a Protestant community so old and so set in its patterns of privilege and exploitation that no faintly reasonable solution could be found. The fiendishly hard negotiations of the early 1920s that had seen the mainly Catholic south become an independent republic and a small northeastern rump remain British had, while satisfying nobody, seemed to hold together more or less until the late 1960s. But by remaining in the United Kingdom, Ulster had to share the same horrors—mounting unemployment, a loss of pride, a loss of economic vigour, a despairing, radical unionization—and its own unique retreat into virulent sectarianism. The final great imperial disaster was played out in pitiless bombing campaigns across Northern Ireland, occasionally spilling into England.

The 1970s in Britain came to be exemplified by endless grim television news pictures of soldiers, burnt-out cars, smashed shop windows and funerals, both British and Irish. We were all filled with a near universal murderous hatred of the IRA, but this was part of a long tradition of murderous hatred. The same newspapers had urged the British essentially to go into a sort of berserker frenzy of imperial repression in the 1930s in the fight against the satanic "Mad Mullah" on the Indian Northwest Frontier or against the equally satanic Haj Amin al-Hussaini in Palestine, criminal mastermind behind the Arab Revolt. In the 1940s, once the War was over, we all hated evil Jewish terrorists or appalling Burmese nationalists, who had made a mockery of British sacrifice in fighting the Japanese. The 1950s were spent urging the secret execution of tremendous numbers of troublemakers, from the atrocious

Mossadeq in Iran to Archbishop Makarios in Cyprus to Jomo Kenyatta (the Mau-Mau Prince of Darkness) in Kenya to Gamal Abdul Nasser himself, the spider at the heart of the web. All of these men, and many others, were viewed as mentally unstable murderers with their strings pulled by Moscow, which now seems a bit strange, to say the least.

Hate figures had thinned out a bit by the end of the 1960s but every *Daily Express*–reading family, such as my own, knew exactly what to make of the IRA. This is not to say that their hideous actions should not have been condemned, but from this distance it does seem to be part of the ongoing disposal of the old imperial state rather than something new or uniquely unacceptable. The tragedy of Ulster lay in the way that, unlike in all the other cases, Britain could not simply duck out when things got rough. Unlike in the Irish Republic—where quite small numbers of remaining Protestants had been ruthlessly chased out years before—there was no solution beyond the sort of vast mass movements of people seen in Algeria in the early sixties or in Angola in the mid-seventies. The dynamics of the United Kingdom and the profound roots of the Protestants never made that seem a plausible option. But put in its place a generation of savage fighting and gangsterism which took decades to wind down was ultimately set to be viewed, in Thatcher's phrase, as "an acceptable level of violence": once again, as with all the previous terrorists, Britain wound up, after many years of tough talk, shootings and human rights abuse, making a deal.

It was striking then but it seems even more so now that one of the most disturbing facets of IRA power was its strongly informed historical dimension—its sense that it was Britain that had done such damage over the centuries, a view received with incredulity or anger by most British people but seen as almost banally true and obvious in many parts of the world. Dialectically this was to be played out in many acutely managed symbolic-historic bombings—perhaps most startlingly in the murders of Lord Mountbatten, the living embodiment of heroic Late Empire, and Airey Neave, an adviser to Thatcher but nationally famous as a *beau idéal* British officer, who had repeatedly tried to escape from the Nazi super-camp for POWs at Colditz castle. And so, in an outcome that would have seemed wonky fantasy only thirty years before, two exemplary figures from the old, now near-vanished Britain met terrible ends at the hands of the Empire's scruffy bin-end.

It was therefore a Britain with its news programmes crammed with bombings, mass strikes, unemployment and financial ruin that I happily sat in, swinging my legs, enjoying the candles' intimate light, reading comics, picking my nose, little realizing that 1973 would bring me face to face (together with millions of traumatized British adults) with the faltering majesty of *Live and Let Die*.

GROWING UP we knew all the principal actors in the Bond films and—operating from childhood's restricted base—I always assumed that they were rather remarkable people. Yaphet Kotto, aside from having a great name, was an actor I loved in *Live and Let Die* and it was always a bit of a surprise to me that he did not follow it up much. I even sat through the daft *Raid on Entebbe* because he was in the cast, but he then rather fell from view with the towering exception of *Blue Collar*. Gert Fröbe was another giant who seemed oddly absent from other films—except as a Nazi in a catastrophic Terence Young–directed movie, *Triple Cross*. And

Joseph Wiseman? Even a completist could not find much further earlier or later than *Dr. No* to watch with him in it. Ilse
Steppat? Richard Loo? Rik van Nutter? Adolfo Celi? If you
can follow these people's pleasurably marginal careers you are
an even sadder figure than I.

The reason, of course, that they are in the Bond films is that
they were outside the Hollywood circuit and therefore very
cheap—and sometimes quite excellent, of course—snatched
from Central European theatres or American TV. This
makes some of the Bond films into a sort of Tower of Babel,
a deranged *macedonia di frutta. From Russia with Love*, for
example, features a German playing a Russian, a Mexican a
Turk, an Italian a Russian, a Scotsman an Englishman, a Pole a
Czech, a Hungarian a Bulgar and an Englishman's hands and
an Englishman's voice a criminal maniac of loosely Central
European origin (Blofeld). Gert Fröbe's voice in *Goldfinger*
being dubbed in by an English actor is fairly characteristic
of the sorts of fixes needed when dealing with inexpensive,
non-English-speaking European actors. But in Fröbe's case
this was a decision of genius—so many profoundly enjoyable
lines, immeasurably improved by being rendered in a sort of
German accent that can be fully realized only by an English
actor camping it up.

The idea that these iconic figures were bussed in and spat
out again because they could be had cheap is profoundly
upsetting to any sense of the Bond cult. I used idly to assume
that the actor playing Felix Leiter was different in every film
for symbolic reasons—because it stopped him from becoming
a rival pole of attraction to Bond, albeit at a high continuity
cost (how does Connery keep recognizing him when he loses
height, gains twenty years, turns blond, puts on weight?). But

could it in fact have been just to keep the pay cheques down? No need for contract renegotiations with Rik van Nutter: replace him in the next movie. Once this thought gets lodged, the films rapidly fall apart in a wilderness of budgetary guess-work. Lotte Lenya agreed to a role she perhaps viewed with shame in *From Russia with Love* only because her voice had gone and she needed work; the man playing the gangster could double up as a waiter in the next scene if given a moustache; Donald Pleasance was in a further seven bits of international co-production nonsense in the same year and was beyond indignity; poor Charles Gray, a fine man frantic for work; Christopher Lee swallows his pride, yet again.

Crashing down into a further sub-sub-basement, how-ever, must be the thought that the actors themselves didn't even value their appearance in the films very highly. What for a Bond fan is Joseph Wiseman's isolated peak was for him, perhaps, his isolated trough. Many had vigorous and interest-ing stage and film careers in their own countries and became involved with Bond simply because they were undiscerning or filling time or fancied a trip to Thailand. Roger Moore has happily admitted to not seeing any of the Bond films since he left the role—not, it is fair to say, because they would give him a tremble of memento mori but just because, being an affable, charity-gala kind of guy, he is not interested. But where does this leave fans, flipping tearfully through *Bond on the Run: Inside the Magical World of 007*? The films imply a desirable lifestyle, a way of looking at the world reflected in men's magazines, but what if in practice nobody involved ever "lives the life"—even a tiny bit? Fleming, far from being the cruelly sensual gun-toting masterbrain one might hope for, in practice most enjoyed chatting with golf buddies over a Scotch at his club. What if Gert Fröbe valued only Schiller's *Wallenstein* or put all his energies into collecting small paintings by Paul Klee? (Although Fröbe, mind you, would be on shaky ground here, having destroyed himself in all worlds by appearing in *Chitty Chitty Bang Bang*.) What if Charles Gray felt his best work was in *The Rocky Horror Picture Show*? As the actors jokily chew their cigars in their canvas chairs between takes, laughing at what rubbish it all was, fussing with their make-up and idly wondering about lunch, what is left to us? In the end the motives of anyone involved in making a film are only marginally relevant, if fun to speculate on. The actor's experience of a film is of being surrounded by lights, heaps of wires, people with cups of tea. Their experience of the set includes using their sense of touch, warmth, smell, all the aspects a film screen shuts us out from. They film it in a completely different order, they film things that are dropped, they film against blue screens. They are perhaps bored to tears—or they are chiefly animated by knowing that later that day they are almost sure to have sex with a lighting technician.

In the end all that matters is the performances—and the Bond films contain some great performances. Almost everybody involved in *From Russia with Love* is operating at full tilt and it is a spectacular movie for actors, even in small roles: Lotte Lenya, Pedro Armendáriz, Vladek Sheybal, Anthony Dawson's hands. But above all it is Robert Shaw's almost wordless assassin, biting his gloved finger, stepping back and forth in the shadows, studiously bored, which is the role of redeeming greatness and one that totally justifies an otherwise patchy career. Gert Fröbe in *Goldfinger*, even if dubbed, is unimprovably excellent. Well, to be honest that is about it.

I was going to make some specious claims on behalf of Telly Savalas in *On Her Majesty's Secret Service* or Charles Gray in *You Only Live Twice* but staring at the evidence on screen I simply don't have it in me to fight in their corner.

FROM THE AGE of ten I went to a boarding school in a freezing, dreary part of east Kent. I never established why I was sent there and it was quite possible that my parents, like most of the other parents whose children were at this school, had been misinformed. It was a tiny place with about a hundred boys. There were children of former maharajahs, of Anglo-Argentinian ranchers, of parents in grisly bin-end imperial jobs in the Arabian Gulf.

The entire point of the school was, in its titchy way, to do with Britain as a Great Power. We assembled each morning in a hall lined with photos of head boys and with enormous wooden boards listing the—disturbingly few—winners of scholarships to major—or indeed any old—public schools. There were also panels of War Dead, and the focus of the entire hall was a glass case holding a school presentation Bible found on the corpse of a luckless Old Boy killed in Palestine in 1917. We used to wish that there was a little more to it than this: that a bullet had been stopped by the book—or that there was some proof that it had held him in good stead. Perhaps the book's weight had in fact fatally impeded his movement, struggling over some dune?

Sports and my hatred for them filled hour upon hour. As the rain poured down we would stumble about chasing a football, while the more fine-limbed and tousle-haired boys would enjoy themselves enormously. Only later, of course, could I appreciate the marvellous aquifer of loathing these years were filling for me, inexhaustible and entirely based on being unable to kick a ball accurately.

The dormitories were all named after British heroes—Wellington, Drake, Raleigh and so on—with the tinies starting out in relatively marginal heroes such as Gordon while thirteen-year-olds at the top of the heap lolled in Churchill. Some of the masters I think felt sorry for us and all the staff were clever and thoughtful people who could only have swapped notes on our frightful predicament over their coffee and biscuits. Anyone with even the least tingle of sensitivity would have had grounds for anxiety. Here was a school training its children about empire and pluck, about team sports and clean living, in a country that no longer had much need for it. We were coming off a leadership conveyor-belt straight into a recycling bin.

We were all dimly aware of the comatose endgame of mid-seventies Britain. Idi Amin loomed as a nightmare figure. We heard about Harold Wilson's resignation but were not sure what it meant. What really mattered was endless discussions about sweets, masturbation and James Bond. The first two of this trinity are constants in any time and place but James Bond was our undoubted hero, shaping our games and our dreams. I can hardly believe this is true, but this devotion extended even to elaborate attempts to re-create the opening credits of *The Man with the Golden Gun*. These credits had featured silhouetted nude girls dancing around in front of the usual explosions, synchronized loosely to Lulu's hopeless theme song. These were lovingly re-created with some of the younger boys forced to dance nude on the beds with a powerful torch playing on them as everyone sang along. The torch gave reasonably crisp silhouettes on the wall alongside the big portrait of—I seem to remember—Sir Walter Raleigh, but the suffocating potpourri of motives that went into this tableau means we should probably move on.

The school's imperial flavour implied, as it did in hundreds of other similar tucked-away little homoerotic idylls, something to do with *leadership*. Women and families were not relevant: what mattered was male camaraderie, an elite corps raised in effect in a barracks. Probably the majority of boys in the school had direct colonial links (aside from two American brothers of great charisma, who we all felt even at the age of twelve probably represented the future, with their expansive talk of Disney World and oral sex) or lived in the shadow of such former links. Many boys went on to senior schools such as Haileybury, which had been set up purely to supply recruits to work in India (I wonder what Haileybury's heavily retooled mission statement is these days?). In retrospect, the atmosphere was that of a larval version of some hideous tropical club. This take on the world was summed up for me by a pug-nosed, haughty child looking like a blend of Droopy Dog and a parody Indian Army officer, who once, black with rage, spat at another pupil, "How dare you, how dare you, you, you, you *JEWBOY*." Ah, golden days.

What is so heartbreaking is that the entire structure in which we were drilled had melted a generation before and that in any event, this little school was hardly turning out an SS *Schloss*-style military spearhead, but rather also-rans and bits-and-pieces—the people who, quite good at football and knowing a bit of Latin, would have footled around in cantonments across Africa and Asia, occasionally getting killed, the dim filling of white rule. We may have been told we were future leaders and our dormitories might have been named after heroes but our role was, in the end, just to do as we were told.

In a sense, then, James Bond mattered so much to us because he was the same, albeit in a seemingly terrific way. Far from being a leader and a public inspiration, his job was to do as he was told and to do it secretly: a murderous, priapic civil servant but a civil servant nonetheless—or as Dr. No less kindly put it, "a stupid policeman." The heroes after which our dormitories were named and whose fly-blown images in flimsy frames adorned the walls were nothing if not self-starters (or loonies such as General Gordon, but we knew all about him only later). The hero of Britain's decline was a mere tool, albeit a tool with an enormous expense account and a great deal of luck, wholly reliant on M, Q and the strange failure of his megalomaniac adversaries to shoot him. He seems to be a fantasy of powerfulness, but it is the fantasy of those who themselves have *no* power. Indeed, at the heart of it all it is the secrecy itself that is so powerless. Wellington was out in the open, blew up stacks of Frenchmen, and got made prime minister for it. In the era of James Bond only backstairs furtiveness, however jauntily handled, is possible. We all adored that secrecy and now it seems more poignant than ever. As we lay there, organizing dubious living tableaux, reading *Live and Let Die*, hearing about the snow-blower in *On Her Majesty's Secret Service* which squirted out blood and with no idea that our Swedish drill, cross-country running, Latin grammar and marks awarded for most crisply made beds had had *no* bearing on British society for at least a generation.

THE BOND FILMS accompanied Britain through terrible times and provided huge and delusive comfort, a comfort accentuated by the near disappearance of the British film industry, putting an almost intolerable weight on Roger Moore's safari-suited shoulders. As one of the handful of British actors remaining on cinema screens (setting aside, perhaps wrongly, the casts of *Carry on Dick* and *Confessions of a Window Cleaner*), his sleep-walking woodenness is fraught with a lack of self-belief, and barely suppressed panic. Each of the Moore films is an achingly implausible attempt to pretend that nothing is wrong. In scene after scene, as he seduces Egyptian girls or quips with CIA operatives or faces off against remorseless Indian industrialists, the tension is almost intolerable—will they or won't they all just start laughing at him? At his clothes? At his country? Will they deride the wonky, poorly engineered little gadgets that the senescent Q slips into Bond's incompetently stitched coat pocket? Will whole streets of extras collapse into gales of cruel laughter as his Lotus Esprit pops and burps along with Moore gripping the wheel, looking grimly ahead and praying the engine doesn't catch fire? Perhaps (and this is a recurrent fantasy of mine) the soundtrack itself would go wrong, the orchestral texture becoming, as the movie progresses, ever thinner and more eccentric as the players one by one simply leave the recording studio in protest at the whole shameful business? Could the grand finale then consist of Moore opening fire on the usual dozens of boiler-suited security guards, but who would now be openly laughing, prat-falling, belching and mooning and all accompanied by a chalky, out-of-tune school piano?

Indeed, by the late 1970s, unless he followed a patriotic and indeed actively dangerous consumer policy, James Bond would have substantially worn, watched, driven, used, flown in, sported, fired and lit only foreign things. It is outside the scope of this book to discuss the painful way that Britain rebuilt itself in the 1980s—a process so recent that its success or failure is still too hard to engage with. But what *is* certain is that by the 1970s a particular kind of country had vanished completely, taking with it, like the *Titanic* (onetime pride of Belfast shipbuilding), a tremendous number of passengers. Whole communities based around coal mining or cotton or shipbuilding simply gone. Together with them went the illusory hopes of the many thousands of South Asian or West Indian immigrants enticed in by the Macmillan government at a time of full employment—all chucked on the same awe-inspiring slagheap of some three million jobless only twenty-five years later. These industries ended for many reasons but at the heart of it was the "decompression" from Britain's global role having come to an end. It is both conventional and correct to point to the suffering imposed by Britain's decolonization on peoples around the world, but the final lashings out of a dying system left plenty of victims at home, too. Like one of the artworks by Jean Tinguely which were popular at the time, complex, anarchic machines which noisily destroyed themselves, so Britain, before the eyes of the world, ripped itself apart.

Many of these victims continued to watch the 1970s Bond films. I usually just feel angry and defensive about these films—*Live and Let Die*, *The Man with the Golden Gun*, *The Spy Who Loved Me*, *Moonraker*—because this was the high noon of my own childhood fascination with Bond and because these films are so palpably bad. But in the context of looking at what life was like for adults in Britain in this period they take on a terrible poignancy. Roger Moore really is the last man standing, surrounded by the same trusty but now startlingly old gang of regulars (Bernard Lee, Desmond Llewelyn, Lois Maxwell) in an ever more quixotic attempt to save a world now merely appalled by or indifferent to Britain's fate. The affection and value of James Bond was still felt by huge audiences—but there is a feeling watching these films now that they must have been watched almost as a patriotic duty. As one perceptive critic of the *Carry On* films said: "They may be rubbish, but by God they're British rubbish." Champagne glasses clink, people are pushed off buildings, formerly well-respected actors—scarlet with shame below layers of pancake make-up—deliver their lines, there are car chases in a variety of countries. But none of it is interesting, sexy or diverting—at their best they are like a travelogue and the viewer can at least look at the textures of walls, roofs, passers-by, glimpses of the sea.

Some years ago there was a very successful children's board book called *Spot's Noisy Walk*, in which Spot (a little dog) visits his farmyard friends. Each page had a button to press that activated a farmyard sound matching the picture on the page: an oinking pig or a tractor's engine starting. The Roger Moore films—and indeed the Dalton and Brosnan films—have a similar air, and some publisher ought perhaps to bring out *Bond's Noisy Walk*, in which Bond, drawn in simple, bright colours, goes to a casino, has sex with someone, shoots a foreigner and so on, all with the right noise buttons (*"Neuf à la banque,"* "Oh, James," "Bang").

AT ABOUT AGE seventeen, I sat in class next to an enterprising boy whose weary dislike of all the lessons and all the teachers I found invigorating and surprising. He went on to become a journalist for various magazines and I have not seen him since we left school. Flicking idly through a glossy magazine the other week I was glancing at photos in the "About our contributors" section when I froze. There was this same boy—but since we last met he seemed to have suffered from some disfiguring illness which had sloughed away much of his face and hair, like a science-fiction mutant hit by a napalm strike just for good measure. I at first felt overcome by a sense of how brave he was to have his picture taken and how we can all learn from this. This sense then got hijacked by thinking that he looked like one of those once-evil-but-now-good aliens in movies, who stay behind, pulling with their decaying fingers the lever that destroys both the evil spaceship and themselves while giving their new friends just time to get clear. "For God's sake save yourselves; I'm finished anyway," and so on. This shameful interlude was followed by realizing that nothing had happened to him at all: that he simply looked like anyone in his forties. In fact, he looked pretty much like me—a far cry from the tubby yet alluring hopeful of the late seventies.

James Bond may not look much like Peter Pan but they both in effect fight Captain Hook, and they both must always remain the same age. Peter Pan shows if anything more career development, as while he may not grow older, he does decisively see off Hook, while Bond's enemies must always bob up again, Hydra-like, under a new name. In the books it is deliberately never quite apparent what age Bond is: clearly it is an impossible age—an attempt to fluctuate between different dates which both allow him a depth of experience in the Second World War but do not make him superannuated by the late fifties. If his age is on hold then so is his level of experience—he is never notably more skilled (beyond a single pistol upgrade) in the next adventure over the previous one—until his marriage, his wife's murder, his mission of revenge and his brainwashing in the final three novels. Indeed, a substantial part of the frustration with the final books lies in this botched sense of development—that the character does not have sufficient pit-props to carry the ceiling made up of such ideas as, for instance, a developing character or greater maturity. How much more appealing and reassuring he is when, like a hamster with his wheel, he performs the same narrow set of functions over and over—the scenario, the seduction, the foiling of the plot, the killing of the villains. Bond then is someone we can cling to both in the books and the films because he is not subject to age and change. In the end Fleming veered away from the consistency imposed by the inventors of Biggles and Sherlock Holmes simply from his own boredom and irritation, and this was a mistake.

The filmmakers have been more consistent—Bond never learns anything: he ought to be a squalid, scar-caked debauchee in psychiatric care three or four movies in, but mercifully he is not. We are spared the six-ton doughnut-munching burn-out staring at daytime television and refusing to answer the phone. The plotlines keep him the same age, but we must nonetheless live out the actors' tragedies of real time passing with them on screen. The feral, just right Connery of *Thunderball* (1965) becomes the querulous fatty of *You Only Live Twice* (1967) and then the frankly seedy figure of *Diamonds Are Forever* (1971). One of the shocks, one of the many shocks, of watching *Live and Let Die* (1973) is to see Roger Moore exactly *à point*: reasonable figure, likeable face, bright eyes, good teeth, a very good Bond, in fact, in a bad film. What we all remember now though is the Bond of

A View to a Kill (1985), in which he looks like some burst-open yogurt found at the back of the fridge.

I have not talked about Timothy Dalton at all in this book because there seems to be nothing to say—but in this context it *is* worth saying that he appears to be about the right age for the role. The same applied initially to Pierce Brosnan, although it must have been obvious to all that his contract was up after the ill-judged scene in *Die Another Day* when he walks across a hotel lobby in a soaking wet shirt: suddenly his torso implies a nasty decrepitude, only too apparently non-threatening to villains and spine-crawling to young women; a poor combination.

This struggle to maintain Bond at the right age is rather moving and an interesting side effect of the phenomenon's longevity. He has seen off generations of now dead fans but still he smiles back.

I WAS ONCE walking through Greenwich Village when a white limo whispered up to the curb, the rear door opened and the tiny figure of Hervé Villechaize stepped out, or rather alighted, onto the pavement to the chorus that must have unvaryingly greeted him: "Jesus! It's Hervé Villechaize," and "De plane! De plane!" Poor Villechaize came to a sad end but for years he was famous in a very provisional and asterisked way as the fiendish sidekick Nick Nack in *The Man with the Golden Gun* and then in the long-running TV oddity *Fantasy Island*, in which his job was to say, as the plane filled with the island's visitors came into sight, "De plane! De plane!"

There is an argument for saying that this entire book is a junk-food, short-attention-span version of *The Anatomy of Melancholy*, but if there is to be only one area where we really should all start blubbing at once about the leaky little pedal-boat that is human life then it must be in meditating on those casually caught up in the Bond machinery.

Entire books can be written about the oddness of, for example, hereditary monarchy: the process by which through accident of birth some nitwit finds himself in charge of palaces, warfare and so on. Something of the same arbitrary cuffs of fate can be found in figures such as Villechaize. This remarkably small man was given the role of villain's sidekick in *The Man with the Golden Gun* solely in order to offer a witless contrast to the black giant who had been the villain's sidekick in the previous film. And so his whole life changed. Nick Nack himself is such an offensive concept that viewers simply stare at the screen waiting for it all to stop (for a moment there I was going to say that a midget villain is simply too implausible, but the films are clearly now way beyond such nice distinctions). Nick Nack's final attempt to kill Bond is thwarted in a climactic chase around a ship's cabin with Bond hitting him with a chair, popping him into a suitcase and hauling it up into the rigging, followed by the film's closing credits and the dejected audience stumbling from the cinema. Interestingly, well slightly interestingly, Nick Nack is left alive—not crushed or boiled or fried up as is traditional. The writers must have felt that in the end a tiny, almost helpless bad guy was quite awful enough as an idea and that it would be the final excrement-found-in-the-salad to witness his killing on top of it all.

All discussions of *The Man with the Golden Gun* are acutely embarrassing because in truth this was the film that, at the time of its release, found me as the purest flame among Bond's adherents. I sat through it as someone at the feet of some yogi or sage: an eleven-year-old acolyte. Compared to the experience of this film, all that has followed has been mere weary cynicism and havering.

One of the truly horrible scenes in this movie features the eponymous assassin's lair, where he practises his skills by inviting in other gunmen who, for a huge fee, hope to kill him, or themselves be killed. A sort of hall of mirrors under the control of Nick Nack is set up and filled with strange traps. Annoyingly, just to write about it is to make it more interesting than the thing itself, which is not for a moment plausible or enjoyable. I feel almost angry at my eleven-year-old self for watching this, swinging my little legs back and forth. A friend and I spent a happy summer at his house reconstructing the hall of mirrors scenes. We would stalk around allowing our faces to be distorted by a fishbowl (containing two fish, Bit and Bot), disorientate ourselves with a strobe (well, turning on and off the sitting-room light), creep past a mildly erotic Javanese sculpture in the hallway and then: the sickening finale as the one elected to be the Man with the Golden Gun would swing round in one of those big black swivel chairs favoured around 1974 to gun down his helpless stalker.

These Toytown renderings of a weary film allied to extensive reading of the books provoked this friend, Andy, and me to write several Bond novels each. I can hardly remember their details now, beyond one called *The Blucher Conspiracy* and another called *All That Glitters Is Not Gold* (after an intensive afternoon leafing through the Book of Psalms for inspiration: how could I have been so irritating as to know even at that age that the Bible was the best source for sonorous yet daft book titles?). It is possible that these books' "lost" status could be reversed with some lucky attic find one day, but I sincerely hope not. There are dim memories of a cobra pit with Bond cleverly waiting until enough of the snakes' weaving heads line up for them all to be shot in a single go. There was certainly no sex and no plot development. Perhaps if one of these books were to be found it would read as a sort of super-condensed, wholly unreflexive essence of Bond: a collection of the genuine salient absurdities free of later rationalizing and pretentiousness. But perhaps not.

DESPITE BOND's being a global traveller, both in the books and the films, his itineraries are in practice rather narrow. The early films are about elite tourism (Istanbul, the Bahamas) because so few people travelled at all, but in the seventies mass tourism flexed its muscles and the films pointed the way. Oddly the film with the feeblest voltage, *The Man with the Golden Gun*, had the most impact, effectively introducing much of the world to Thailand, a country which had barely featured in people's minds until then. *The Spy Who Loved Me* is packed with straightforward tourist shots of the Alps, the Pyramids and so on and, because of Moore's increasingly patriarchal appearance, implies that such destinations are readily accessible even to older relatives. But it is interesting to see where Bond *doesn't* go—never to black Africa, never to South America (beyond a Rio scene in *Moonraker* so pitiful that it hardly counts as location shooting), as these continents are a shorthand in viewers' minds for poverty, not luxury and, like some highly specialized insect or flower, Bond cannot survive without an emperor-size bed and smirking bar staff. Mexico sneaks in (or a small bundle of clichés loosely approximating to Mexico) because it provided financial backing for *License to Kill*. Any environment that sets off hygiene, disease or deprivation issues in the audience's mind will have the filmmaker running thousands of miles.

In this context it is very odd that Bond hasn't visited Australia. He couldn't in the books, as it was too far away (Japan was an amazing, implausible stretch in the books—otherwise Fleming never sends his hero east of Istanbul, west of Las Vegas, north of Berlin or south of Jamaica, beyond fragmentary and scarcely visualized little outings to Sierra Leone and the Seychelles). This is particularly odd on the face of it, for some of the more traditional aspects of white Australia would seem to appeal to Bond. But of course Bond can only travel to places which are a shorthand for glamour and criminality. Only very recently could Australia rustle up a bit of the former and crime (let alone super-crime) forms no part of its cliché. It is possible to imagine a catastrophic Bond film in which he settles in a beach house outside Perth, chats with his neighbours, goes to the shops, comments on how friendly everyone is and has a nice cold drink around six o'clock—such a film would become hard going after the first ten minutes or so (with the pre-credit sequence perhaps entirely taken up with Bond fussing over the menu in a gorgeous seafood restaurant?).

Australia is therefore off limits for Bond—it is simply impossible in the popular imagination to think of Australians as mean, and it would be upsetting to see Bond shooting such genial people, however macabre in practice their country's origin may be. There are also, of course, of course, more sinisterly racial issues. Bond is simply far better at killing people with darker skin or who are ethnic/outsider in some other way. This is choice even when he is in the United States, fighting for choice black people (*Live and Let Die*), gay people (*Diamonds Are Forever*) or Southern crackers (*License to Kill*), who in the books too form a sort of sub-species. This resolves a central problem: if Bond were up against, say, a fit Canadian, he would have no visual advantage—there is no reason on earth why a safari-suited Roger Moore should defeat anyone. What the films need to do, therefore, is allow the white viewer to draw on a vast file of unpleasant thoughts which make Mexicans (*Goldfinger*) squalid and impulsive, Japanese (*You Only Live Twice*) immune to pain and fanatical, Russians (*The World Is Not Enough*) unstably treacherous, terrible shots and so on. It is implied that they die because of these traits and on the very rare occasions when Bond is straightforwardly fighting unmediated (un-gay, un–Deep South) white people there is a confusing air of race transgression. This is clear in his handling of the rather glum Swiss people in orange ski suits in *On Her Majesty's Secret Service*—perhaps the only Swiss people to die violently in nearly two centuries. This is also, incidentally, another good example of Bond lashing out at current British obsessions—with the currency speculations that ruined its economy blamed by Wilson on the financial machinations of Swiss bankers, "the gnomes of Zurich," there must have been a lot of pleasure in seeing a Swiss heavy impaled by Diana Rigg on a piece of modernist sculpture.

Bond's theoretical Australian or Canadian opponent would also have a background of such tremendous and unthinking state-backed prosperity that Bond would be punching someone whom viewers would immediately equate with pension plans, sports interests and a healthy young family. Hordes of crazy ninjas, Korean security guards, Spetznaz psychos, sword-wielding Sikhs, etc., may all equally be in their line of work to support aspirational families in modest comfort in some liveable suburb, but culture, history and thousands of films have all conspired to make their deaths appear acceptable, indeed inevitable.

Of course, omnivorous national stereotyping soaks all the Bond films. When in the last Bond film, *Die Another Day*, Bond goes to North Korea, the audience can relax, knowing that this is a sort of shorthand for unspeakable cruelty, carelessness with human life and enjoyment of torture: how pleasurable to find the entire population complying so energetically. Indeed, in the space of about ten minutes the North Koreans *do only* what they are meant to do—lash out crazily—rather than what they really spend most of the time doing, glumly digging around the shelves of poorly stocked supermarkets while listening to piped martial music.

THE WHOLE PROCESS by which we watch filmed simulacra of killing, however stylized, is something that has vexed some viewers since film was invented. Our whole relationship with murder, like our whole relationship with sex, has been changed so totally by film that it could at least be argued that nothing else in the twentieth century is as startling. These endlessly fascinating issues around film—about the nature of the viewer's gaze, about film's shaping and transforming role within societies and so on—apply to Bond in curiously pure ways. The idea that almost all forms of human intimacy were private—or at least as private as possible within the confines of, say, a small encampment or an overcrowded tenement—is so completely basic to how we used to see ourselves that the switched assumptions in seeing intimacy enacted on a vast screen are bewildering.

If murder is the most extreme and terrible form of intimacy then its happy embrace by movies marks a really odd change.

Someone reading about the Jack the Ripper murders in the 1880s, say, would have encountered them through highly censored, stylized printed accounts or in stage melodramas which, however chilling, had a static, distanced relationship with their audiences. If that someone had been in his twenties at the time of the murders he would only have to be in his sixties to see the astoundingly strange, unnerving Jack the Ripper finale to Pabst's silent masterpiece *Pandora's Box*, in which Louise Brooks's murder is handled in a way that makes the audience almost seem appallingly complicit in a sexual nightmare. Clearly some massive if almost indefinable boundary has been crossed.

The killings in the Bond films are of course closer in spirit to stage melodrama than to Pabst's hysterical claustrophobia. The films are also finely balanced between making the killings graphic and believable and securing a family-based film rating. Like a figure leaping and raging in a straitjacket each Bond film yearns to be nastier, cries out to be more salacious, but in the end the camera always turns itself away from the action on the viewer's behalf—no falling figure is ever shown impacting, no flesh and bone fly through the air: just as every embrace about to get genital provokes a slow fade and saxophone music.

Clearly as the films have been wearyingly churned out, the issue of how to kill people has vexed the scriptwriters more and more. Like someone hogging and cramming himself at an extravagant buffet, the first films gorge on the most exciting and obvious ways to kill people—they are electrocuted, harpooned, strangled, slurped out of jet windows, eaten by sharks (of course). The sense of despair on this front is shown even by the fifth film, *You Only Live Twice*, where several of the methods of death show a growing panic, most strikingly a lamentably under-realized piranha pool: the unseen, finny killers are rendered as less than satisfying little green bubbles. This question has impossibly undermined all the later films—they are doomed by their need not to repeat what has gone before, and the splendid deaths of the early films shut off any question of reusing—except in a perfunctory and sheepish way—a harpoon gun, say. By the time the films are setting up ever more absurd scenarios to justify villains falling into rock-crushing machinery or down industrial chimneys or being torn to bits by a weird drill-like gadget, it is impossible not to sit there in mute contempt for what is unfolding on the screen. Like the tubby, jaded audience at a Roman gladiatorial gross-out with steel-shod giraffes fighting coelacanths or whatever, we can simply be impressed no longer. But, like that audience, we are too fat and battered to move. When a giant ice chandelier landed on top of a bad guy in *Die Another Day*, the bad guy having been tricked by Bond's—for goodness' sake—invisible car, people should have torn up their seats and flung them at the screen, but instead they stayed and will no doubt, as I will, attend the next Bond film. At least, in fairness, North Koreans being crushed by ice chandeliers was something new.

THERE IS A cosiness about the formulae of the Bond films that has given them for many years now an attractive, narcotic quality. The formulae mean that each film is taken up with almost mantra-like elements: seeing aeroplanes landing and the Bond theme tune striking up, the chit-chat with Moneypenny and her successors, the session with Q, Bond's initial sexual partner being killed in some appalling way. These became through the 1970s the equivalent of idly watching a cricket match ("Oh look—she's been shot by a gun hidden inside a scarecrow!"), a British ritual on a par with reading about the activities of the royal family or buying Genesis albums. The excitement of the initial films was long gone, but it was impossible *not* to go to the predictable range of thrills laid out for our pleasure every two years.

This became less sustainable as Roger Moore became ever odder looking in the part and the filmmakers clearly rather lost interest, as it was inevitable they would. Looking back I feel like a decent, long-term member of some cosy, traditionalist church who attends year in year out, turning an ever more wilfully blind eye to what is going on at the altar. From *Moonraker* onwards the church analogy implies carrying on sitting in humble prayerfulness while the vicar hauls in rare animals to sacrifice and defecates, gibbering, on the altar. Looking back: when did I completely lose my self-respect? I would guess with the speedboat gondolas in *Moonraker*. But I was happy enough at the time and have still watched each new one on its release so, as with all self-esteem issues, it becomes really almost impossible to pinpoint the exact moment when it would have been best to have walked out.

But what did the rest of the world see in these films? Their global popularity is in many ways a complete mystery. Indeed, given how over time the films manage to patronize and offend much of the planet it is amazing that they are not more publicly condemned. Their success in America seems straightforward enough: they are viewed as comedies of self-delusion. When at the Cold War summit meeting in *You Only Live Twice* the British representative pooh-poohs Soviet and American anger over their rockets being hijacked, claiming that Britain's own secret service was on the job, American audiences must have roared with happy laughter: by 1967 *the*

British wouldn't even have been invited! The beautiful tension between Bond's swaggering around with Felix Leiter and the reality, that the CIA had thousands of better-trained, home-grown, properly equipped, less wonkily priapic agents of their own to draw on, makes Bond a figure to trump even Inspector Clouseau in America's pantheon of amusing British imports.

For non-American and non-British audiences, however, what can the films offer? Given what Britain has done to much of the world in recent centuries, for many audiences watching Bond movies must have the same pleasure as a rectal probe. The honest old Spanish patriot in his favourite armchair at home, tears pouring down his face as his heartbroken sons pin down his convulsing form, beyond all anger at the smirking Gibraltar shenanigans in *The Living Daylights*. Some fine-featured Indian nationalist propped up in his sickbed to watch *Octopussy* and, seeing his entire culture witlessly lampooned, simply turning to the wall and dying. The uncontrollable waves of nausea and massed hissings in the world's cinemas in almost any conceivable time zone whenever Big Ben chimes and there is the traditional long shot of Whitehall. Are there in fact respliced variants of the films, discreetly removing all the scenes offensive to specific cultures? Or—better—perhaps even stopping the films at the point where the evil criminal genius appears triumphant? Are there crude (or now perhaps not so crude) reedits with additional material to show Bond tripping up, collapsing in a cowardly heap, suffering some erotic dysfunction? Is there a two-minute version of *Moonraker* where in the opening scene Bond jumps out of the plane, fails to snatch the parachute and simply jellifies on landing, accompanied by cinematic ovations not seen since *Rock*

Around the Clock? It would almost be a lack of initiative *not* to do such drastic pirate reedits, playing to packed, smoke-filled houses, menfolk gesticulating obscenely at the screen: "This murderer, this drunkard, this sexual butterfingers, this *Englishman*."

So many of the signs and symbols in the Bond films which we find reinforcing and rather lovely—the effortless ability to master languages, cultures and womenfolk—must in other contexts act as a virtual Radical Islam recruiting poster. Indeed this, in conjunction with the gross materialism, the palpable sense of spiritual failure, the workaday profanity and contempt for human life—particularly differently coloured human life—may ultimately prove to be the Bond films' most lasting legacy. Bond's enormous, grossly sybaritic Las Vegas hotel room in *Diamonds Are Forever* alone should goad even the most backsliding madrasa student to feel insulted. What is it about a society that produces such films and such values?

James Bond can exist only *because* he is British. No other country has developed an ideology over so many years that makes every other nation so available, so pitiful and funny. This has come from either ruling them or attacking them at various points. This pitiful *and* funny is important: it shares with the United States the deep-seated feeling that everyone else's cultural, economic and social histories are "wrong" by numerous criteria, but Britain is unique in also finding those histories simply uproarious. The world is a mass of accents, foods, bottom shapes, moustaches and gestures there to be laughed at but also enjoyed. There are no barriers of dialect or custom which Bond cannot jump: he is as at home in a gypsy camp as in a Jamaican rum shack, in the Florida everglades as in a sumo arena, in a Greek monastery as in a maharajah's palace. All hilarious, all enjoyable. This would simply not be plausible if Bond were Italian, say, or Chinese or Mexican. Of course, it is completely absurd anyway, but the British genuinely see the world as something over which they have proprietary control: the world is simply an enormous outdoor estate for its owner to wander around.

As I have tried to show in this book by matching Bond's actions with Britain's global behaviour there is an absolute sense of superiority for both which in its practical implications we have spent the past sixty or seventy years dismantling (or rather having dismantled for us). But Bond continues (with the Queen) as a fossil remnant of something that has been otherwise beaten out. The Queen must presumably spend some part of each day moping about how her dad had been King-Emperor, had the allegiance of a quarter of the planet and had been treated in some quarters as a god, whereas *she* has to wander around the streets expressing interest in the lives of ladies holding plastic flags with ice cream dripping down their fronts. Bond shows no such introspection or reskilling. It is a very odd aspect of contemporary Britain that a country which is almost unrecognizable from the one which nurtured Fleming (aside, of course, from the occasional survival, such as a seemingly unstoppable urge to despoil Iraq) should still, for so much of the world, remain the country of James Bond.

It is worth taking one final look at a James Bond film: *The Spy Who Loved Me*, which premiered in 1977. As a cultural artefact it is dead on the slab, but the Britain in which it opened and dominated the box office all summer was a truly terrible place. The one scene for which the movie is now remembered, when Bond skies off over a precipice with a parachute sporting a huge Union Jack, must surely have provoked some incredulous laughter at the time. Or perhaps just respectful surprise that the Union Jack didn't fall apart, plunging Bond to his doom?

The previous year had seen the resignation of an exhausted and ill Harold Wilson. His successor, James Callaghan, a traditional Labour Party bruiser and fixer, had to deal immediately with horrific financial disasters. This was the point where Britain appeared on the verge of imploding. Every country had had to deal with the amazing blow of quadrupled oil prices, but in Britain this fed into a tornado of nightmares: enormous inflation, mounting unemployment and a completely overwhelming sense that the United Kingdom was a country with no future. Callaghan himself came up with the unhelpful joke to his government colleagues "If I were a young man I would emigrate," thereby effortlessly bringing together a number of themes, the fundamental one of course being that there was nowhere anymore for British people to emigrate to. The enormous IMF loan of 1976 rescued Britain from financial meltdown but it was itself an overwhelming critique of what Britain had become: a country teetering on the brink of becoming another Argentina, a ruin surrounded by tatters of former glory. At the time it seemed that it was the mass strikes that were the problem, but now they seem much more of a symptom—a scream for help from people whose wages were being destroyed by inflation, working in a range of industries hanging on by their fingernails. This friendlessness, despair, lack of plans, the hideous sense of the country ripping itself to pieces (quite literally with the relentless shower of IRA bombs thrown into the mix) makes this period depressing beyond measure.

Some odd signs later could be seen as pointing to the future, though. One of the major destabilizing issues remained the colossal debts Britain still had from the Second World War, which had been squirreled away in various colonies that now—as very much ex-colonies—speculated in those debts, making sterling crazily unstable. The IMF loan at last wound up this issue, and thus ended the last big and tangible link with the War and with the Empire.

The summer that saw *The Spy Who Loved Me* also saw the far, far larger event of the arrival of *Star Wars*. I think it is incontrovertible to say that at the time for every boy in the country this amazing film simply blew to pieces the entire war-obsessed hangover—the generations of children who had relentlessly re-created the Battle of El Alamein or built minutely detailed models of the *Bismarck* suddenly stopped. The Afrika Korps lay neglected in their box as everyone started practising Darth Vader breathing noises. The minutely detailed Lego rendering of a Berlin flak tower was overnight smashed up and reassembled as the Death Star.

Even as a fourteen-year-old fan I sat dutifully through *The Spy Who Loved Me* but jumped with delight at *Star Wars*. We were there at the birth of the modern, globalized Hollywood blockbuster and just loved it. Britain did not yet actively participate in the future implied by the selling and marketing of *Star Wars*, but the IMF deal fixed and closed down part of the past. *Star Wars* (and is it possible to imagine a film more remote from the values and experience of, say, James Callaghan?) was a pointer towards a strange and new planet.

As an already rather puffy and decayed Roger Moore rescued the world, as usual, this time from Curd Jürgens' fish-obsessive maniac, James Bond had reached the outer limit of his reassuring, restorative role in his nation's life. He could comfort Britain for the loss of empire and status in the fifties, he could comfort Britain for the loss of its remaining prestige and the collapse of its industries in the sixties, he could offer a poignant and daft counterpoint to the early seventies, but nobody could do much for the utterly ruinous late seventies. As Roger Moore lies in the arms of Ringo Starr's future wife (oddly), *The Spy Who Loved Me* appears to be one of those stories which turn out at the end to have been a fantasy in the mind of a criminal lunatic or someone about to be executed. It seems wholly appropriate then that it should have been followed by *Moonraker*, a painful bid to trump *Star Wars* with Moore heading off into outer space, taking with him both the cultural icon created by Fleming twenty-five years before, and an entire national history now, mercifully, wound up.

Conclusion

TWO WALKS

MOST DAYS I have the doubtful privilege of walking across London's Covent Garden. This used to be the city's fruit-and-vegetable market but after all the fruit and vegetables left it was converted into a setting for a clump of depressing shops. Its great role in the capital's life now is as a meeting place for tourists—tourists who in countless European cities and towns drift, almost helplessly, towards any windswept open area which can provide a sense of being at the heart of things. London's lack of a clearly defined heart really upsets people, even to the point where they risk the psittacosis-laden nightmare of Trafalgar Square—or the in many ways even worse Covent Garden.

Not the least problem with Covent Garden is its being filled up with surely Europe's lowest-self-esteem street performers. There must be a pecking order in everything, and just as a superb Italian pastry cook will find work in Milan, a less good one will get work in New York, a rather hopeless one will gravitate to Berlin and a flailing, tear-stained, disaster area will slink into London, so there must be some comparable, invisible hierarchy within the world of jugglers, stilt-walkers and people dressed in metallic paint pretending to be statues. You would expect Europe's tourist streets to be jammed with jugglers, but in fact, like a liquid, they seem to find a level—an even distribution across the several hundred environments in Europe willing to tolerate them. One odd recent disappearance has been the groups of Peruvian Indians playing selections from "Bridge Over Troubled Water" who, to their anger and surprise, at last found themselves attracting absolutely no money at all after some years of being quite flush. But then perhaps this is part of that subtle redistribution and they are now happily drawing the crowds in Pinsk or Kaliningrad? Is there *really* some hidden hierarchy? Are there scratch marks on posts in travellers' code indicating a vacancy for a fire-eater in Córdoba or Stuttgart? How do they avoid two or more people dressed amusingly as the Tin Man from *The Wizard of Oz* wrecking things for each other in Ljubljana or Antwerp?

I mention this only because wandering through Covent Garden, anyone who is British comes face to face with the odd truth that this is a country which people visit. Just as we will talk in ecstasies about the crusty bread or peasant carts of the Abruzzo or how the Aegean really is a slightly annoying insistent blue, so there must be droves of non-British people returning home and sounding off about: what? And who are they? I always like to think that Covent Garden is thronged with fellow cosmopolitans—that we catch one another's eyes with nods of high-gloss recognition. New Yorkers, Milanese and Madrileños smile with inward respect as—connoisseurs of the urban—they enjoy the little £5.00 squares of oat flapjack they are eating or admire the just-out-of-treatment stilt-walker having an attack of the shakes. But what if there is another hierarchy to which we remain blind? Just as there is for the street performers? What if London is a magnet only if you are from, say, Schweinfurt or Besançon, Straubing or Langres? What if New York dreams are filled with Rome, and Indianapolis dreams are filled with London?

I don't say this at all in a spirit of self-hatred—I love London. But when I think of some time-pressed Dane or Mexican flipping through brochures and plumping to spend her time and money here, it does not seem quite rational. We are alive for only so long. We are simply not given enough hours of life even to begin to spot a glint from a reflection of an understanding of the human mystery. Go to Pisa, go to Dresden.

The tourists who are spat out by enormous coaches onto the Embankment and who meander up to Covent Garden—buying postcards of Prince William or of a woman's nipple hilariously disguised with crayons as the nose of a cheeky mouse—are spat there because they want to be spat. London may be first on their list of essential destinations or it may trail somewhere behind Kiel or Toulon, but something is dragging them here.

Presumably, in practice, the most powerful non-cultural magnet for visitors to London must be the freaky presence of the royal family, the flags and the pageant history associated with soldiers dressed in bearskin hats (so different from the compromised militarism most tourists enjoy at home), tangled up with a vague sense of sadness about Princess Diana. An early ability to play "Hey Jude" on the recorder probably lurks in the background too. But into this heady mix must come James Bond. Can there be any more iconic moment in the films than the grainy shot of Westminster with Big Ben donging and Bond being briefed on which country this week needs its population count adjusted down?

The books and films have (I fear, in darker moments, more in Besançon than in Paris) been an immensely success-ful form of propaganda for Britain. We can of course never balance out such disparate things—but the wan, humiliated, failing country of the fifties and sixties, watched with incre-dulity by the French, Germans, Japanese, Americans and Italians as their own economies and cultures raced along, was in effect propped up and made viable and desirable only by the monarchy, the Beatles and James Bond. Of these it is James Bond that has roots most specific to the crisis of the period and which to an outsider best crystallizes what was viewed by others with genuine admiration during and after the Second World War.

In effect, what mainland Europe had suffered could not allow such insouciance—and indeed Britain's experience could barely permit it—but through the insight of a cynical, depressive Old Etonian something new and modern had been created which could express the romance of Britain and which generated a good will and a sense of openness that continues to make London so alluring. The books and films were and remain extraordinarily successful across Europe and are as much part of the mainland bloodstream as else-where.

And so, however irritating Covent Garden may be, it is also harmless and quite happy. A space in which, as in much of Western Europe, people merely circulate, accumulating needless accessories, in a defanged, declawed, neutered sort of way; it is a good response to the last century. And in light of how Britain *could* have turned out if the War had been lost, if the Empire had been fought for more violently, if the economy had not ultimately recovered, it is also cheerful. In the end, the more history you experience or the more history you know, the more shopping for face cream or Sardinian dog-milk ricotta and watching people fall off unicycles seems like a pretty good result.

JUST A FEW YARDS south of Covent Garden there is a very different walk. Covent Garden may be dopy but it is at least a sort of hymn to harmlessness. Its parallel street, the Strand, is different.

I have always sort of loved the Strand because of the comic gap between its being one of the most historically supersaturated streets in London and its being so dreary. As the principal land route between the political world of Westminster and the mercantile world of the City of London, the Strand has through its long existence been exceptionally important. So many serious events in London's existence have involved kings, writers, soldiers and an infinity of messengers and gossip-mongers navigating the Strand. And yet it holds almost no traces of this: it is ruthlessly workaday and fumy, crowded with office workers—and with tourists heading for a rendezvous with the stilt-walkers they love so much.

On a closer look the Strand does have a heart, however, and it is not an appealing one. It is impossible to imagine Richard II's perfumed court trotting up it from Whitehall to visit John of Gaunt at his palace, or even imagine young and excited David Copperfield scampering across it (and ideally being hit by a passing cab). But there *is* an accretion of things which in some lights are inspiring and in others horrifying. Once I found myself stuck in London for the night having missed the last train and decided to spend the time walking the ceremonial areas of the city. With no company and a need to stay alert I stared at everything in a way that has since become habit. It then struck me (helped of course by exhaustion, drink, the pleasurable City-of-Dreadful-Night lighting effects and the lack of living people) that the Strand and its surroundings are simply a monstrous necropolis which I am doomed always to wander in, overwhelmed by the wreckage left by family, culture and politics—by projects I can only ever faintly sympathize with or understand.

Walking west from Fleet Street there are endless buildings in gloomy dead-white stone which form a sort of litany to Britain's weird impact on the world, all built from the spoils of that impact. The humourless monster of Australia House stares across at a statue of a man who ordered the invasion of Egypt. On every side there are buildings rooted in the Empire—either directly (different Australian states, Zimbabwe, Gibraltar) or indirectly (the BBC World Service, the Stanley Gibbons stamp shop, the old Shell-Mex House); the Wellington pub looks out, reasonably enough, on the approaches to Waterloo Bridge.

By the time you get to Trafalgar Square things have got completely out of control. Nelson's Column itself—looking like a stone-and-bronze Regency conception of what a rocket launch might look like—flanked by statues of people who mainly killed Indians. The square is dominated by three gaggingly oppressive ziggurats—South Africa House (vicious white rapacity) and Canada House (welfare-oriented white rapacity) and Admiralty Arch (British naval rapacity). Leading out of the square there are lasting pleasures in every direction—a wilderness of statues offering walkers a macabre counting-game: people who killed immense numbers of Indians, fairly large numbers of Indians, a lot of Chinese but in a Christian spirit, lots of Indians, heaps of Africans and so on. Alongside these are the far more sympathetic monuments to the two world wars, which in many ways simply reflect the pigeons coming home to roost for the actions of the earlier bronze gentlemen. The only really clear run is the Mall, once you are past the statues of Captain Cook (unwitting dispossession of the inhabitants of an entire continent) and various soldiers (Chinese and South African campaigns). This is only, however, because the Mall then becomes lined with morally neutral trees, all framing the approach to Buckingham Palace, once a place for many of the peoples of the world, rather like a pilastered oblong Death Star. So mesmeric is the palace that it's easy to miss the reappearance of statues after the break— this time an allegory of South Africa as a nude white cupid with a miniature ostrich tucked under his arm (or, no less witlessly, the ostrich is perhaps not miniaturized and, to scale, the cupid is meant to be thirty feet tall). Anyway—time to turn back.

Ian Fleming spent the War at the Admiralty and the area around Horse Guards with the government bunker, the radio masts scattered around the roofs, the scrunch of gravel, the guards on duty cannot have changed at all beyond the addition of a statue of Lord Mountbatten, which Fleming would have commented acidly on.

What is really very odd about all these places, streets, buildings, monuments is that they now all belong to a different country. There is something of the same effect in the other European capitals but these have all gone through such overwhelming regime changes that it is easier to understand that their governments and peoples are snipped off from their pasts—their surroundings purely decorative and instructive. Britain has managed to elude this. Street names rarely change, the statues stay untoppled—although quite a few of the latter commemorate strikingly nasty looters and killers.

How we managed to reach this point, in the early twenty-first century, with our institutions still intact and our self-belief as enraging to other nations as ever is one of the extraordinary stories of the modern age. No empire can be wound up without vast pressures on the ruling nation. Other twentieth-century empires have ended in invasion, desolation, immense, radicalized convulsive fits. Britain in the end suffered a decade of humiliation and two decades of economic horror before emerging again, like something from a cocoon, as a new, localized, well-off part of Europe with an enthusiasm for coconut milk, korma and pesto—and with the Queen still sitting there.

Of course it would be awful if it were really built, but surely a statue either of Fleming or Bond belongs around here—over by the buildings where Fleming worked and to-wards Whitehall. Nobody else—writer or writer's creation— has more powerfully engaged in managing that vast shift from Imperial state to European state. Fleming somehow, through some final heroic version of his wartime work, moved everyone on. He comforted, entertained and distracted people who had lived with assumptions which within less than two decades became completely outmoded. The magic, the romance and the often squalid reality of dominion over the world which had animated millions of emigrants, sailors, soldiers, traders, journalists for so many generations came to an absolute, unrecoverable, bewildering end. But secretly, *secretly*, in a luxury hotel somewhere in the world, one man (a man who would today be in his eighties) was slipping a .25 Beretta automatic into his chamois-leather shoulder holster, examining his rather cruel mouth in the bathroom mirror, putting on his dinner jacket and going out into the night to save their world.

ACKNOWLEDGEMENTS

It is both routine and just for any writer to acknowledge debts towards those who have preceded his own work—to state that you have been able to see so far only because you are standing on the shoulders of giants, striding towards some golden upland. Fleming studies do certainly include some giants and I could blithely (and defensively) claim to be standing on the shoulders of such figures as David Cannadine and Umberto Eco. However, I have a niggling feeling that this would just be an imposture and that in reality I am lying face down in quite some other part of town. This is an entertainment on British themes rather than a major contribution to any debate.

I am enormously indebted to several books. Most crucially, of course, to Andrew Lycett's superb *Ian Fleming*, a biography that can be read with enjoyment even by people with no interest at all in its subject; David Cannadine's *The Aristocratic Adventurer*, John Darwin's *Britain and Decolonisation*, David Edgerton's *England and the Aeroplane*, Niall Ferguson's *Empire*, Leslie Halliwell's *Film Guide*, even when it is wrong, Peter Hennessy's *The Prime Minister*, Geoffrey Owen's *From Empire to Europe*, Lee Pfeiffer and Dave Worrall's meticulous *The Essential Bond*, A. J. P. Taylor's *English History 1914–1945*, Polly Thomas and Adam Vaitilingam's *Rough Guide to Jamaica* and David Thomson's *New Biographical Dictionary of Film*.

I have a profound and genuine intellectual and professional problem with acknowledging the many historians whom I work with and whom I have talked to about this project. It seems to me that to mention them would be both to imply their approval (which has not been sought) and to invoke their protection, which even I really cannot sink to. Writing this book has been a freelance (indeed, teetering on rogue operative) project and needs to be kept separate from my life as a history publisher. Nevertheless, I am really most grateful to them all. The one exception to this anonymity, though, has to be Robert Bickers, whose *Empire Made Me: An Englishman Adrift in Shanghai* has, more than any other book, shown me new ways to think about Britain's imperial past.

I would also like particularly to thank for often very considerable or indeed essential help with the actual writing of the book: Andrew Bell, of course, Malcolm Bull, Chloe Campbell, Sarah Chalfant, Jill Foulston, Helen Fraser, Alison Hennessey, Peter Hennessy, Jim and Sandra Jones for supplying the world's finest writing space, Tony Lacey, Barry Langford, Stefan McGrath, Adam Phillips, Carole Tonkinson (not least for the *Water Babies* joke), Corinne Turner, Zoë Watkins, Barnaby Winder (who, not least, rescued me from a catastrophic *Goldfinger* plot error), Felix Winder, Martha Winder and Andrew Wylie. Jonathan Galassi and Andrew Kidd have been, from my own professional viewpoint, rather disturbingly prompt and perceptive editors. Above all I have to thank the infinitely inspirational Christine Jones, my marvellous piece of luck. I have an irrational hatred of effusive acknowledgements, but here have to crack very slightly. Whatever its other, often insuperable deficiencies, this is a happy book, entirely thanks to her and our children. I cannot begin to thank her enough.

Potsdam, Sequim, Meißen, Wandsworth Town,
2004–2005